Communication and Medical Practice

Communication and Medical Practice

Social Relations in the Clinic

David Silverman

⑤ SAGE Publications

London ● Newbury Park ● Beverly Hills ● New Delhi

SAGE Publications Ltd
28 Banner Street
London EC1Y 8QE

SAGE Publications Inc
2111 West Hillcrest Street
Newbury Park, California 91320

SAGE Publications India Pvt Ltd
C-236 Defence Colony
New Delhi 110 024

SAGE Publications Inc
275 South Beverly Drive
Beverly Hills, California 90212

British Library Cataloguing in Publication Data
Silverman, David
   Communication and medical practice: social relations in
   the clinic
   1. Physician and patient
   I. Title
   610.69′6   R727.3

ISBN 0-8039-8108-2
ISBN 0-8039-8109-0 Pbk

Library of Congress catalog card number 87-062028

Printed in Great Britain by J.W. Arrowsmith, Ltd, Bristol

Contents

Transcription Symbols

/	overlapping
( )	untranscribable passage
(conflict)	guess at unclear utterance
(0.5)	silence, in seconds
(. . .)	passage not transcribed
wa-a-tching	drawn out word
exceedingly	stressed word (except where noted 'my emphasis')

Transcript Markers
These markers appear before each passage of transcript as a guide to its origin. Some explanation is given below.

Transcript 67:23	transcript number and page of transcript
12/11/80	date of transcript
P7	Private clinic and number of clinic in sequence observed
H	Hodgkin's clinic
L	Leukaemia clinic
NT	New town clinic
SC	Suburban clinic

Explanation of the additional markers in Chapter Three is given in that chapter.

Preface

This is a book about medical encounters in hospital clinics. The research reported here took in a wide range of conditions — heart disease, hare-lip/cleft palates, various kinds of cancers and diabetes. It also extended over a nine-year period, from 1976–85.

Inevitably, then, this is a somewhat heterogeneous collection of studies, influenced both by the varying demands of paymasters and by my changing intellectual biography. Fortunately, from the point of view of the reader, these coincide with influential ways of formulating medical encounters: from theories of medical communication in the seventies to responses to Foucault's account of disciplinary power in the eighties.

The research coheres at three principal points. First, with the exception of the cancer patients, I was dealing with paediatric clinics. This generated a continuing interest in the moral field that envelops doctor/patient/child relations and discourses. Second, as I explain in Chapter One, no one working with doctors, parents and patients can remain blind to their pressing practical problems. So this book is not simply an example of using encounters as data upon which to engage in sociological theorizing. In the pages that follow, I continually return to the practical and political aspects of these encounters — albeit viewed in rather less optimistic ways in Parts 2 and 3 of the book. Finally, although the frame of reference shifts from interactionism to Foucaultian discourse analysis, the perspective remains consistently sociological. Throughout, I am concerned with forms of discourse and the sites in which they arise rather than with styles of communication or the psychological attributes of doctors and patients.

I owe a special debt of gratitude to David Hill of Sage who suggested that I write the book in this form and to Stephen Barr for his support at the later stages of its production. My fellow research workers, Geoffrey Baruch, Robert Hilliard, Mary Kirk, Annette Murphy and Geof Rayner, know that this work would not have been possible without their support and insights.

Many others also made useful comments and suggestions: David Armstrong, Zygmunt Bauman, Robert Dingwall, Barry Glassner, Jaber Gubrium, Anne-Louise Kinmonth, Tina Posner, Linnie Price, Mary Simms, Gerry Stimson, Phil Strong, Brian Torode and Terri Walker. The Social Science Research Council (as it then was) funded the studies of the paediatric cardiology and hare-lip/cleft-palate clinics and Goldsmiths College Central Research Fund supported the oncology clinic study. I gratefully acknowledge their support and also the provision of sabbatical leave from my teaching duties in the 1986–7 session. At different stages, Sarah Montgomery, Olive Till and Jane Firmin typed the manuscript and always met deadlines.

Finally, I would like to express my gratitude to all the medical staff, parents and patients who made this research possible but whom I cannot name.

David Silverman
London

1
Introduction

A much-repeated complaint about research reports is that they are too polished. They read as if researching were just a matter of going from A to B, a direct path without diversions or doubling back from cul-de-sacs. As we all know, this is a gross misrepresentation of how most research is done, particularly qualitative sociological research which, traditionally, is rich on observation and poor on hypotheses.

The unrealistic character of the polished research monograph is a serious matter. It conceals the cognitive, temporal and political processes through which a relationship was constructed with the parties in the setting, and how sense was read into (what came to count as) data. This is confusing and frustrating for apprentice-researchers who cannot understand why their own material will not so readily speak for itself. It also represents a sad wastage of data. As Dalton (1959) showed many years ago, that one is let in to study an organization and that certain people vouchsafe information is not only a matter of satisfaction to the researcher but should also be an occasion for puzzlement. Why on earth should anyone want to have an outsider nosing around their private territory? Who reveals confidences and why? What do they want from you and what do they do with it? Surely such questions need to be addressed in research reports themselves rather than safely secluded in collections which tell the 'inside story' of different studies — the sociological equivalent of the gossip column?

In this opening chapter, I want to try to answer some of these questions about my own research. The aim is to reflect upon how the 'findings' represented in the next nine chapters emerged over time, as the predispositions of the researchers meshed with their responses to the settings and their relations with the people whose behaviour they were observing.

Despite this cognitive and political to-and-fro, I believe that the studies reported here have a clear thematic line of development. This will need some demonstrating since this was not a study of a single setting but a series of studies of many settings, based on a number of initially disparate concerns. So a second aim is to reconstruct a logic which reveals the analytic linkages between apparently disparate work extending from interviews with parents of cleft palate children to observation of a private medical oncology clinic. Here the purpose is not to produce a rationalized gloss on the research but to reflect upon the omnipresence of certain themes so the pages that follow are about what I later call 'the discourse of the social' — the situated nature and consequences of an appeal to the social or everyday realm by both participants *and* researchers. Contrary to first impressions, a recognition and a use of social discourse is by no means a straight-forward strategy for reducing professional power.

This brings me to the third and final theme of this book. Whatever the researcher's intellectual interests, the experience of being involved with the day-to-day work of medical staff and the occasional tragedies and joys of patients and parents tends not only to encourage a measure of humility about their energy and adaptability but also a tendency to question whether 'things' (interactional matters, institutional settings) need to be organized in quite this way. Even the most hard-bitten researcher who resists such a response and is eager only for an additional paper on the curriculum vitae, to be followed by a rapid exit from the field, will still have to cope with the understandable curiosity of medical staff, patients or parents about what the anonymous person in the corner, complete with tape-recorder and notebook, is making of everything. Amiability and a dead-bat to enquiries will only succeed for a limited period even in so reticent a culture as is to be found in England.

However, whether one is motivated by pragmatic considerations or by worthy intentions, prescription for practice is a minefield. Wholesale critiques of professional practice often suffer from under-analysed data and from under-developed alternatives (see Rayner and Stimson, 1979; Strong, 1979; Silverman, 1985; 185–90). Conversely, closely-arranged attempts to reveal the 'functions' of apparently irrational procedures (see Atkinson and Drew, 1979), may lead in the direction of an unhelpful conservatism of the kind that 'things wouldn't be this way unless they served some purpose'.

In such circumstances, it is tempting to opt for a variety of modest reformism often based on an appeal for a more patient-centred medicine (Byrne and Long, 1976). Things only start to go awry when you realize that use of 'the discourse of the social' is not an alternative to contemporary professional practice but its very form. In preaching 'humanism', the researcher is reinforcing a central contemporary strategy of power (this is discussed at length in Chapter Eight).

So the third theme of the book is my attempt to come to terms with the powerful deconstruction of reformism found in Foucault (1973, 1977, 1979) and his followers (Armstrong, 1983; Arney and Bergen, 1984). The history of these studies charts a movement from this optimistic reformism of the 1970s towards the apparently pessimistic relativism of the 1980s.

In the pages that follow, I will take up these themes by looking back chronologically at the studies reported here. I begin with the point of entry into the setting, discuss the original research design and the preliminary themes and findings. I then move on to later studies in a range of medical settings, drawing out their point of contact with the original work, before concluding with some reflections on the politics of research.

Point of Entry
My own experience of how research gets started is that chance factors play a far more important role than conscious planning. So it was in this case. I was introduced to a doctor at a party. It turned out that he was a paediatrician treating children with congenital heart disease. He mentioned his worries about how adequately he managed communication with parents. Since I was a sociologist, would I be interested in taking a look at his hospital?

In 1976, when this happened, I had barely any knowledge of the literature in the area of the sociology of medicine (or as I later came to call it, using a rather less 'loaded' term, the sociology of health and illness). I taught courses in the sociology of language and in methods of sociological research. I had published a textbook on the sociology of organizations (Silverman, 1970) and a research monograph on selection and promotion committees in the Administrative Section of the Greater London Council (GLC) (Silverman and Jones, 1975). The approach from the doctor, however, came at a convenient time. The GLC work had been written up and I was eager to establish another research site, so I pointed out my lack of background knowledge to the doctor but agreed to 'take a look'.

The doctor was a physician at a large London teaching hospital which specializes in chest and heart disease. Although not a children's hospital, there was a separate ward with beds for children with congenital heart disease. The doctor was one of two consultant paediatric cardiologists and, of course, there were also a number of surgeons. The catchment area for patients covered much of the South East of England and patients were referred from general practitioners (GPs) or from paediatric or maternity hospitals. A number of patients came from abroad and some British patients came long distances from outside the main catchment area, usually because of personal links between the doctors at each end.

Over several months in 1976–7, I sat in on the Wednesday out-patient clinic which could last anything from two to four hours and involve between six and fourteen patients. I also followed the doctor around on a couple of ward rounds and chatted with parents on the ward or in the mothers' room. I was given a tour of the facilities of the Paediatric Cardiology Unit (PCU) but declined the offer to watch heart surgery in progress! I had no stomach for things of this kind and, fortunately, my sociological interests did not require such observation.

The work of the PCU directly involved three floors of the hospital. On the ground floor, the out-patients' clinics took place. There was a crowded waiting room and a separate playroom for children. Appointment times were usually all around 10 a.m. which could mean a very early start for those travelling from country areas. Parents who drove to London also had the additional frustrations of coping with parking restrictions on crowded streets. When children arrived they were X-rayed and had an electrocardiogram (ecg). The clinic consultation might not then take place until after 2 p.m. if it was a crowded session. However, special efforts were made to see new patients first and, if consultations were getting behind, a Registrar would often take a share of the cases.

With the help of Geof Rayner, then Research Assistant in the Sociology Department of Goldsmiths' College, and Robert Hilliard, a PhD student from the Department, I began to piece together a body of information about the social organization of the clinics and about medical decision-making in the treatment of congenital heart disease (CHD). Children reach the PCU through two main routes: either they are diagnosed soon after birth and are admitted in the first few days of life as neo-natal emergencies, or they are picked up later on by GPs or at baby or school clinics. At this later stage, suspicions are typically aroused by a heart 'murmur' heard on the stethoscope or, less commonly, by signs of breathlessness on exercise or of blueness (cyanosis) on fingers or toes.

As it turns out, many 'murmurs' may be 'innocent' or non-pathological. Together with worried parents, we were reassured to hear that many people have such murmurs and they often do not indicate the presence of heart disease. Where CHD is detected in a child, the outlook is not as bleak as popular mythology would lead us to believe. The normal procedure then was for children to be admitted overnight for an invasive investigation (cardiac catherization) — although I understand that now this has been largely replaced by an echocardiogram which can be done at the out-patient clinic. Many conditions are readily repaired surgically and certain kinds of CHD (for instance small ventricular septal defects, holes-in-the-heart) will actually repair themselves without any need for surgery. In these cases, doctors stress that the children can subsequently be regarded as 'normal' and only require infrequent check-ups and prophylactic penicillin cover for dental work. Only in a relatively small number of severe conditions is repair impossible or too risky. In such cases, shunts or holding operations may be carried out to try to keep the child relatively free from symptoms, while, in the long run, risky surgery or even heart transplants may be contemplated.

As might be expected, clinics can be very difficult for parents. As some were later to tell us, they come expecting to hear a life or death sentence on their child. The heart is often seen as the centre of all life and parental anxieties about the outlook are made worse by the guilt many mothers feel at having produced an 'imperfect' child. The first visit to the PCU is generally, then, a fraught occasion, with the doctor often trying to reassure and calm very frightened people who later, so they told us, blamed themselves for not having asked the right questions.

Conversely, some out-patient consultations can be relaxed, even jolly, affairs. Experience of clinic routines and knowledge of your child's condition seems to build parents' ability to cope and to participate. Predictably, successful surgery is an occasion for congratulations all round — to doctors for their technical wizardry and to parents for having looked after their child so well.

In-patient stays, however, are not all plain sailing. Children are admitted to a ward on the third floor which also houses a playroom, offices for medical staff and a 'mother's room'. Mothers told us that they appreciated the opportunity that was provided for many of them to stay overnight in hospital apartments. The nursing staff also seem to have responded well to the emphasis, following the 1959 Platt Report, on open visiting on childrens' wards. Mothers seemed neither to be totally excluded from looking after their children nor deserted and thrown in at the deep-end without advice. They reported that they were encouraged to do as much for their child, in terms of feeding and so on, as they wanted. This was a far more satisfactory situation than that reported by Stacey et al. (1970).

Nonetheless, in such an anxiety-generating situation, problems remained. Mothers who could not stay overnight, normally because of the presence of other children at home, sometimes found transport to the hospital difficult and expensive and suffered problems connected with their employers (see also Earthrowl and Stacey, 1977). For those who did stay, the mothers' room could offer support but also worry. Crises of morale seemed to shake the parent community when bad news descended from the fourth floor where the Intensive Care Unit (ICU) was located. The crucial bench-mark for parents was the announcement of the decision after surgery to move their child out of the ICU and back on to the ward. However, everybody was also affected by the news of the progress of other people's children. Low morale would set in when a child died, although one mother admitted very guiltily to us, that, as she had been told that there was a one-in-five risk from her child's surgery, when she heard that another child had died she felt strangely relieved. Her comment says something about the different ways in which parents and doctor hear percentage risk figures. As one parent told us: 'If you've only got one child, what does a twenty per cent risk mean?'

My initial interest centred, however, not on these accounts generated at interviews but upon our tape-recordings and transcripts of out-patient consultations. I will shortly discuss in detail why these tapes came to be so central to the research design. I need only mention here the fashion in the 1970s for collecting 'naturally-occurring' data coupled with my original interest in the sociology of language.

My first attempt to analyse the data focused on exchanges between two different mothers and our paediatric cardiologist. In one case, I tried to show how the doctor managed the exchange by translating the mother's queries and doubts into his secure clinical realm. In the other case, both parties seemed to negotiate the relevance for them of what I called 'technical' and 'familial' discourses (Silverman and Torode, 1980: 332–47).

The analysis of this material was contexted in a discussion of different theories of language rather than conventional issues in the sociology of health and illness. Nonetheless, even in the former context, I now see certain problems with it. First, it was based on a purely abstract theory of communicative competence developed by Habermas (1972) and I am now doubtful whether any universal theory of linguistic practice can do justice to the range of settings in which talk goes on (see Dingwall, 1980). Second, relatedly, I had merely referred to the fact that the second 'negotiated' encounter occurred after unsuccessful surgery. Surely, consonant with my observations on the clinics, we might expect significant variation in the way consultations proceeded according to contextual features like this. Thirdly, was it entirely in order to select two consultations in order to prove a point? Shouldn't systematic analysis investigate variation in consultations across a large number of cases and contexts?

The time had come to delve into the social science literature in the area to examine the prevailing models of medical encounters. Much of this is discussed elsewhere in this book (particularly in the Introduction to Part 1 and in Chapter Eight). I need only mention that, at this time, we were particularly struck by a book that had just been published by two doctors working at Manchester University's Department of General Practice (Byrne and Long, 1976). This sought to demonstrate that doctors tended to work to rigid agendas and that this precluded proper listening to patients' stories or open discussion of treatment options. Instead, they called for a 'patient-centred' model of practice where the doctor became as much a listener as an initiator.

Byrne and Long's analysis seemed to have much to recommend it. It was based on detailed quantitative analysis of over 100 consultations and it fitted neatly into a liberal, humanist position that was acceptable to many social scientists in the 1970s. However, it was limited to general practice consultations. The obvious thing seemed to be to find out whether their model applied to the very different setting of high-technology, hospital medicine. This indeed was how we set out to draft our research proposal to the Social Science Research Council.

The Original Research Design
The title of this research proposal was 'The Patient-Centred Model in a Hospital Setting'. From the start, we opted for multiple sources of data and methods of data analysis. The research was designed as a longitudinal study centring around 100 out-patient sessions which eventually were to generate over 1200 taped consultations. This had the advantage of allowing us to follow through, over time, a series of consultations with the same participants, unlike Byrne and Long's consultations which were one-off affairs.

It was, however, also necessary to compare the sort of high-technology medicine practised in the PCU with other forms of hospital medicine. In order to preserve the longitudinal element in the research design, we had to find a condition which required continuing out-patient contact over at least a two-year period and a continuing programme of treatment. Eventually, access was negotiated with a consultant surgeon who ran a clinic for hare-lip and cleft-palate children at a suburban London Childrens' Hospital.

The aim was to see how the conditions of practise shaped the format of the consultation. Comparison was also aided by the opportunity that arose during the course of the research to observe a limited number of consultations at a provincial PCU and a cleft-palate clinic in Australia as well as PCU's in both Australia and the United States (see Rayner, 1981).

The data, however, do not speak for themselves. Decisions had to be made about how these 1200 tapes were to be analysed. A strategy was called for. It was decided to reject the sophisticated methods of conversation analysis (ca). (See Silverman, 1985, Chapter 6). I had already had difficulties with one approach concerned with universals in talk and it seemed best to avoid a focus on formal methods of conversational sequencing in a study which was concerned with variations within specifically *medical* consultations. Moreover, the time needed to prepare the precise transcripts used in conversation analysis would have been so great that only a tiny proportion of our tapes could have been used in this way.

As an alternative, it was decided to use a Goffman-based model of the 'ceremonial order' of the clinic which focused on displays of identities within rules of etiquette, in particular:

> Who is to be what . . . and what sorts of rights and duties they may expect, exert and suffer (Strong, 1982: 3).

Some of the limits of such an approach are touched upon in the Introduction to Part One of this book. Here I need only point out the advantages of concentrating on variations between medical encounters using a large number of transcripts which were adequate for the purposes at hand. Considerable attention could thus be paid to deviant cases (see Chapter Six) and simple forms of quantification could be used to test hypotheses. (see Chapter Four).

The reader will note that in this study and the subsequent studies reported in this book, the focus is always on data derived from out-patient clinics. As I have already implied, the impetus behind this was a rejection of the value of much survey research data in favour of material gathered from interactions that would occur without the researcher's presence. Such 'naturally-occurring' data, I then felt, was less suspect than the contrived responses elicited in survey research. I am less sure now about this distinction, trading as it does on a form of 'naturalism' which assumes that some body of data can exist 'untouched by human hands' (see Hammersley and Atkinson, 1983). Nevertheless, it informed the early work.

Even if you take this argument seriously, however, out-patient consultations are not the only naturally-occurring encounters in hospitals. What about what happens in waiting-rooms or on the wards in encounters between nurses, doctors and mothers, individually and together? Indeed, our attention was drawn to the central importance that parents attached to ward interviews with consultants after cardiac catheterization and surgery.

There is a simple, practical reason for micro-sociology's concentration on the dynamics of clinic or GP consultations. The reason is convenience. First, consultations, unlike most ward encounters, are scheduled occasions. This means that researchers, who often have teaching commitments, can timetable research days when they know that they will be rewarded with sizeable chunks of data. Compare this to hanging around on a ward waiting for something to turn up. Only the most earnest researchers, with plenty of time on their hands, would be likely to choose the latter setting. This was precisely the reason that the research neglected an important route for admission. Neo-natal emergency cases, by their nature, could not be timetabled conveniently.

Second, out-patient clinics have the advantage that they allow the researcher to assume a non-problematic role. Of course, there is the issue of patient consent (to which I return later). But, within this constraint, researchers can become flies on the wall, unnoticed among the many faces sitting around in a crowded clinic. There is time to set up a tape-recorder and no problem in making notes when this is what medical staff are doing too. Compare this to the observer on the ward who has a most problematic situation in terms of identity. Who is this creature, people may ask, who is clearly not a member of staff and yet doesn't seem to have any connection with a particular patient?

These studies have convinced me that such pragmatic factors explain the focus of much interactional work. Rationally, who would choose a day hanging around, without a role, and having to sneak off to the lavatory to make notes should anything turn up, particularly, when the alternative is a secure place in a comfortable room for a couple of hours once a week, with a tape-recorder set up and even a desk on which to lean a notebook?

Despite my analytic and practical reservations about other kinds of data, I was concerned, however, that a purely out-patient study might not recommend itself to a funding agency. Therefore, albeit reluctantly, Hilliard, Rayner and myself decided to attach an interview study to the proposal. The aim, as we put it, was to add to the *extensive* study of clinics an *intensive* study of the experiences of a limited number of families. Originally, the plan was to compare the responses of a number of parents of children with cleft palates or heart disease with those of a 'control group' of 'normal' parents. Fortunately, this plan was abandoned at an early stage. Not only did it present insuperable problems in selecting and interviewing such a control group (How were we to find them? What would we talk about?) but it also misconceived the nature of family dynamics. As a perceptive ward sister pointed out, the parents she saw *were* 'normal' parents.

The issue of displays of 'normal parenthood' in the context of a child's congenital illness was eventually to become central to how the interview data were analysed. When the research proposal was submitted, however, I was deeply doubtful about how we could use the interviews. The plan was to interview a sample of twenty families, with children at our hospitals, after each hospital appointment. At that time, however, we were not at all clear about the status to be attached to parents' talk. Coming from a tradition where observation of what people were doing was central, what were we to make of their talk about what they had done? If we could expect only rationalizations, what was the place of rationalization in social action? Furthermore, given that the last thing I wanted to do was to use the interview data to make an ironic comparison with the events described (as if what parents said necessarily showed how imperceptive the doctors had been), did we need the interview data at all? Even as we began the research, we had no answers to these questions.

Early Research Themes
In summer 1978, we learned of the success of our research proposal. The Social Science Research Council (SSRC) would fund us for two-and-a-half years. Two graduate students from Goldsmiths' were appointed as research officers: Robert Hilliard would focus on out-patient clinics and Mary Kirk would be mainly concerned with the interview part of the study.

From the start, it became clear that the comparison between the PCU and the cleft palate clinic would have to take account of many more factors than the level of medical technology. Certainly, the care of cleft palate children was far less mystifying to parents. The defect was visible and the anatomy non-problematic. Knowledge of methods of diagnosis and treatment were also easily accessible to parents.

Compared to this, heart disease was an unknown, terrifying quantity to most parents. Knowledge of the anatomy of the heart was usually very limited and heart disease perceived as a unity, no distinction being made between a heart murmur and gross cardiac anomalies. Moreover, unlike the cleft palate child, the heart patient could appear well and still have a life-threatening condition. Such a diagnosis was dependent on high-technology means of assessment, from electrocardiograms to cardiac catheterizations and echo-cardiograms.

The clinics revealed, however, that this knowledge gap became less significant over time as parents became more familiar with cardiac disease. In both settings, the stage of the career trajectory set the context for the consultation and could largely erase factors associated with the technology of treatment. For instance, after successful surgery, post-operative consultations took on a similar 'congratulatory' format in both cleft palate and cardiac clinics. Doctors encouraged parents' displays of satisfaction with the transformed appearance of their baby (lip repaired, no longer blue and thriving) and played up the future years of normality ('looks like any normal child', 'can be a professional footballer').

In order to account for the variation of the consultation format, Robert Hilliard coined the notion of the 'site' of the encounter. The site encompassed matters relating to the stage of the child's medical career and is fully discussed in Chapter Two, while Hilliard's original draft hypotheses are set out in Appendix One.

At this stage, we felt we had added usefully to Strong's (1979) trail-blazing account of the 'ceremonial order' of paediatric clinics. Like him, we found that National Health Service (NHS) consultations took on a 'bureaucratic' format in which authority was claimed by an interchangeable medical team but where the moral probity of parents' conduct was rarely challenged by doctors. In addition, however, our tape-recorded material allowed quantitative and qualitative analysis of variability in the amount of parents' interventions and in the form of the diagnosis statement and of the decision about treatment.

The specification of the concept of site allowed further analysis of a set of deviant cases in the PCU clinics. The apparently more 'democratic' consultations for Down's Syndrome children seemed to be associated with a flattened career trajectory and a medical policy designed to achieve purely medical (i.e. non-surgical) treatment. Similarly, the 'consumerist' medicine practised with adolescent cleft-palate patients established a number of concealed double-binds for both patients and their parents (see Chapters Six and Seven).

These two spin-off studies provided a link with earlier and later work. The smaller number of cases involved allowed closer attention to be paid to the language of the encounter, while being sensitive to how the 'site' constituted a context for the talk. In particular, I bracketed off issues about the personality or motivations of patients and parents in order to examine how they were constituted as 'subjects' in the talk. This worked in very different ways for Down's Syndrome children and cleft-palate patients as Table 1 shows:

TABLE 1
The Constitution of Social Subjects in Two Clinics

| | Child | |
	Cleft-palate adolescent	Down's Syndrome child (any age)
Patient	Rational consumer	Silent social object
Parents	Passive observers	Compassionate decision-makers

The link with later work arose out of the problematic politics of these encounters.

As I remarked in earlier publications (Silverman, 1981, 1983), in many respects these consultations approximated to those recommended by liberal reformers. They were unhurried, focused on the emotions and social concerns of patients and their families and allowed 'consumer' choice. At the same time, these very particulars served as intended or unintended strategies of power, establishing double-binds and/or producing medically desired outcomes. I make some tentative responses to this situation in Chapters Six and Seven but I was forced to return to these kinds of issues in a later study of diabetic clinics.

This still left the problem of the interview data. The material on our twenty families started to pile up. Contrary to some expectations, nobody seemed to feel that our request to interview them in their homes was an intrusion. On the contrary, we were welcomed into the home and often did not leave until well after two hours (and many cups of coffee). We decided to adopt an open-ended interviewing strategy and soon discovered that an initial request (at first interview) to 'tell me the story' or (at later interviews) a question about 'what has happened since I last saw you?' was quite sufficient to produce an extensive account, which could be sustained more or less indefinitely by a few requests for clarification.

Carrying out the interviews therefore constituted no problem. We arranged interviews in the evenings when both parents would be at home and the children safely in bed. Parents seemed delighted to talk, several commenting on the pleasure of being able to 'get things off their chest' to someone who was not linked to the concerns of medical staff or family.

We still, however, lacked an analytic framework and a methodology for addressing the interview data. We were clearly not doing survey research, nor did we want to use the data in a purely illustrative or anecdotal manner. Eventually, we discovered a way to 'crack' the problem. In 1979, Geoffrey Baruch replaced Mary Kirk as the research worker concerned with the interview study. During that year, the matter was brought to a head as Geoffrey was aiming to get a PhD out of the interview data. No longer could we hope to avoid the problem by playing down the interview part of the study. After much discussion, we adopted an approach derived from Margaret Voysey's (1975) work on the families of handicapped children. Voysey noted how what such families said was to be seen less as a direct picture of unmediated 'feelings' and more as an expression of an 'official morality' about parenting. Similarly, Baruch (1981) discovered that parents were telling him moral tales which painted a picture of valiant struggles against adversity. Stories of 'atrocities' were told about the lack of early detection of the heart condition, despite parents' sense that 'something was wrong'. Later on, mothers would produce accounts of a hospital stay when only their intervention prevented an accident or emotional crisis. Throughout, we were presented with a picture of responsible parents, initially feeling guilt over the birth of an imperfect child, then toying with thoughts of 'going private' to get the best treatment for them. Parents continually reflected over what was in the children's best interests as regards such issues as 'spoiling', and how much they should tell their children about what was wrong with them.

There were powerful cultural forms at work in these stories and it was not our aim to treat what we had been told ironically. As societal members, we could see the 'good sense' of these tales, but that did not mean that we had to treat them as simple statements of events to be contrasted with what we observed or with other people's accounts. In many respects, an 'atrocity story', for instance, is no less powerful because there is no corroborating evidence.

The approach, however, still left unresolved two further issues. First, how was Baruch to demonstrate the omnipresence of these moral tales? Second, what was their implication for communication at the clinics?

The first question was resolved by the use of simple counting procedures derived from Sacks's (1974) work on membership-categorization devices. Put in a nutshell, Baruch (1982) took a sample of parents' 'first stories' and classified and counted the norms appealed to and the parties involved. As predicted, stories were told largely in the format of mother-child rather than doctor-child relationships. A deviant case proved the rule: a medically-qualified parent was alone in telling her story from the point of view of the doctor-child pair. The policy implications of this finding were initially obscure. If parents' accounts were not to be used as an ironic commentary on clinic practice, how could we apply our analysis? The issue was postponed.

Later Studies
By late 1980, our research team had grown. Annette Murphy had joined us on a 'linked' SSRC studentship to research further the experiences of cleft palate teenagers. I had focused on the interactional problems associated with these patients being asked to talk about their appearance in the context of possible cosmetic surgery. There was also some interview evidence that they concealed their hospital stays for surgery from their friends.

The original intention was that Annette should conduct extended interviews with these young people. However, despite attempts to make them feel comfortable, experimenting with interviews in their rooms on their own or in the presence of trusted friends, these encounters proved fruitless. Just as families and medical staff found difficulty in talking to young people, so did researchers.

An alternative strategy was adopted. First, the clinic data were re-analysed and additional comparative material derived from another London cleft-palate unit. Second, a larger sample of the families of cleft-palate adolescents was obtained and the forms of their tales studied over time. A surprising uniformity was found once again in descriptions of parenting. This led, thirdly, to a content-analysis of the advice pages of a number of womens' magazines and to the identification of points of contact between them and the mothers' narratives. Thus an important link was established between the 'micro' particulars found in interview accounts and 'macro' cultural structures.

In late 1980, however, with funds running out, we were more concerned with the practical problems of preserving our research team! It was decided to apply for renewed funding on the basis of an action research study. The study emerged out of two sets of findings. Our interview data suggested that parents formulated their child's experience in moral terms and welcomed an opportunity to do so in a public setting. The analysis of clinic sites had demonstrated that parents participated most in consultations under certain conditions, particularly where they were given time to reflect on what they were told.

We were reluctant to suggest changes in communication methods in the early traumatic cardiac clinics. First, despite differences in 'style' between different doctors, parents reported similar problems. Second, parents recognized that many useful medical matters necessarily took up much of the doctor's time at a consultation with a new patient.

On the basis of discussions with staff at the PCU, we decided to recommend an additional voluntary pre-inpatient clinic for families. Funds were obtained to evaluate the role of this clinic and the responses of parents and medical staff. The study is reported in Chapter Four.

The research team were now funded until late 1982. However, an eighteen-month project meant that almost as soon as we had begun the evaluation study, we needed to cast around for another topic that could form the basis for further funding. Here another chance set of factors entered the picture. An undergraduate student at Goldsmiths' was taking time out from a job as a nurse-researcher at an oncology unit in a London teaching hospital. She introduced me to two consultants there and the seed of an idea for further work was planted.

In 1982 an application was made to the same funding body for a further grant to apply the concepts of 'site' to a number of oncology clinics and of 'moral career' to the accounts of cancer patients. As it transpired, this ambitious application, involving four years of funding for an international comparative research programme, was unsuccessful. The unfortunate effect was that apart from Ms Murphy, the research team was broken up. Nonetheless, the contacts at the oncology unit had been made and I decided to undertake a small study of out-patient clinics, funded by the Goldsmiths' College Research Committee.

Comparative work was done on a leukaemia clinic and a clinic treating patients with Hodgkin's Disease. This study is reported in Silverman (1982). However, another chance factor meant that the work eventually took a rather different turn. I had noticed that one of the physicians whose clinics I had been studying was absent from the hospital on one or two afternoons a week. I discovered that this was when he undertook a private clinic in consulting rooms near Harley Street. Now I was aware of the literature on the statistics of private practice in the UK. There was also Strong's (1979b) work on encounters in a fee-for-service clinic in the USA. Without expecting a positive answer, I requested permission to attend this physician's private clinic. Most unexpectedly, permission was granted. The results of this study are reproduced in Chapter Five. I believe they substantiate and enlarge the saliency of the concept of 'site' as well as Strong's observations on the 'ceremonial order' of private practice.

In 1984, an opportunity arose to return to a paediatric setting. At another social gathering, I encountered a paediatrician who was working at a hospital in a New Town outside London. He mentioned the problems he had at his monthly clinic for diabetic adolescents. I asked if I could sit in and so during the next year I found myself present at a dozen Tuesday afternoon clinics. As I point out in Chapter Nine, two factors made this clinic unusual. First, the doctor concerned was an unusually 'progressive' figure among medical practitioners, his office being lined with books on the latest psychological theories about 'transactional analysis'. Second, this clinic was for 'problem' patients and less problematic children were seen by the Registrar. I therefore built a comparative element into the research design, observing a number of consultations at a more 'standard' suburban clinic.

This research is discussed in the last two chapters of this book and I will limit myself now to a few observations. I discussed earlier my interest in Foucault. The dilemmas for intervention studies suggested by his work were given an added twist by this paediatrician's practice. This was no authoritarian clinic. Despite the risks that many of these young people were taking with their health, the doctor imposed few solutions; instead, he preferred to negotiate what he called 'deals'.

Yet, of course, negotiation and the appeal to what Donzelot (1979) has called the 'psy-complex' is itself a strategy of power. When the doctor took an early draft of my paper as a hint that he ought to stick more consistently to a negotiating format, I must admit I winced. Chapter Nine documents my attempt to think my way out of the impasse apparently created by a Foucaultian discourse analysis.

A less problematic area also opened up at these clinics. My earlier work on cleft-palate consultations had discussed the dilemmas of mothers who want to intervene to formulate their child's best interests but are prevented by the cultural norms of the 'autonomy' of 'young adults'. Another form of this dilemma was present for the mothers of adolescent diabetics. Not only did they have to concede their child's 'autonomy' but they also wanted to display that they had acted 'responsibly'. In this no-win situation of incompatible aims, they juggled with defences to potential charges of 'nagging' and 'irresponsibility'. Contrary to some of Strong's (1979b) observations about respect for the moral infallibility of motherhood in NHS medicine, these mothers seemed to engage in extensive interactional work to rebut actual or, more usually, potential charges about their behaviour. These dilemmas and their skilful responses to them are discussed in Chapter Ten.

The Politics of Research
The past few pages have implied how fund-raising provides a tacit backdrop to the work of a research team. I have also discussed some of the explicitly practice-oriented questions that arose in these studies. However, there is a third broadly political area that I have so far neglected: relations with people who are the subjects as well as the objects of study. A few fugitive comments are in order.

I earlier remarked that I had been invited in to study 'problems of communication' at the PCU. Things are rarely that simple. In this case, I soon learned of a political battle being fought in which the research might figure. Suggestions had been made that the PCU might be closed down in the interests of 'rationalization' and of maintaining child-care entirely within *paediatric* hospitals. In an earlier study (Silverman and Jones, 1975), I had suspected that the research was being used in order to establish a precedent for outside observation of work routines, leading to redundancies. Here a far less worrying political agenda was involved. If it could be demonstrated both that communication practices were 'good' and that the PCU had nothing to hide from an outside team of researchers, then that could be used to support its survival.

In fact, the PCU still survives today and I have no way of knowing whether the study played even a small part in its reprieve. Giving a paper at an international medical conference and publishing a paper in a medical journal (Silverman et al., 1984) certainly gave the research some publicity. On the other hand, as other researchers have noted about such professionals, medical staff in the PCU and the oncology clinics were uniformly suspicious of any data that were not based on a large sample and expressed in quantified terms. In some respects, this had useful consequences as it encouraged us to test our findings in a rather more rigorous manner than is found in some interactionist studies. Perhaps we sometimes pushed things too far. Ironically, an editorial in the *International Journal of Cardiology* commented that our paper, which followed it, concentrated too much on quantitative data and that some qualitative discussion of different cases would have been useful!

Another problem that some sociological work creates for people trained in the natural sciences is the absence of a logic of hypothesis-testing. Sometimes this can be turned to the researcher's advantage, as when making the sensible claim that it would be inappropriate to formulate hypotheses before considerable familiarity with the setting had been established. On other occasions, it creates considerable suspicion about what precisely you are up to and confusion when the purpose of the study gets redefined at a very late stage.

This certainly happened in the oncology research when the focus suddenly switched to a comparison of private and NHS practice. Admittedly, this was a fascinating analytic and political issue. However, it was difficult to explain this to medical staff who had quite a different agenda. This came to a head when anger was expressed over a paper on the topic which I later published (Silverman et al., 1984). Although I had sent a copy of it beforehand to the doctors concerned, they claimed not to have seen it. Then it turned out that their main complaint was that I had referred to an 'Oncology Clinic' when I should have referred to a 'Medical Oncology Clinic'!

The issue of passing on research reports to medical staff is tricky, not only for political reasons. Traditional research design seeks to avoid the danger of contaminating the data through people altering their behaviour as a result of finding out about your conclusions. Yet what is one to do when doctors press you for some 'feedback'?

In such cases, I would pass on research papers without regrets. First, as Bloor (1983) found, sociological reports on medical settings are often unintelligible or less than fascinating to medical staff. Second, if the kinds of social processes discussed have any salience, then they are unlikely to be significantly changed by doctors receiving any additional piece of information. Finally, providing one has gathered a substantial body of data prior to the release of a research report, then, should any change take place, one is in a good position to compare and contrast behaviour before and after exposure to the report in question.

However, doctors are not the only people one relates to in medical settings. Where one is engaged in work on the wards it is essential to develop a good relationship with nursing staff. Put purely negatively, nurses should not feel that you are an additional agent of medical authority. More positively, as I have already mentioned, the nursing staff can be a source of valuable insight about patient-staff relations.

We are back to the issue of how the research is presented to the people in the setting. Doctors are very much geared up to the issue of 'obtaining patient consent' as part of the design of their own research protocols. In the case of these studies, I have to admit that I fudged the issue by allowing the doctors concerned to introduce me and to obtain consent in the ways they found most comfortable. These varied in practice from a written note distributed to patients and families before they entered the consulting room to a brief statement (in the private clinic) that 'Dr Silverman is sitting in with me today if that's alright'! Nobody objected. Two doctors for the price of one is not to be sneezed at. Eyebrows were only raised when I failed to accompany the doctor during his physical examination of the patient.

I think I would avoid such deceptions in future. However, contact with patients and their families need not be restricted to the clinic. The interview study allowed some feedback (at a late stage) about our findings. Visits to parents' groups for heart and diabetic patients proved a useful exercise, at least for us, encouraging us to eliminate some jargon and to focus on the practical implications of what we had been saying.

Two final observations: first, it is a truism of participant-observation fieldwork that researchers should be sensitive to their own responses to settings. This is true in medical settings even for the apparent fly-on-the-wall researcher sitting behind a notebook. For instance, at the private clinic, it was when I began to reflect on why I was standing up and shaking hands with each patient and why I had dressed, unusually for me, in a business suit, that the power of its ceremonial order first struck me. Second, it will be noticed that the studies reported here have involved a very wide range of medical settings. This was stimulating practically and analytically. But how legitimate is it to hop around from one setting to the next? May it not encourage an instrumental attitude towards research (the next-paper-on-the-C.V.syndrome)? I still get invitations to address parents' heart groups or Down's Syndrome groups many years after I have left that area. What are the responsibilities of the researcher?

I
THE CLINICAL SITE

In many ways, the twentieth century may be seen as the era in which the modalities of language use became a central cultural concern, extending from literature and philosophy to sociology and anthropology. This 'linguistic turn' had many favourable consequences for the social sciences, replacing a somewhat empty positivism of 'variable analysis' with closer attention to the observation of everyday settings and to the formal structures through which they were constructed.

Like most 'breakthroughs', the new-found emphasis on language also had its drawbacks. To what extent could a discourse analysis, based on conversational 'interpretations' and 'interruptions' (Silverman and Torode, 1980), handle the institutional context of talk? Again, how far could the sequential organization of talk, discovered by conversation analysis (Sacks, Schegloff and Jefferson, 1974), provide an all-inclusive model for anything more than ordinary conversation? In particular, was 'social structure' to be treated as nothing more than participants' 'sense of social structure' and any appeal to 'structural' factors to be regarded as naively reductionist?

Now, of course, a recognition of the context-boundedness of accounts had always been central to one of these new tendencies: ethnomethodology. It had little difficulty in acknowledging, for instance, that scientists' discourse was situationally specific to the laboratory (Lynch, 1984) or that descriptions were constructed for particular audiences (Gubrium et al., 1982). Rather more troubling were suggestions that 'access to the procedures of talk is asymmetrically distributed' and related to 'a low structural position' (Molotch and Boden, 1985:285) or that non-discursive phenomena, like wage payment systems, constituted a silent background to talk, being particularly relevant to what was not talked about (Clegg, 1975).

What consequences should this have for a research study based on data drawn from naturally-occurring clinic talk? The position I take here is guided by two assumptions. First, there is a need to understand the context of talk as provided by a particular institutional setting. Here I can do no better than quote Manning's perceptive comments:

The fundamental problem in pragmatics ...: how does one understand

talk's context, things unstated but assumed in the course of speech? ...
The doctor-patient relationship is a socially sanctioned, institutionalized
encounter governed by mini-rituals of opening and closing, by a logic of
information exchange, by time, place and task constraints, and by setting
specific diagnostic aims. It is not, in short, a telephone conversation, the
locus classicus of CA's *aperçus*. (Manning, 1986)

My second point develops out of the first. If analysis must be
concerned with the setting-specific factors from which the talk
emerges, it cannot *reduce* that talk to a mere product of those factors.
I have pointed out elsewhere the minefield that Waitzkin (1979), for
instance, creates when he attempts to explain a few fragments of clinic
talk as the simple determinations of economic structures (Silverman,
1985: Ch.9). Context provides the space or site in which people
interact; it constrains but it does not determine their behaviour.
Indeed, people may make strategic use of their knowledge of
constraints such as time (see Bourdieu, 1977).

One response to these arguments would be to re-define
conversational analysis to focus on the varieties of institutional
conduct. A fine example of this response, geared to a clinical context,
is provided by Fisher (1984). She focuses on how doctor-patient talk is
shaped by medical control of turn-allocation and by a three-part
sequential organization of initiation-response and comment. She
finds that 'comment' sequences are used by doctors to correct and
assess patients' talk, while patients comment mainly through 'back-
channel' talk and overlaps. Fisher's work exemplifies a fruitful,
context-sensitive application of conversation analysis. Later on in this
book, particularly in Chapter Ten, I attempt such an application in
the context of what I call 'charge-rebuttal' sequences in a diabetic
clinic.

In this section of the book, however, my concern is with rather more
traditional sociological issues. My aim is to highlight the varieties of
setting in which clinic talk occurs and to show the variability across
settings. This closely follows Freidson's rejection of a single model of
medical work:

The question is, how stable and complete is the professional's role in the
varied circumstances of practice and if it is not entirely stable, which
elements vary and which do not. (Freidson, 1970:18)

The impact of variation in the 'circumstances of practice' has also
animated such studies as Strong's (1979b) account of ceremonial
orders in the clinic, Calnan's (1984) discussion of the varied
importance of clinical uncertainty in doctor-patient relations and
Davis's (1982) study of the relation between medical work and clinic
task and clientele. In a more general sense, I appeal to the later

Foucault's recognition of the non-discursive conditions of knowledge — for instance the role of institutional sites, professional statuses, trained capacities and technologies (see the discussions of Foucault's work by Dreyfus and Rabinow, 1982 and Cousins and Husain, 1983).

The notion of 'site' is central to this analysis. It was first developed for the analysis of the clinic date by one of my co-workers, Robert Hilliard. It is used less as a refined theoretical concept and more as a way of sifting data from the clinics. Sometimes it is used in a purely territorial sense — for instance the impact on parents of carrying out examinations of children at the desk, couch or in a side-room or the consequences of the organization of space in private, compared to NHS, clinics.

Elsewhere, especially in the next two chapters, site refers to time-related factors (particularly the previous medical career of the patient) and to forms of clinical practice in the context of medical technologies (in particular, the disposal that ordinarily follows in cases of a particular kind). Mobilizing our longitudinal and comparative data, I attempt to show how 'site' explains significant variation in doctor-patient relations. To illustrate how we used the notion of site, I have included in an appendix a schematic working paper prepared by Robert Hilliard.

Inevitably, I must concede that, in highlighting situational factors, I have drawn tacitly on everyday knowledge about forms of talk and what they mean. Thus, if readers are able to detect the patterns in talk which I depict, this will be because we are using the same commonsense resources. This could potentially be disabling if one's interest were in topicalizing these resources for systematic analysis. I would merely argue that, if I can demonstrate crude variability between sites, this is something of importance which is relevant both to more refined accounts of conversational forms and to clinical practice.

2
Decision-Making Discourse: Part 1

Only relatively infrequently do we find that sociology's conventional wisdoms accord with a popularly-based consensus or even approximate the position of significant interest groups. Grand theory (whether Parsonian or Althusserian) is an obvious example of this lack of fit. But the same holds for respectable empirical studies. Looking at examples of the latter, the affluent worker debate may have obsessed British sociology in the 1960s but it hardly rang any bells in the popular imagination or shed any impact on practical politics, apart from being in tune, for a while, with revisionist social-democratic theories. Bernstein's work on linguistic codes and his later analyses of the social organization of the 'open' classroom were certainly read by policy-makers but proved to have too awkward implications to be integrated into popular debate or administrative decision-making.

However, the recent discussion of patients' rights in health services, growing out of decades of sharp but unfocused lay complaints about the professional practices of doctors, seems at last to offer an opportunity for a convergence between the versions of reality held by sociologists and by significant interest groups. For over a decade, medical sociologists have been trumpeting about 'professional dominance'. Now, at last, the beginnings of a movement for 'patient power' seems to hold out a prospect of a sociological diagnosis being accepted and of remedial action being undertaken.

As Wiener et al. (1980) have pointed out, the debate about 'patient power' is coming from all directions. They write that:

> The awareness that patients need to have more of a say in the medical decisions that are going to affect their lives has surfaced in discussions ranging from 'informed consent' to 'access to medical records' to 'the nurse's role as a "patient advocate" '. Previous acceptance of the medical expert-lay person relationship has been translated, in today's language, into *'power imbalance'* ... To a large extent, the patient-power movement is part of the general *consumer movement*. (30–31, my emphasis)

Unfortunately, a congruence between lay and sociological accounts of medicine is no guarantee of their correctness. A theme of this chapter echoes that raised in the sub-title of Wiener's paper; entitled 'Patient Power', it is sub-titled 'Complex Issues Need Complex Answers'.

Professional Dominance

Let us begin by briefly looking at accounts of medical dominance. A broad spectrum of opinion from the political centre (Freidson) to the Marxist left (Navarro) agrees in its critique of Parsons' account of the supposedly consensual basis of medical encounters. Freidson (1970) has forcefully shown the extent to which professionalism is less an exercise in shared values than a concealed power-play. In many situations, he argues, doctors do not need to persuade their patients. They rely instead on their control of access to desired services (certificates, medicines, operations) and on their tacit appeal to the patient's 'faith' in their knowledge and competence. Additionally, according to Freidson, they manipulate their client's apparent freedom of choice to 'go elsewhere' or to reject advice in order to 'put the burden of compliance on the client and to avoid the burden of having to persuade the client that compliance is in his interest' (1970 : 120).

This picture of manipulation seems to be supported by a range of empirical studies spanning two decades. As early as 1963, Davis was pointing out that genuine clinical uncertainty was only one of many factors which prevented patients receiving information. His study of child polio victims revealed that parents were kept in the dark long after the prognosis was quite clear. The doctors justified their secrecy by arguing that it was 'better for parents to find out themselves in a natural sort of way'. The real gain, however, he suggests, was made by the doctors themselves for, by failing to reveal 'bad news', they avoided unpleasant 'scenes' with distraught parents.

We would expect that information-control would be associated with control over decision-making and, indeed, professional control over medical disposals has been well documented in Bloor's work on Ear, Nose and Throat (ENT) clinics (Bloor, 1976a, 1976b). Bloor shows that doctors in these clinics employed three kinds of working practices or 'routines': (1) search procedures, used to discover signs and symptoms whose significance was hidden from parents; (2) decision rules about the implications of these signs and symptoms for diagnosis and disposal, and (3) modes of clinic organization governing access to the clinic, seating arrangements and access to data. In turn, these routines had two functions. First, they expressed or 'embodied' the doctor's claim to professional or 'functional' autonomy. Second, they were used as a means to deny parents any potential influence through delaying tactics and determining the sense of what other doctors had said.[1]

The empirical documentation of professional dominance has received a further boost from recent work in the history of medicine by

Foucault (1973). He shows vividly how the development of hospital-based medicine from the nineteenth century onwards, coupled with the vast increase in specialization and technical sophistication, created a new clinical discourse which was more than ever inaccessible to the patient. With some concealed disagreements, Jewson (1976) has taken up Foucault's argument.[2] In hospital medicine, he suggests, we witness the institutionalization of an alienating 'object-oriented medical cosmology'. This has had three main consequences: (1) the focus of medical knowledge has shifted away from the person of the patient to esoteric technical entities defined in terms of the doctor's perceptions; (2) the profusion of speculative systems has been replaced by an ongoing consensus maintained by senior members of the medical hierarchy, and (3) the eighteenth-century sick-man was granted a new role — that of 'patient':

> As such he was designated a *passive* and *uncritical* role in the consultative relationship, his main function being to *endure* and to *wait*. (Jewson, 1976 : 235)

Professional Dominance and Decision-Making

Judged by any ideal standards, say 'democracy' or 'non-distorted communication', professional dominance over health and illness appears either morally inexcusable or the predictable outcome of a system of economic exploitation. It all depends upon the writer's political position.[3] However, we must remember Wiener et al.'s (1980) point about the complexity of the issues raised by professional dominance and its apparent opposite 'patient power'. Two immediate questions arise. First, to what extent does professional dominance express realities of technical expertise which, as the Chinese are discovering, will not be wished away by political reforms or revolutions? These realities, of course, do not legitimate each and every asymmetry in medical encounters, but they do suggest that a certain inescapable asymmetry may be at the heart of the matter. The second question immediately follows. To what extent should we seek to establish more realistic standards than 'democracy' by which to assess medical encounters and, relatedly, how far is control over decision-making a serious aspect of the movement for patient power? Let us make some initial observations about these questions.

1. The asymmetry at the heart of doctor–patient relations is suggested by the legal requirement for 'informed consent'. In the United States this principle implies that:

> in proposing a therapy or a diagnostic procedure, the physician must disclose all relevant information that a reasonable person would need to make an intelligent decision about his proposal. (Wiener et al., 1980:32)

The principle itself, of course, assumes an asymmetry of knowledge. I need to be *informed* because I know less. I give my *consent* to another's proposal because he has the knowledge to make such proposals. So the law itself does not operate with an idealized assumption of equality but assumes asymmetry. The point is, naturally, obvious. As Wiener et al. later note:

> it is ridiculous to deny that even with the best patient education there still remains in the physician–patient relationship an unequal distribution of knowledge. (p. 36)

This basic inequality is the necessary backdrop to the realizability of any proposals for 'patient power'. Furthermore, recent technological developments have heightened the doctor–patient knowledge gap. As Wiener et al. point out, these developments are stretching out the trajectories of many chronic illnesses, thereby making decisions about treatment much more complex. They continue:

> Second, technology (including drugs and machines) has produced options that did not exist before. What technology is to be used? How? When? Who decides? Intricate technology requires specialized knowledge and has led to a proliferation of experts. (p. 33)

In such a context, where any one physician is often stretched to the limits of his knowledge, the scope for patient decision-making is minimalized. Any realistic proposals for modifying professional dominance over decision-making must, therefore, recognize the knowledge explosion which is placing many professionals in the role of a layman confronting experts on the borderline of his own knowledge.

2. It is also important to avoid making the assumption that all patients want, or should want, to be partners in decision-making. Wiener et al. cite an anecdote about a patient who complained about a doctor who *agreed* to her proposal that minor surgery should be performed in his office rather than in the hospital. The patient's complaint was: 'He's the doctor. Why was he so quick to change his mind?' (p. 35).

The very jokiness of this story suggests that the patient concerned was being unreasonable. However, we see an altogether more serious instance of lay acceptance of medical decision-making in the treatment of children with serious congenital heart disease. Here the situation is complicated by the fact that professional and layman are deciding the fate of a third party, a child. Children are blessed with an elevated moral status ('innocence') but are held to lack the theoretic capacity to decide their own fate. Normally, that is decided by their parents. But imagine the situation where a wrong decision can mean the death of a child. Understandably, many doctors at our PCU feel that parents do not want to be left alone to play God with their child's fate. So, usually, they will offer heavily loaded 'advice' to parents about which treatment option they themselves recommend.[4] Generally, this advice will be gratefully received and accepted by parents who are thereby partly freed from the moral consequences of having to make a decision which might turn out to mean the death of their child. Parents do their duty by bringing their child for treatment to the people best placed to decide (doctors at a reputable hospital) and by nursing the child at home and caring for him/her in hospital.[5]

Two examples drawn from out-patient consultations readily illustrate this common parental aversion to decision-making. Both children are diagnosed as having a moderately serious but remediable condition (tetralogy of Fallot). The initial instance is drawn from the first out-patient visit of a sixteen-day-old girl. The baby is clearly blue. She is accompanied by both parents and a nurse from the Maternity Hospital where she is still a patient. The doctor has offered a tentative diagnosis and suggested that the baby be admitted immediately for catheterization and assessment. The baby's father has just asked about the nature and risks of corrective surgery and the doctor has answered:

> (Transcript 3:3)
> F: Mm. Well that's all we can do. I mean we gotta leave it in your hands anyway. Is it common . . . or what?

Very similar sentiments are expressed by a parent in a second example. This time the child who is eighteen-months old is asymptomatic. Once again, there has been a lengthy discussion of the prognosis although the doctor does not propose to admit the child for catheterization.

> (Transcript 26:4)
> F: Well we'll certainly be guided by you.

Especially at these early encounters, parents struggle to get some hold on an area which is initially fairly incomprehensible to them. It is very difficult for them to take in all the information offered to them, let alone to make a decision. Nonetheless, they display their 'responsible' parenthood by (1) bringing an obviously well-cared for child to the consultation; (2) behaving towards him/her in a patently caring way during the consultation; (3) meeting and, sometimes, anticipating doctors' instructions regarding the preparation of their child for examination (e.g. quietening, undressing him/her, etc.); (4) answering doctors' questions in a way which reveals their close attention to their child and to any drug regime determined by the doctor; (5) asking 'sensible' questions about diagnosis and prognosis.[6] Even though parents will not really take the decision, the question and answer session does important moral work both by expressing their proper concern for their child's fate and by reassuring themselves that the doctors do indeed seem to display competence and authority.

A second out-patients consultation for the latter child, now aged almost two, expands on the father's earlier expressed need for 'guidance'. Responding to a researcher's comment on his child's 'liveliness', given while the doctor is temporarily out of the room, the father comments:

> (Transcript 21:2)
> F: I mean in the past sort of doctors have um brought up the point of having to operate on er sort of thing. The trouble is I wouldn't like to 'ave to make the decision. I mean. You know, it's very hard to make, you know, an unemotional decision because you think, oh I don't wanna see er cut open for that. I don't know, I think we'll 'ave to sort of leave it in the hands of the specialists, as it were, because obviously they can make an objective decision whereas ours is coloured by our feelings towards S. (the child's name), as it were.

It transpires later that he has mistaken the researcher for a doctor (a common feature, it would appear, in such research). Subsequently, however, after the real doctor has returned, a long period of questioning about later possible treatment is followed by a repetition of the theme of 'objective' decisions:

> (Transcript 21:4)
> F: As I was saying, you can't actually understand.[7] You know, to be honest, I hate the idea of an operation but I would obviously leave it in the hands of someone who could make an objective decision, i.e. yourself or one of your colleagues.

Still later, he returns to the same phrase about objectivity in the context of his own perceived incapacity to judge:

> (Transcript 21:6)
> F: Yeah, well I mean, I'd be quite prepared to leave it in the hands of the experts who can make an objective decision. Because obviously, you know, I mean, I can't assess her.

It would, of course, be wrong to assume that an announced lack of preparedness to engage in decision-making necessarily reflects an unalterable reality of incompetence or an inbuilt unwillingness to make decisions. It is possible that we are witnessing here a parallel with the well-documented phenomenon of the 'deferential' voter who defers to his betters as a matter of faith. Alternatively, it might be suggested that parents withdraw from the decision-making process, in order to be better able to criticize after the work. A parallel here would be trade unions' lack of sympathy for moves towards appointing workers' representatives on the Boards of industrial corporations.

With only one or two examples of the kind of explicit statements used above, it is not possible to refute such alternative explanations. Nevertheless, the transcripts do suggest that it is very hard to read the parents' actions as either 'false consciousness' or deliberate strategic behaviour. It is more convincing to argue that they seem to reflect a rational response to a situation which is totally outside their knowledge or experience and which involves choices with grave implications for the life of a loved child. It is less a case of blind faith than a recognition that, in terms of points of referral, they have reached the end of the road. They appear to have no alternative but to accept what they are told by professionals whose answers seem to demonstrate their knowledge and experience. At other stages of their child's career, as I will later show, things may look very different. At this early stage, any demand for 'democracy' looks misplaced: at best, it would be an example of 'conceptual puzzlement'.[8]

3. If professional dominance over decision-making sometimes reflects a realistically based consensus between doctor and parent which assigns the latter to a largely passive role, much of the critique earlier noted would seem to fall away. However, this only happens if we assume that medical consultations are exclusively concerned with diagnoses which lead to disposals. Fortunately, many doctors now accept that medical encounters also involve such issues as the transmission of information and the relief of anxieties. However, doctors do not always recognize that the information-flow is two-way and that patients often want to convey their own concerns and experiences as well as to learn clinical diagnoses and prognoses. Research at the PCU indicates that a particular concern for parents at the early stages is the nursing at home of a sick child. It is very difficult for mothers to know whether a baby is sick or 'difficult' and accordingly whether any special measures should be employed.

Take the case of an asymptomatic baby with a possible moderate-sized hole in the heart (ventricular–septal defect or VSD). At the first out-patient visit, after a follow-up appointment is arranged, the mother explores the issue of the child's likely 'normality'. She then raises a crucial problem that arises for her in nursing the child when he finally leaves the Maternity Hospital:

> (Transcript 70:5)
> M: When I get him / home
> D: / Mm
> M: What sort of signs should I be looking for?

One month later, at a second consultation, she explores her problems in feeding her baby at home:

(Transcript 67:2–3)
1. D: Right. So he's feeding well?
2. M: Well, feeding often.
3. D: Feeding often. / There's
4. M: /(   )
5. D: There's no need to be too rigid about it
6. M: No, it just kills me that's all, every two hours in the night. Is it more difficult to feed them with a hole in the heart?

These brief extracts suggest that, at least in the early stages of the career of a child with congenital heart disease, participation in decision-making is not at issue. Nonetheless, parents do want to play a part in the consultation, particularly by raising issues connected with the home-nursing of their child in the context of the information they receive about the medical diagnosis and management-plan. 'Patient power' would here refer to the right to be informed and to be able to get answers to practical problems. Consequently, we cannot say that a one-sided decision-making process is 'undemocratic' or an example of 'distorted' communication. Distorted communication only becomes an issue where one party illegitimately attempts to silence debate by an appeal to unnegotiated, naturalized 'realities' (Habermas, 1970). Here we might detect its presence by a consultation which limited itself to purely clinical matters and offered no scope for parents to raise and to talk through their problems in coping with a sick child. 'Professional dominance' and its presumed antithesis 'patient power' cannot then be measured by the presence or absence of 'democratic' decision-making forms. Certainly, in some consultations, especially at later stages of a medical career or in cases of handicap requiring social as much as clinical judgments, control of decision-making is a fair index of patient power. Elsewhere, however, we should look to the varied needs of the parent or patient and the extent to which they are accommodated within the routines of the consultation — and sometimes *outside* those routines.

Limits to Professional Dominance
Shifting the focus away from decision-making towards broader social issues does not immediately minimize the applicability of a model of professional dominance. Strong (1979b) observes that clinic business centres around the diagnosis and communication of medically defined 'conditions'. He goes on:

> The vague and circuitous nature of everyday talk about illness had no place here, nor could there normally be any mention of the ways in which that particular illness had a meaning in parents lives. How they felt about their child, the practical problems of its condition, their ups and downs . . . were normally excluded. The transaction was rapid, focused and, above all, impersonal. (p.152)

Strong notes that this concentration on medical matters was a production of the constraints of time and of an interview setting with a hidden agenda. The model of professional dominance thereby re-asserts itself even if we no longer exclusively focus on decision-making.

Moreover, we cannot even assume that a more socially-oriented encounter is itself a guarantee that the parties are on more equal terms. I show in Chapter Six that a move into social territory may, in certain circumstances, be a strategic ploy used by medical staff to produce a demedicalized model of a child and hence to preclude tests and operations which they do not favour.

The picture is, however, not quite so one-sided. For instance, the transcript we last examined shows a broadening out of the consultation into precisely 'the practical problems of (the child's) condition' which Strong has suggested is 'normally excluded'. It is only fair to note, however, that this broadening of the agenda normally arises, as here, as a result of *parental* interventions (the question in Transcript 70:5, the comment 'feeding often' at Utterance 2, Transcript 67:2–3).

Nonetheless, this example and others that will be introduced later suggest that constraints may not only operate in one direction i.e. in favour of professional dominance. In short, we need to look at the kind of constraints which limit the salience of purely medical agendas. I will call two such constraints 'bureaucratic forms' and 'parent resources'.

Bureaucratic Forms
Strong (1979b) has argued powerfully that NHS consultations, although focused and impersonal, are structured by an appeal to reason and politeness. Doctors portrayed those present: 'As allies who had come together in a common cause. Decisions were not imposed but discussed' (p.100).

Strong refers to this body of interpretive work as a 'bureaucratic' role-format. Unlike the 'charity' format that he observed in American public hospitals, degradation ceremonies and other lesser kinds of 'character-work' were not a feature of the NHS consultations. Although parents were expected to have faith in the staff's ultimate competence and authority, they were not cast as passive spectators. Strong found that doctors portrayed parents as moral, rational and intelligent. Parents were treated, therefore, as people with whom a rational discussion about the condition and its treatment could take place. Parents were addressed as theoretic actors, able to understand choices and able to be persuaded by evidence — once they knew the facts.

Strong's work is concerned with the 'ceremonial order' of the clinic, the maintenance of the surface appearances of an encounter. However, it is not permissible to deny the relevance of these surface appearances simply by appealing to a deeper and hence more 'real' level of medical encounter e.g. professional dominance. First, our observation of more than 1000 out-patient encounters wholly accords with Strong's findings about the appeal to reason and politeness. Second, such appearances are treated as real by the participants. Where a doctor steps beyond their bounds, that step will become in Garfinkel's immortal phrase 'observable—reportable' and sanctionable. For instance:

> (Transcript NB1 1/10/80 Patient 1)
> [*Baby is accompanied by father, the examination has just been completed*]
> D: Where's your wife?
> F: At home. Why?

It is only necessary to note that doctors' questions about the child's condition or development never elicit a question from a parent about why they are being asked. Doctors are just assumed to have good reasons for such questions. Here, however, a question about the absence of a wife has no apparent grounding in matters which doctors have in hand. Moreover, it might infringe the politeness rule which implies that parents' home circumstances are either not topicalized or topicalized very gingerly. For example:

> (Transcript 30:3)
> [*Disposal statement is being completed. Mother is a single parent*]
> D: OK. We'll see her in six weeks. Are you managing alright at home?

Although the 'bureaucratic' role-format can co-exist with highly medicalized consultations, it nonetheless serves, as we shall see, as a constraint on medical decision-making and as a lever which parents can use to create discursive space for their matters-at-hand. For example, only a parent granted 'reason' or 'theoreticity' could sensibly ask 'What sort of signs should I be looking for?'

Parents' Resources
It is a tried and trusted sociological truism, established in studies ranging from Goffman (1968) to Crozier (1964), that even people at the foot of hierarchies of authority have certain strategic counters to play. With no attempt to be systematic at this stage, we can note a number of such counters or resources that are brought into play at the paediatric consultations we have observed. First, parents can and do draw upon their increasing familiarity with staff, medical routines, diagnoses and treatment options to satisfy themselves that all possibilities are being thoroughly explored. Although they rarely attain the competence or *esprit de corps* attributed by medical staff to parents who are themselves doctors, doctors' wives, nurses or foster-mothers, they are attributed a much increased level of competence as their child's medical career

lengthens. They do not fully enter into what Strong calls the 'collegial authority' of the team of doctors but they become relatively more equal partners.

A second strategic counter arises where medical interventions produce a poor result, especially where this goes against the balance of risks earlier stated to parents. As we shall later show, this kind of outcome or the kind of condition which concludes its treatment trajectory by the drying-up of all possibility of useful medical interventions, restores, in sad circumstances, a strategic balance to doctor–parent relations. Finally, parents can and do latch on to *competing* versions of their child's conditions offered by different referral agencies. This, however, is probably the weakest resource they possess, since the PCU stands at the end-point of the referral process and medical staff can afford to be unconcerned by or even dismissive about medical opinions generated elsewhere (say by the GP or even by a referring hospital).

At this stage, such a discussion of the limits to professional dominance is necessarily sketchy and programmatic. It is hoped that the later detailed analysis of decision-making in a range of contexts will deepen the argument. Before beginning that analysis it only remains to set out briefly the form that it will take.

Making Sense of Decisions: The Chauffeur's Model

The rationale underlying the data-analysis that follows may be set out in summary as a concern to discover the everyday routines used to organize the discussion of decisions, according to the 'site' or the encounter and by reference to a model of the parent as a chauffeur.[9] Let me briefly unpack this telescoped statement of purpose.

1. *Everyday routines:* A few years ago, Wadsworth introduced a reader instructively entitled *Studies in Everyday Medical Life* by a call for:

> More investigations that base their empirical evidence in everyday life situations . . . such studies will set out to investigate the rules, routines and procedures that doctors and patients use to organize consultations . . . '
> (Wadsworth and Robinson, 1976:11)

Three years later, in the first major fulfillment of this research programme, Strong prefaced his study of out-patient consultations by a rationale beginning from:

> the myriad ways in which doctor and patient both present their behaviour and read that of another as each attempt to make sense of and to control the situation. (Strong, 1979b:5)

A central feature of such an approach is that it draws its material from naturally-occurring medical settings and does not rely directly upon data generated by research-initiated questionnaires or interviews. The point about this is not to deny that the latter kind of material has some relevance for analytic purposes but to recognize that it gives access to a reality with its own form of social organization which is in no way competitive with what happens in the naturally occurring settings which participants report. Responses to a research interview in no way may be used analytically to do 'ironies' upon what is said or unsaid in naturally occurring settings (or, indeed, vice versa).

Such a focus on 'everyday life situations' carries with it two harsh requirements. First, the data-base should be publicly available to other researchers and, because it exists independent of any initial analysis, should be able to be reworked both by others and by the researcher herself. Ideally, this would demand a video and audio-recording. Where this is not permitted, the researcher must make do with a tape-recording or with notes written at the time. Despite the elegance of his analysis, Strong (1979b), for instance, was hampered by the lack of any recording. He was therefore usually unable to count instances of subsequently generated analytic categories.

The second requirement is that competing explanations of the data are taken seriously and that a sufficiently wide range of encounters, encompassing the variety of relevant contexts, are used to test out these explanations. What must be avoided is the merely anecdotal use of favourable examples to suit an argument. Where anecdote is coupled with mere assertion about the determinate sense to be read into a transcript, one is left with polemic rather than analysis.[10] Simple counting, where permitted by the data, can serve as a limited but simple check on the applicability of explanatory schemes (cf. Silverman, 1985, Ch.7).

2. *The 'site' of the encounter:* It is now almost a conventional wisdom that medical encounters cannot be fully understood through a single interpretive scheme which flattens out differences between settings. For instance, Freidson's critique of Parsons' account of the 'sick-role' refers to the 'varied circumstances of practice' (1970:18) and argues that:

> what is needed is specification of a set of roles corresponding to important and potentially final organized stages of the process of seeking help. (p.13)

Again, few *sociologists* would argue that such variety can be explained by reference to the psychology of patients or to the consulting styles of doctors. Indeed, what Strong (1979b) calls 'the structural context' is the primary explanatory frame.

Researchers, however, are also conscious that there are different levels of structure and that it is difficult to control for all of them in any one study. In particular, we may analytically distinguish 'macro' structures, such as national systems of health care with their attendant legal and economic forms, from 'micro' structures such as the social organization of patient careers, the social status attached to the condition concerned (e.g. clinical research interest, popular stigma etc.) and the relevance of different forms of medical technology for its assessment and treatment.

Whether the focus is macro or micro, the researcher needs to take seriously the process of interpretation through which the impact of these structures is mediated and avoid the simple determinism of variable-analysis. As Strong puts it, when talking about role-formats:

> (these are) not structures which totally determine action but are instead routinized, culturally available solutions which members 'use' to solve whatever problems they have in hand. (Strong, 1979b:13)[11]

Within the micro framework of the present research, we have to take for granted the NHS pattern of consultations with its associated legal, economic and moral forms. However, this allows us to examine systematic variance *within* this pattern.

In the context of out-patient encounters, earlier studies have revealed how consultations vary according to their place in a patient's career-trajectory. West (1976) shows how the first out-patients session for possible childhood epilepsy had a fairly rigid structure which offered little opportunity for the initiation of topics by a parent. Consequently, parents appeared very passive. At later contacts, there was much more bargaining and questioning by parents as they became more experienced in coping with and evaluating their child's epilepsy. Here, West comments:

> the doctor cannot rely solely on routine solutions to substantiate the medical definition of the situation. He has to 'work' increasingly to maintain his claim to competence. (West, 1976:26)

West notes that the strategic balance is particularly changed when treatment is unsuccessful or when the doctor is seeking to suggest a major reorganization of the child's life, for instance in terms of schooling. This accords with Strong's finding that when things 'go wrong', there is a move away from an 'easy alliance', based upon doctor's decision-making, towards a more openly democratic form.

West and Strong's work suggests that the patient's previous treatment history offers one important context for members' interpretive work. A second such context is the 'disposal' that the doctor wants to suggest or, more rarely, the parent wants to obtain. As Strong, once again, shows, a proposed immediate discharge is associated with a speedy 'search and destroy' campaign on parents' doubts. On the other hand, where the patient trajectory is drawn-out or uncertain, doctors observed by Strong used a 'step by step' approach, amplifying parental doubts slowly and indirectly and only elaborating on the prognosis if challenged.

If we combine 'previous treatment history with 'preferred disposal', we can begin to talk about what Hilliard (1981) refers to as the 'site' of the encounter (see also the appendix). We can then start to assess significant variability in the character of decision-making according to its site. For instance, if we simplify and take only two possible values for each variable, we produce the following 2 by 2 table:

TABLE 1
A Simplified Model of the 'Sites' of an Out-Patient Consultation

| | | Preferred Disposal | |
		Discharge	Treatment
Previous Treatment History	None (first out-patients)	(1)	(2)
	Post-operative follow-up	(3)	(4)

It is easy to predict that the character of decision-making talk will vary significantly from a first out-patients' leading to a discharge (cell 1), to a post-operative follow-up which reveals the need for further treatment (cell 4). The task of this model is to map such variance.

3. *The chauffeur's model:* In order to get some initial hold upon the data, I searched for an analogy that seemed appropriate to the circumstances of decision-making talk at paediatric out-patients' consultation. The first thing to be borne in mind was that, unusually for medical encounters, both doctor and lay-person were directing their talk at a third party who, while always present, rarely played any role in talk about disposals.[12]

There is a parallel here, it seemed, with what happens when a motorist takes a car to a garage workshop. Although one may assume that a parent's presumed care for a child has an altogether deeper moral and emotional basis than a motorist's care for a car, both forms of caring-relationship, at hospital or workshop, are organized between outsiders for a silent third party (although of course, the child may cry and the car-engine make troubling noises).[13]

The question now arises: even if this is a possible analogy, what work will it do? I began to see the power of this analogy when I reflected that motorists bring cars to the workshop in two major types of situation. Either they believe that there is something wrong with their car or they require the car to be given a 'service'. In the first case, they are expecting the garage to repair a fault; in the second case, they are expecting only routine maintenance work to be done.

The significance of the initial referral situation is that, in the light of it, the motorist will respond differently to what the garage decides to do. For instance, if there is a fault recognized by the motorist and the garage-owner proposes to undertake a minor repair or a test, then we would hardly expect the motorist even to be consulted or, if consulted, to dissent. On the other hand, if a car is brought in for servicing, with no apparent fault, and the garage-owner proposes further tests or repairs, then we would expect the matter to be fully discussed. In both cases, where repairs are likely to be costly and/or may not be successful, we would also expect consultation to take place.

Although the matter is complicated by the lack of a fee-for-service payment system in the NHS consultations observed, there are clear parallels between decision-making talk in garage and clinic settings. All we need to do is replace 'fault' with 'symptoms' and 'no fault' with 'asymptomatic'. Concretely, we would here be talking about children who are referred because they are recognizably blue or breathless ('fault') or because a murmur is heard by a GP or some other referral agency ('no fault', as far as the parent can see). If we distinguish three possible disposals,[14] 'discharge', 'test' (usually catheterization) and 'surgery', we can predict that the character of decision-making talk will vary significantly according to whether the child/car is defined by its parent/owner as running well/faulty (see Table 2).

TABLE 2
Decision-Making Talk, Referral Status and Preferred Disposal:
A Simplified Scheme

Doctor's Preferred Disposal	Referral Status	
	Faulty	Running Well
Discharge	'Search and destroy' if perceived status still maintained by 'owner'	Non problematic
Test	Non-problematic: owner's assent presumed	Problematic need to change perceived status
Repairs	Non-problematic if repairs are cheap or non-risky	Highly problematic: probably not discussed until after test

Table 2 is simplified because it treats a parent–child relationship in the same way as a motorist–car relationship. Particularly relevant for our purpose is the fact that parents do not generally claim ownership of their child in the same way as the motorist claims ownership of his car. Consequently, the motorist may feel perfectly free to care or not to care for his car, and if it looks worn out, to sell it or even 'write it off'. Conversely, parents display sensitivity to moral obligations to care for their children: in both clinics and research interviews parents are keen to display their moral adequacy in this regard (Voysey, 1975; Baruch, 1981).

Furthermore, write-off decisions, while not unknown, may leave parents and doctors open to legal action. It follows that a better analogy of the parent–child relationship may be that of a chauffeur and car. Unlike owners, chauffeurs do not have the right to dispose of the car as they see fit. Nonetheless, they have an obligation to care for it and to display it looking its best. Consequently, in the rest of this analysis I will use a 'chauffeur's model' of the parental role and see how far we can get with it.

It is also worth considering three kinds of rarer cases excluded from this analysis: (1) where the garage-owner/doctor concludes that, while there is a significant fault, there is nothing further that can be done; (2) where the garage/hospital may have already carried out an ineffective repair and (3) where there is a significant fault but this pales into insignificance in view of the overall, irreparable faulty construction of the car/child.

Each of these additional cases is interesting because it modifies the normal structures of professional dominance present in the more routine situations presented in Table 2. In cases 1 and 2, the relation between professional and parent becomes more equal, either because there is no resource the professional can offer or because his competence is threatened by an earlier mistake. Case 3, which approximates to Down's Syndrome children and, ironically, to cars which a garage may recommend to be written-off, may generate discussions expressing sympathy (for having been sold 'a dud one') and directing the parent/motorist to count their other blessings (see Chapter Six).

In the discussion that follows, these three additional 'sites' of the encounter will be investigated, together with the three disposal situations set out in Table 2. It will be recalled, however, that the 'site' of the encounter encompasses both the preferred disposal and the previous treatment history (Table 1). In turn, various conditions will have typical career trajectories. So a patient's place on a particular career trajectory will be reflected at any one consultation in the past treatment history and preferred disposal.

Decision-Making: The Variables

We are now in a position to set out the main argument and to map out its implications in terms of independent and dependent variables. This can be done schematically as follows:

1. The 'site' of the consultation is constituted by the previous treatment history and the doctor's preferred disposal. Different conditions have particular career trajectories associated with the past (treatment history), present and future (preferred disposal).

    1.1 The site of the consultation does *not* determine what will happen; it maps out a field of possibilities, each of which may be actualized.

    1.2 These possibilities of action apply to both doctors and parents.

    1.3 Doctors will associate each site with certain appropriate responses i.e. normal-things-to-be-done-at-this-stage. They will also attribute a growing level of technical competence to parents as the career trajectory unfolds, particularly after the first in-patient stay (see the appendix).

    1.4 Parents will generally have indeed gained in technical competence as their child's career progresses. The site of the consultation will also provide them with the possibility of more active decision-making where a choice is to be made about invasive treatments involving significant risks to life or where previous interventions have been unsuccessful (see the earlier discussion of parent resources).

2. Courses of action actually adopted from the field of possibilities constituted by the site of the consultation will depend upon a number of intervening variables.

    2.1 Doctors and parents will both attend to whether the child is symptomatic i.e. whether the condition is 'patent' (see the appendix). The patency of the condition will shape the way the doctor proposes disposals and will influence the parents' response, especially where invasive treatments are involved (see the earlier discussion of the car-owners' model).

    2.2 The data available to the doctor (X-ray, ECG, height and weight data), the physical examination and the current referral letter, may reshape the patient's career trajectory e.g. it may move from a smoothly flowing case of normal-things-to-be-done-at-this-stage back to special measures.[15]

    2.3 Parents may or may not intervene in the consultation to express doubts or to show anxiety about the diagnosis or preferred disposal. In turn, the doctor will respond according to the options implied by 1.3 and 2.1. Depending upon the extent to which expressed doubts and anxieties persist, the doctor may postpone or revise his preferred disposal.

3. The site of the consultation, as modified by the intervening variables 2.1 to 2.3, will shape the form of the consultation. The dependent variable is, therefore, the character of decision-making that occurs. This arises in three ideal-typical forms (cf. note 4).

    3.1 Decision-making where only the most formal reference is made to parents' wishes and consent or where no such reference is made ('doctor's decision-making').

3.2 Decision-making involving the active 'selling' of a preferred disposal to parents or the use of delaying tactics ('persuasion').

3.3 Decision-making based on joint assessment of the opportunity-cost of different disposals ('democracy').

The relationship between these variables may be represented schematically as in Figure 1.

FIGURE 1
Decision-Making: The Variables

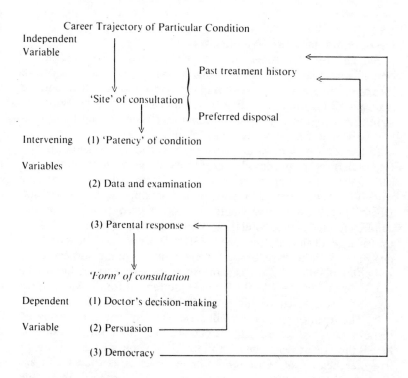

It will be noted that 'feed-back' arrows have been indicated between all three sets of variables. This recognizes that any 'intervening' variable may change a patient's career trajectory and that the 'form' of the consultation can act back on the intervening variables (especially 'parental response') and, thereby, on the career trajectory. The 'feed-back' is a further reminder that the variables should *not* be viewed as structural determinants of action but as providing a modifiable field of possibilities for action. This notion of a strategic field, influenced both by the chronology of sites and by mutual response to the other's tactics is foreshadowed in Bourdieu's (1977) important discussion of the dialectical relation between objective structures and actor's improvisations. As he puts it:

> the fact that there is no 'choice' that cannot be accounted for, retrospectively at least, does not imply that such practice is perfectly predictable ... the agents ... find in the relative predictability and unpredictability of the possible ripostes the opportunity to put their strategies to work ... the agents remain in command of the *interval* between the obligatory moments and can therefore act on their opponents by playing with the *tempo* of the exchange. (1977:15)

Decision-Making: The Hypotheses

It has already been suggested that the 'patency' of a condition is centrally related to decision-making discourse. As was shown from the chauffeur's model, a parent is likely to respond very differently to a suggested disposal according to whether his child is recognizably symptomatic ('faulty') or 'asymptomatic' ('running well'). Accordingly, the major hypotheses are as follows:

1. Decision-making will accord with a medical decision-making form wherever the proposed disposal 'fits' the patency of a condition. Thus a discharge of an *asymptomatic* child with an innocent murmur will normally be imposed by a doctor and not opposed by the parents. Doctor's decision-making would also be expected on asymptomatic children following successful surgery or being offered a routine follow-up for a small hole-in-the-heart (VSD). The same will be true for a decision to catheterize or perform relatively minor surgery on a *symptomatic* child.[16] In all cases, the reference to parents' wishes will be purely formal (rather like the formal requirement for the Monarch to give the Royal Assent to duly processed Acts of Parliament).

2. The form of persuasion will arise typically where the proposed disposal does *not* accord with the patency of a condition. An example here is the case of *symptomatic* children, whose purported episodes of irregular heart-beat (*arrhythmia*) cannot be substantiated and are discharged or whose parents are offered a placatory test. Again, the parents of *asymptomatic* children whom it is proposed to catheter will usually undergo some kind of selling process.

A less active form of persuasion than selling is the use of delaying tactics. These seem to arise in two kinds of circumstances. First, where active intervention (via catheter or surgery) is still elective and the child is asymptomatic, the doctor may hold it off, expecting that the subsequent greater patency of the child's condition may make the parents more amenable to intervention (cf. Bloor 1976b). Second, in the relatively unusual case of unsuccessful surgery, the normal doctor's response is to buy time by delaying further invasive interventions as long as possible.

3. Decision-making will approximate to 'democracy' usually only where surgery is likely to remain elective or where there is a choice between low-risk palliative surgery or high risk corrective surgery. The former case is typical of children with moderate-sized VSD's or children with complex anomalies. Here much will depend on the parents' sense of how the child is 'coping' with the condition. The latter case arises in those complex anomalies where there does exist a form of corrective surgery with a fairly high risk.

Two other far rarer 'sites' are associated with 'democratic' forms. As has already been noted, Down's children may be constituted as 'write-offs'. Here the 'persuasion' form will come into play via a stress on the child's apparent 'enjoyment of life'. This tends to be coupled with an unusual insistence that decision-making about both catheterization and surgery may be left to parents and the use of 'democratic' forms. Finally, at the end of the career trajectory of children with complex, uncorrectable conditions, after palliative operations have been tried, we encounter consultations where the range of surgical options has dried up. Here, as in the case of severely handicapped children studied by Davis and Strong (1976), parents meet doctors on equal ground and review together the remaining possibilities of drug therapy and of caring for the child at home.

Objections and Limits

We have almost reached the data. Before finally doing so, I must respond to some possible objections to the analytic framework already established. Thereby, I will present some of the limits that I perceive to arise in the present research enterprise. I will briefly list four points.

1. One possible objection to the analytic framework employed above is that it *already presumes* medical dominance. Instead of beginning on a *tabula rasa* of discursive symmetry, it begins from medical definitions of conditions and treatments. Consequently, it assesses decision-making from a standard already imbued with medical perceptions.

Now this kind of objection can come from two kinds of source. First, it might be generated by those Marxist critics of medical practice who are disposed to treat any aspect of a medical encounter as a surface indicator of a deep societal structure of exploitation (cf. Waitzkin, 1979). Second, however, it might also be made by students of language, like Habermas (1970) who argue that discursive symmetry is guaranteed by the very structure of language itself.[17]

My response to both these (potential) critics is the same. It would be unrealistic to fail to recognize the differential knowledge and resources of doctors and parents and not to appreciate the limits created by the interview-format assumed at out-patient consultations. I do not need to develop this point as it has already been considered earlier in the paper. I would only stress here that it makes more sense to recognize the asymmetries *necessarily* present in out-patient interviews rather than to employ decontextualized models of either ideal-speech situations or systematically-distorted communications. By being 'realistic', moreover, we are able to analyse situations where there is variance from the normal form, and to consider the basis and consequences of parental interventions which move the decision-making form away from 'doctors' decision-making'.

2. One obvious limit of the framework is that it makes the career trajectory of conditions the major independent variable. As already noted, this excludes comparative work on 'macro' factors, in particular the national system of health care, although this has already been picked up indirectly with reference to Strong's work on 'bureaucratic' role-formats. More seriously, however, it limits variability due to varying treatment practices at different hospitals.[18] There is also very little attention paid here to the impact on decision-making form of such variables as the hierarchical status of the doctor (it may well be that less senior staff are more inclined, for structural reasons, to delay finalizing decisions) and the occupational status of the patient (in particular, the different form taken by consultations with parents who themselves have some outside connection with medicine).

3. The analysis is further limited by its exclusive concentration on decision-making at out-patient consultations. We have some evidence to suggest that the post-catheter *in-patient* interview is at least as significant a setting for discussing decisions. As noted in Chapter One, we lack the data for an analysis of this setting.

4. Finally, it would be wrong to pretend that the hypotheses established above in any way preceded in time the analysis itself. However, there is an established case for allowing working hypotheses to emerge out of the data and, thereby, to 'ground' theory, in Glaser and Strauss' (1967) sense. More dangerous would be any attempt to seek out data which seemed to confirm preconceived hypotheses. Two simple defences against this have been used here. First, where several cases drawn from the same site exhibit the same form of decision-making, we can be more confident that variance is not due to chance factors. Second, some simple quantification will be attempted to test the claims made in the qualitative analysis.

Notes

1. Bloor (1976b) does, however, note variance in medical practices. The elicitation sequence can vary from a closed elicitation of symptoms whose significance is entirely

hidden from the parents to a form of open-ended questioning ('What's the trouble?') which can allow them to open up the hidden agenda of the consultation. Such variance together with doctor's attention, noted by Bloor, to the 'patency' of symptoms in making decisions about elective surgery, will be examined systematically later in this chapter.

2. While Foucault (1973) suggests that the new clinical discourse replaced the old classification of disease 'types' with a conception of an 'individual's' illness, Jewson (1976) argues the other way round. For him, it is the *old* discourse which is 'subject-orientated', while the new discourse is 'object-orientated' i.e. concerned simply with the data of the body.

3. Campbell and Duff (1979) is an example of the moral position, Navarro (1976) an example of the economic position.

4. This is a big generalization. As we will see later, there is great variability in the character of decision-making. The 'advice' or persuasion mode mentioned here as at the middle of a continuum, ranging from open democracy, where parents are left free to choose, to the most formal kind of consent, based entirely on medical decision-making. This continuum is illustrated below:

FIGURE 2
Modes of Decision-Making

| Medical | 'Persuasion' | 'Democracy' |
| decision-making | | |

5. For an account of parenting as moral activity see Baruch (1981) and Voysey (1975).

6. Sometimes these various duties conflict, thereby producing role-conflict for the parent and (conceded) moral disapproval from the doctor. For instance, the child may be examined on a couch in a side-room. Is it proper for one or both parents to accompany the child? In one case we have observed a mother torn between attending to the consultant's diagnosis offered at the desk and quietening her crying baby who was still being examined by other doctors on the couch. Eventually, the baby was picked up by a doctor and returned to its mother. When the parents left, the doctors engaged in lighthearted but disapproving remarks about the mother's presumed lack of competence! This reveals how the concept of 'site' may have a purely territorial reference (see the appendix).

7. The father's lack of understanding is probably related to the contradiction between his daughter's 'healthy' appearance and the serious diagnosis being offered. I will later take up the issue of the relation between the 'patency' of a condition and the character of decision-making.

8. Wittgenstein used this term when attempts were made to take a word out of the language-games in which it had its home and to apply it, indiscriminately, like a coin which has the same value in any transaction.

9. It should be noted that I am at best only indirectly concerned with an analysis of the decision-making rules actually employed by doctors (for an example of this see Bloor 1976a). My concern here, as in Chapter Six, is with the social organization of the discourses in which decisions are announced, disputed or confirmed.

10. This is the sense I have when reading work such as Waitzkin (1979) which, despite its provocative theoretical analysis, uses transcripts in a purely anecdotal way.

11. My only quarrel with Strong here is that I would refer to culturally and *situationally* available solutions.

12. For an important exception concerning teenage children attending a hare-lip/cleft palate clinic see Chapter Seven.

13. There is a further related parallel here with medical encounters. Just as the parent will be presented with a consent form authorizing surgery so the motorist will need to sign in advance an authorization which will allow the garage to undertake certain specified work but which also may or may not allow the garage to undertake repairs if faults should be discovered during work on the car.

14. I have deliberately excluded routine follow-ups because the analogy with the garage begins to look awkward here. In fact, I would expect routine follow-ups to produce decision-making talk similar to that predicted in the 'discharge' cell.

15. It must also be borne in mind that there is often great variability between the career trajectories of patients, with similar conditions, depending partly upon the intervening variables discussed here.

16. Here, for purposes of simplicity, we are not taking account of the overall career trajectory associated with particular conditions. The later analysis will look at the impact of 'patency' across a range of conditions.

17. This line of criticism has a parallel with the position Torode and I take in an earlier book (Silverman and Torode, 1980). It will be seen here that I take a much more *contextual* view of discourse than that proposed in that book.

18. Such a comparative analysis is attempted in Chapter Five.

3
Decision-Making Discourse:
Part 2

Introduction

This chapter documents the variability in doctor–parent interaction according to factors specific to how the parties concerned define the child/patient's condition. This process of definition occurs within a number of general constraints at which I have only so far hinted.

The Paediatric Cardiology Unit (PCU) practises a form of 'high-technology' medicine. It is helpful to differentiate the particular features of such a setting, and to look at the several ways in which these imposed constraints upon discourse. These particular features are:

1. Specialist medicine. Patients are referred to a consultant cardiologist, at a hospital for diseases of the chest and heart. In two ways, this limits the ability of families to affect the structure of the consultation. First, they do not initiate the consultation by bringing a problem to the doctor's attention, and second, doctors may invoke the specialist character of the clinic to exclude discussion of concerns raised by the parents.

2. The treatment is centrally located in a London teaching hospital. This implies that there is no continuing relationship between the family and the hospital and its personnel over a range of routine and non-routine medical contingencies. There is no close contact between the hospital and other agencies dealing with the child's care: clinics, GPs etc. Other agencies often leave families with a confusion of information and expectations which are easily overridden but less commonly explored at the apex of the referral network.

3. Sophisticated medical procedures. Consultations involve a wide range of technical diagnostic aids and a variety of specialist medical and paramedical personnel. The relevance of these, apart from their general intimidating character, is the ability and obligation they give to the consultant to structure the interaction. Teaching and consultation functions allow the doctors a separate, free discursive area in which discussion can take place in terms partly or entirely opaque to the family.

4. The complexity of the medical issues involved imposes an immediate barrier to lay understanding and involvement. Lay medical knowledge in the case of current paediatric cardiology may be

inappropriate and misleading. Even serious congenital heart disease is in many cases asymptomatic, making the parental equivalent of 'self-diagnosis' impossible.

5. The diseases and their treatment often involve a high risk to the child's life. As well as being a generalized constraint on open dialogue, this means that risk and seriousness tend to be expressed and defined in terms of the relevances of the hospital, this being the only available frame in which life-and-death decisions can routinely be taken.

6. The relatively high status of the unit studied and its personnel, compounding the traditional status unbalance of doctor and patient, implies an asymmetry of discursive rights. Here, cultural factors reinforce and are reinforced by the medical ones noted above.

Despite these constraints, many parents were able to equip themselves with special resources, chiefly in the form of an extension of their prior medical competences, to cope with the special situation they found themselves in. Common lay understandings of heart disease were dismantled, with the assistance of medical staff. Over the course of the child's treatment, but particularly during the first in-patient admission period, this formed the basis on which parents were able to play an increasing and genuine role in consultations. The openness of the discursive structure of consultations was seen to depend on parents' display of such competence. This display often followed the doctor's assumption and hence imputation of such competence at an appropriate (post-inpatient) stage of treatment.

Data-base

The material discussed here is taken from a limited group of consultations. Bearing in mind the danger of using only material favourable to my argument, I have limited the cases considered to three sources:

1. A random sample of seventeen cases, chosen by taking the first two cases from side B of the first tape of a randomly selected out-patient clinic.
2. A sample of six out-patient clinics within a space of a specified ten-week period (approximately sixty cases).
3. A random sample of one joint clinic held by the Unit's consultant at another hospital (twelve cases).

Where longitudinal material from consultations with the same patients could speedily be identified this has been included with the original sample.

Two factors have hindered the representativeness of this account. First, only a fraction of the material has been transcribed and the analysis reflects a bias towards previously transcribed data. Second, it is impossible to refer in a single paper, to all of the nearly 100 consultations without making a selection of certain lines and thereby missing the unfolding of an interview. Hence many consultations in the sample are not discussed here — not because they suggest contrary findings but for reasons of space.

This is balanced by a brief and admittedly crude quantitative analysis of a further random sample of 102 consultations. This is discussed in the next chapter. I also outline there the policy implications of the research.

Notation
In the following review of the data, consultations will be grouped together in order of seriousness of the diagnosis; I will begin with innocent heart murmurs and conclude with serious complex conditions. The diagnosis, together with the stage of treatment, give the 'site' of the encounter, which will be treated as the independent variable, as in Table 3 above. Before each transcript there will be given a summary of the site (independent variable), degree of patency, data and examination findings, and parental response (intervening variables) and the form of consultation (dependent variable). To avoid repetition, the following notation will be used:

Conditions (C)
1. Minor symptoms or conditions 1.1. Innocent murmurs 1.2. Heart arrhythmias 1.3 Patent ductus arteriosis
2. Less serious, self-correcting or correctable conditions 2.1. Ventricular-septal defect 2.2. Atrial-Septal defect 2.3. Pulmonary stenosis 2.4. Valvar aortic stenosis
3. Serious but correctable conditions 3.1. Tetralogy of Fallot
4. More serious, relatively uncorrectable conditions 4.1. Uni-ventricular heart 4.2. Atrial-ventricular canal defect
5. Congenital heart disease with Down's Syndrome 5.1. Tetralogy of Fallot 5.2. Atrial-ventricular canal defect

It should be emphasized that clinical typologies like this, while relevant to doctor's decision-making, often have little or no relation to the parent's perceptions. This does not at all indicate a failure of communication. Rather it arises because parents necessarily begin from the symptoms that the child presents rather than from any typology of cardiac disease. As their child's career trajectory unfolds, doctors will offer models of such typologies and their child's place on them. In addition, in-patient stays will encourage parents to generate a lay typology, offering an overall picture of the seriousness and treatment of certain conditions, while tending to preserve their child's relatively favourable position compared to perceived 'worse-off' reference groups.

Stage of Career (SC)
1. First out-patient visit 2. Second or subsequent out-patients but no in-patient stay 3. Post-cardiac catheterization or 24 hour ECG out-patients 4. Post-surgery out-patients (no further in-patient stay envisaged) 5. Post-surgery out-patients (further in-patient stay likely)

Patency (P)
1. No symptoms 2. Not blue or breathless but other non-heart related symptoms 3. Blue and/or breathless

Examination (E)
1. Confirms expected disposal 2. Changes expected disposal

Parental Response (PR)
1. Passive 2. Active

Form of Consultation (FC)
1. Doctor's decision-making 2. Persuasion 3. Democracy

Let us first look at two consultations involving children with innocent murmurs.

(Case 1, Transcript 5)
C 1.1, SC 1, P 2, E 1, PR 2, FC 1
[*Summary: Baby aged one, referred by GP*]
(5:1)
1. D: And this is John Andrews (2.0) Who is one?
2. M: He's one, he's just one.
3. D: Just one. (1.0) And the problem is?
4. M: I'm not sure. I don't know what my doctor said. (1.0). I seem to recall him saying something to the effect that he'd noticed a murmur the last couple of times he'd examined him.
5. D: Right. That's what he says in this letter.
6. M: Mm. And he just wanted to check it. He's had a succession, I don't know whether it's related, of colds, high fevers, swollen glands, and ear infections which is the reason I was concerned.
7. D: Yes. Right. I think you went to your own doctor because of these things.
8. M: Oh yes.
9. D: And he listened and heard a murmur. Which is really why you're here.

All the while, the doctor is glancing at the referral letter. This creates some apparent difficulty for the mother in finding a discursive space appropriate to the doctor's question about the 'problem'; hence utterance 4 'I'm not sure. I don't know what my doctor said'. She then states what she 'recalls' that he had said and adds in her own concerns about her child's state of health (utterance 6).

Two initial comments may be made about the opening to the

consultation. First, by utterance 9, the doctor's questioning has essentially brought the state of play back to where it began (the referral letter). Although this may be an attempt to check out the congruency between the referral letter and the mother's own perceptions, it creates, as has been suggested, a little initial difficulty for the mother. Second, however, the doctor's questions have allowed the mother to raise *her* concerns (the colds etc.). Notice that she immediately recognizes that these may not be cardiac-related matters ('I don't know whether it's related') and that the doctor refers only to the 'murmur' as the reason 'why you're here'.

Immediately after this exchange, the mother enlarges on her child's series of 'upper-respiratory infections' but reveals that he does not go blue, although he sounds 'totally congested'. For the doctor, this constitutes an asymptomatic child. Even before the examination, he is seeking to place on one side the 'non-cardiac' sides of the child's condition and to assert his *specialist* competences:

(5:2)
1. D: Yes (2.0) I think probably I'm here to deal with the heart bit, if there's anything wrong with it
2. M: Mm
3. D: I won't I won't get involved with the other business
4. M: Fine. Well I wasn't quite sure what my doctor actually meant

By now, the child has been reconstituted as an asymptomatic child with a murmur. If the examination has the expected result (ECG and chest X-ray within the normal range, examination normal), then he can be discharged. However, the medical decision-making form relies on an agreement between the child's 'wellness', as perceived by the parent, and the disposal suggested. In order not to be seen to discharge a 'sick' child, his various symptoms need to be accumulated into a 'non- heart' category.

After the examination by the consultant, the child is passed on to another doctor present:

(5:3–4)
1. D: (To other doctor) Would you like to listen? I don't think there's anything wrong with him basically.
   (To mother) He's very snuffly and his problem is his adenoids. He's got, I'm quite sure, big adenoids there. He's breathing through his mouth, he can't breath through his nose.
2. M: Yes, yes
3. D: And that's what his problems are. As far as the heart is concerned, chest X-ray, ECG, pulses and everything else are normal. The murmur is very soft. Now all children have heart murmurs

Medical decision-making can now operate because, in terms of his heart, there is nothing 'wrong with him basically . . . his problem is his adenoids'. It therefore makes entirely good sense (and does not at all infringe parental rights) to discharge the child. Moreover, the discharge disposal is taken to be so obvious an outcome that it is not even stated by either party.

The mother's concerns do, however, receive their due attention irrespective of the medical decision-making format. Despite the doctor's earlier statement of specialist competences, there is a subsequent period of discussion about the optimum timing of adenoid operations. Additionally, when the mother volunteers a question about why murmurs are not usually heard in adults, the doctor enlarges his earlier statement on the nature of 'innocent' murmurs. He concludes by neatly drawing together the prominence of the murmur with the child's other problems.

The consultation is concluded by a compliment, which, in terms of the analysis in Chapter Two, attests to the fulfilment of the chauffeur's (mother's) role:

(5:5)
1. M: OK right (1.0) Thank you very much indeed
2. D: Nice little boy
3. M: I know. Thank you. Thank you very much indeed.
4. D: OK. Bye bye.

Throughout the consultation, the doctor has established a framework in which medical decision-making comes to be recognized as the most appropriate format. Shorn of all other realities, the mother comes to accept that the proper features to attend to are: 1. Child with heart murmur 2. Referred to specialist hospital 3. Murmur found to be 'innocent' 4. Discharged.

However, this in no way means that she is unable to raise her more general concerns about her child's health nor that, when questioned further, is there any reluctance by the doctor to expand on the nature of 'innocent' murmurs. The concluding compliment neatly conveys to the mother the doctor's sense of a mother who has properly carried out her child-rearing activities. Observed in a number of consultations, it invariably is treated as a compliment by parents.

If this is an instance of professional dominance, it is a form of professional dominance which is legitimated to the parent and which does not prevent her raising her own concerns. It is difficult to see where a critique in terms of 'lack of democracy' or 'distorted communication' would even begin.

The substantial interpretive work required here to transform a 'sick child' into a case of 'innocent murmur' is highlighted if we take another consultation. Here the parent is himself a senior registrar in another Department. Consequently, the presumed relevances of a Cardiac Unit form the taken-for-granted backdrop of all the parent's comments and the consultation has that matter-of-fact tone we have observed in cases where parents are medical personnel. Indeed, the father speaks almost in note form (as if he is dictating an entry into his child's notes):

(Case 2, Transcript 15)
C 1.1, SC 1, P 1, E 1, PR 1, FC 1
(15:13)
1. D: A well child?
2. F: Totally fit. A murmur spotted a year ago (   ) really anxious GP at a child clinic. So we thought she ought to be checked again. But apart from that totally normal and healthy, masses of energy, no more than the usual cuts and bumps.

Here the father, knowing the likelihood that the murmur is 'innocent', practically apologizes for being there at all: the 'really anxious GP at a child clinic' is mentioned as the precipitating factor. Nonetheless, the referral is now presented as a *joint* decision. Compare: (15:13) 'So *we* thought she ought to be checked again'. With the previous mother's comment: (5:1) 'And *he* just wanted to check it' (my emphases).

The elicitation sequence very speedily leads into the examination. The diagnosis of 'innocent murmur' is taken to be self-explanatory and is supported by a statement of the results of the examination usually reserved for the referral letter:

(15:13)
1. D: That's fine. An innocent murmur. She's got normal pulses, normal cardiac impulse, obviously pink and not (   ), not breathless (   ) sound normally split, no accentuation and a very short, early systolic, localized buzzing murmur which is the classical innocent murmur.
2. F: Well this is what we hoped the case was and I'm most grateful to you.
3. D: It's a pleasure. There you go. A very well little girl.

The shared universe of discourse is emphasized by the doctor's reference to 'the classical innocent murmur'. No further explanations or questions need arise because, as the father says, 'this is what we hoped the case was'. By utterance 3, the child is already being dressed. The absence of the mother is not a case for comment, as happens in other cases.

At this point, the whole truncated encounter has lasted *one-fifth* of the length of the previous consultation. It is only extended by some teaching talk between the consultant and a student which occurs while the child is being dressed. On the way out, the father adds a further apology for having the consultation:

(15:14)
1. F: The doctor was extremely alarmed despite the original reassurance from (   ). I'm most grateful to you
2. D: Bye bye. Shall I write a note?
3. F: Um. Yes it might be a good idea.

Such an apology need only arise because medical-men can be assumed to know when not to trouble their doctor unnecessarily. However, all is well because of the 'really anxious', 'extremely alarmed' GP. The appeal is clearly to the 'collegial authority' shared by hospital doctors (see Strong, 1979b) but not necessarily including GPs. The shared basis of this appeal is revealed when, in a unique gesture, the consultant asks the father whether he should write a referral letter to the GP. Later, it turns out that the consultant instructs his secretary to send the letter to the father himself with a *copy* to the GP.

It is important to add that this 'collegial authority' in no way challenges the medical decision-making form. The father–doctor submits entirely to the diagnosis and disposal suggested by the doctor at the Unit. Knowing the ropes as they do, medical families can be assumed to understand what is expected of the parent of a sick child and to await passively the disposal suggested by the doctor best qualified to know.

Our sample also contains four cases of children with suspected heart arrhythmia (tachycardia). This has a similarity to a murmur in that, by itself, it is minor and usually innocent. The elicitation sequence tends, however, to be much longer since the circumstances of the relevant episodes are important in establishing a diagnosis. The disposal options lie between a discharge and the use of a 24-hour ECG which may sometimes require the child to be admitted to the ward.

In the case below, the examination reveals no abnormality but the mother has shown great concern about her daughter's episodes of fast heart-beat and chest pains.

(Case 3, Transcript 15)
C 1.2, SC 1, P 3, E 1, PR 2, FC 3 → 1
(15:9–10)
1. D: Quite honestly, I think it's very unlikely that she's got any anything fundamentally wrong with the heart at all
2. M: You don't think
3. D: Um what we could do, if you would like us to, and you think it would put your mind at rest, with (0.5) quite honestly I don't think there's anything wrong with her heart
4. M: Yes
5. D: But what we could easily do is to get err a recording of her ECG

and her heart-beat over 24 hours, rather than just over a short period of time that it takes to do the child's thing. And we could then look at that 24-hour tape-recording and see if that showed anything. Um (1.0) my prejudice is not to bother. I don't think there's anything wrong, but we would certainly do that if you would feel it was important to rule out anything.

It is clear that the doctor favours a discharge. However, he has noticed the mother's concern and makes an offer of a 24-hour tape: 'If you would like us to and it would put your mind at rest'.

Given the apparent failure of symmetry between the desired disposal (discharge) and the patency of the condition (high), and the fact that a 24-hour tape does not involve the invasive aspect and very slight risk of catheterization, the doctor is prepared to move the consultation into a 'democratic' form. Although the offer is heavily hedged in by his own reported 'thinking' and 'prejudice', it nonetheless is clearly serious.

However, the mother's response to the offer is unexpected, given her earlier expressed anxieties:

6. M: If you're sure there's nothing wrong with her (2.0).
7. D: Yes
8. M: Um (0.5) you know she has (   ) hospitals quite a lot (   ) and nothing's ever been (0.5) you know she goes to the doctor very regular/
9. D: /mm
10. M: And it was just that one time.

It now transpires that the mother's anxieties extend equally to stays in hospitals. It also could be that she has been influenced by the doctor's 'prejudice' that nothing needs to be done. In any event, having made the offer, the doctor has restored a symmetry between disposal and parental anxieties. He is now free to return to a medical decision-making format. So, after another summary of the results of the investigation, he simply defines the disposal himself:

(15:10)
D: Um I think what I'd (0.5) I think the best way to deal with it is to say this. We don't think there's anything wrong and I don't *actually* think she has had a primary episode of a heart beating too too fast. I think we should leave it.

Notice how the earlier democratic discourse of 'I' 'we' and 'you' is now replaced by the purely clinical discourse of 'I' and 'we'. Having formulated earlier a 'you' with a mind that could be put 'at rest' if you 'thought' or 'felt' it important, the doctor returns to his secure clinical home-base. We thus can observe the *situated* nature of the appeal to democratic forms and the *contingent* character of its maintenance. Given a mother who is content with what 'you' are sure about and who even avoids entering the 'I' voice offered by the doctor (utterances 6, 8 and 10 above), 'democracy' becomes a nonsense (a parallel might be with an election in which all the voters abstain).

Elsewhere in cases of arrhythmia, we find that the form of the consultation largely relates to how symptomatic the child is. In two cases, where the child was breathless or had periods of unconsciousness, the doctor meets the parental expectation for action by simply stating a decision to do a 24-hour tape (in one case by an immediate admission into the ward). The medical decision-making form arises simply because the disposal involves no risk and can be assumed to meet the 'customer's' desire for action. The parallel, according to the chauffeur's model, would be with a faulty car that could be given a simple test. However, this need not rule out all forms of parental intervention. In one of these cases, parents and doctor negotiate about whether a non-heart ailment should also be investigated while the child is on the ward or whether he should be transferred to a local hospital.

In a further case, we can see the form that a consultation takes *after* a 24-hour tape with the expected negative finding. Prior to the tape, the child had had two episodes of arrhythmia. Now the parents report him as well and having had no further attacks.

(Case 4, RS 5)
[*Baby aged five months*]
C 1.2, SC 3, P 1, E 1, PR 2, FC 1 → 2
  1. D: He's well. No further attacks, nothing?
  2. M: No
  3. D: No problems. The tape was alright, the baby was alright. I don't
        think there's anything wrong with him.

The examination confirms the expected disposal of a routine follow-up several months later. Given the asymptomatic status of the child a doctor's decision-making format is used, as we would expect:

  1. D: Well management would be playing it safe to leave him on his
        medicine till he is one year old.

Notice the passive voice used by the doctor. Doctor's decision-making is such an obviously apposite form that not only the 'you' disappears but so also do 'I' and 'we'. It is now simply a case of: 'management would be . . . '

Here the voice of the text-book seems appropriate to a text-book case which confirms medical expectations and satisfies parental anxieties.

Where such anxieties arise, the doctor moves in speedily to destroy them:

2. F: Will you stop, will you you have him in hospital when you / stop it?
3. D: no /
4. F: [*laughs*] We were (   ) to find / out
5. M: / I'll just sit there biting my fingernails wa-a-tching [laughing] him
6. D: Ah no he won't do that. Even if he did have an attack then he won't get into bad trouble. I mean he would only get into bad bad trouble if it went on for 36 hours with nothing being done
7. M: Mm.
8. D: That's *exceedingly* unlikely
9. M: Yes.
10. F: Mm. Although we were *rather* worried when he went in the second time, because it took something like four hours for him to come down after we recognized it and got him in, as you as you know. It was only after about eighteen hours approximately / [*laughs*]
11. M: / Yes
12. F: It's a bit worrying when he sits up there all the / time
13. D: / The natural history, for what it's worth, is that the majority of the children who have these episodes in early infancy grow out of them. Not all, but the majority.
14. M: Yes

Here at Utterances 6, 8 and 13 the doctor sets out to reassure both parents about what might happen when the medicines are stopped. He now has to use the 'persuasion' format because the symmetry between (long-term) disposal and (feared) patency of symptoms has broken down. Once more the move is in accord with our model.

The final minor condition represented in the sample is patent ductus arteriosis (PDA). We have four cases in the sample, three are first outpatients and the fourth is post-operative.

I shall only look at length at one, involving the first out-patient visit of a baby referred with suspected PDA. The referral letter mentions the parents giving consideration to using 'private' medicine, a point to which I shall return.

(Case 5, Transcript 117)
C 1.3, SC 1, P 1, E 1, PR 2, FC 2
[*Notice the work that is done on the concept of 'wellness' in the following early sequence*]:
(117:1−2)
1. D: And from Dr S's letter, a well little girl who's got a heart murmur.
2. M: Er well (0.5) er no but er well (0.5) I don't know what Dr S said but

when we first, it was discovered which was in (   ) by Dr N
(0.5) I don't know if you've got his notes. Um, he thought it was a
heart murmur first of all and then he said it was the channel
leading out of the heart didn't shut off at birth. He did call it a
name but I can't remember.

3. D: A ductus. Yes
4. M: Aah!
5. D: Yes. But in the way that the child was picked up, she's basically a
        well girl. Yes?
6. M: Oh yes
7. F: Yes
8. M: It was only through a cold
9. F: That it was picked up
10. M: That they picked it up. They hadn't noticed it before then.
11. D: Sure. So (1.0) a well little girl

Something rather curious is happening here. If it is a PDA, then the
routine disposal is catheter and low-risk surgery. If the parents were to
define the child as unwell, then, according to the chauffeur's model, the
doctor could safely slide into a medical decision-making format
(routine repairs on a minor fault). However, here, as in many other
cases that we have seen, he does extensive work on retrieving a version
of the child as 'well'. As we would predict, this subsequently requires
him to engage in 'selling' tactics appropriate to the 'persuasion mode'
where there is asymmetry between disposal and patency.

What seems to be happening is that the doctor is instating an
essentially 'medicalized' version of wellness which can co-exist with a
heart condition and simply arises 'in the way that the child was picked
up'. In doing so, he is able to generate a selling procedure related to
medical knowledge about 'well' children who nonetheless have
conditions which, although not patent, require to be treated. The
unintended consequence is that parents lose a site from which to talk
about their child and hence to exercise judgment in non-clinical terms.
After all, if they can no longer assume that a child with a diagnosed
heart condition is 'unwell', they have little basis to act as full decision-
making partners. The implication is that the 'persuasion' format which
the doctor himself makes necessary through his generation of
asymmetry firmly asserts the centrality of clinical relevances, even as it
seems to defer to parents' everyday concerns.

Persuasion involves a relatively long consultation. The doctor
concludes his examination and states his agreement with the suggested
diagnosis. He then explains that the heart is 'actually normal' but that it
has a 'tube' which means that 'the lungs receive too much blood at too
high a pressure'. He illustrates his analysis with a diagram and
elaborates the 'long-term' lung problems that might arise without
treatment:

(117:4)

1. D: That's not caused any problems in your little baby so far, obviously, but it certainly will do if left for a long time. And the problems would be firstly that she will be more prone to chest infections and, perhaps more importantly, that (1.0) the lungs don't like having too much blood at too high a pressure for too long and they can in fact be damaged if that is left for a long period of time.

2. F: What sort of time scale are we talking about? A long time, we're talking about some sort of many years / rather than not, yes?

3. D: / Yes, yes

Here clinical understanding reveals that even clinically 'well' children can have long-term problems with underlying but invisible conditions. However, even if parents cannot enter the clinical framework as equals, at least they can assert their role as consumers of clinical expertise: hence the question about time-scale. The rest of the consultation takes the form of *suggested* disposals and further selling tactics by the doctor and further consumerist moves from the parents.

First, the suggested disposal:

(117:5)

D: What I think we should do is that we first need to confirm that that is the diagnosis and that there is nothing else wrong with the heart itself. And to do that we do a special test called a heart catheterization . . .

Predictably, this statement of disposal takes a 'persuasive' form based on 'I' and 'We' but excluding the 'You' earlier found in the 'democratic' format. Examples of these forms are provided in Table 1.

TABLE 1
Disposal Statements

Form of Consultation	Form of Disposal Statement
Doctor's decision-making	Passive voice ('Management would be')
Persuasion	Voices of I and We ('*I* think *we* should')
Democracy	Voices of I, We and You ('*I* think . . . but *we* would . . . if *you* thought . . .')

The 'I' voice used in the disposal statement is invariably cast as passive and reflective — it 'thinks'. It is bolstered by a voice of 'We' which is active — it 'does' things. This is the voice of the medical team. The 'I' voice receives support from its institutional base but also reveals its authority in being able to formulate its proper action — exactly *what* 'we should do'. This combination of authoritative reflection and collective action reveals the power of the persuasive mode.

However, the form of persuasion does not rely simply on appeals to authority. It also demonstrates that its authority is based on rational grounds, available to any sensible person. Here, after the disposal statement, the parents are invited to see the good sense of the catheter:

(117:5)
1. D: Hm (2.0) the the reason for doing the test is, I mean I'm 99 per cent certain that all she's got is a ductus
2. F: Hm hm.
3. M: I see
4. D: However the time to find that we're wrong is not when she's on the operating table.
5. M: No.
6. D: We must know beforehand. And it's a totally unnecessary risk to take.
7. F: Hm hm
8. D: To put her up for surgery without a catheter test
9. F: Right.
10. M: Um.

As the doctor advances his 'reasons', the parents take on the role of chorus, echoing the good sense of the reasoning. Their child has now been successfully re-constituted from an ill child with a heart condition into a well child but with an underlying heart condition that it would be sensible to investigate further.[1]

However, this medicalization of the child does not prevent the parents from seeking to get some hold on the decision-making. Having been ruled out from any participation in the doctor's collegial authority (the voice of 'We'), they can still speak as consumers of a medical service, able to question the *social* organization of the disposal decision:

(117:6–7)
1. M: Um, the other thing er, will it have to be done in this hospital? (1.00)
2. D: Well it would be *optimum* if it was this hospital [*chuckles*]
3. F: Hm
4. M: Well no it's only that er we live down in Countyshire
5. D: Hm
6. M: And er
7. D: No, it's better done in a proper children's heart unit
8. F: Hm.
9. D: And the reason he was sent up here was because that's what the Unit is
10. F: Hm/
    M: Oh/ it is a *children's* hospital up here. I didn't realize that.

Here the parents work at consumerism, 'shopping around' for the best service. The brief silence after utterance 1 and the doctor's chuckle indicate that this may be an unexpected form of questioning within NHS consultations, where families are not normally able to choose between places of treatment. The matter is clarified when, after a further question (about accommodation at the hospital for parents), the father mentions his BUPA cover. However, this sally into the private patient form is resisted by the doctor who points out that the only accommodation available is for the parents of NHS patients!

Nonetheless the parents insist on playing their part as consumers. Precluded from exercising any meaningful choice about the social organization of the disposal, they can at least comment on the quality of the service:

(117:9)
[*After further talk about accommodation*]
1. M: Hm
2. F: Hm. We'll be OK.
3. M: Well that's very helpful.

Consumerism is sometimes seen in NHS consultations among parents who bring in check-lists of questions. Part of the work done by the list is to assert some degree of control over the agenda of the consultation. In turn, this may be resisted by the doctor's refusal to answer questions until after the examination.

Here, however, based upon the future possibility of fee-for-service treatment, the consumerism extends beyond that normally observed. Unusually, the claim seems to be that the agenda of the consultation can be a matter for parents.[2] Witness below how after the doctor has sought to close the encounter, the father concedes but the mother makes it clear that the closure is by *mutual* agreement:

(117:11)
[*The parents have started to discuss when they might have another child*]
1. D: That that's where the conversation is for *you* to decide.
2. F: Yes, that's right, we'll leave. Thank you very much [*laughter*] (1.00)
3. M: [*To daughter*] Are you coming then? [*To F.*] That's about *all* I think then. Isn't it?

Because of the insistent consumerism of the parents, the consultation lasts considerably longer than many others even within the usually extended 'persuasion' format. 'Persuasion' nonetheless remains the continued focus of the encounter. When the doctor at one point moves into a democratic framework (including, for once, the voice of 'You'), the parents, for all their consumerism, decline the offer to take a decision themselves:

(117:9)
[*The doctor has just resummarized the planned catheter disposal*]
1. D: And then, depending on what we find, we can schedule her for surgery, *if you would like** us to then, or have it later on (   )

2. F: Hm hm. Well obviously you're [*chuckling*] it's in (   ) you know
3. M: Well you'd know which
4. D: Well the (   ) is at this age it worries the parents more than
          the child . . .
          (* my emphasis)

The parents have been persuaded that the medical agenda is best left
to the doctor. Having made his 'democratic' offer at Utterance 1, the
doctor is now free to resort to the voice of impersonal authority
(Utterance 4). It remains only for the parents to show their good sense
by assenting to the doctor's rationally-grounded suggestions:

(117:10)
[*The doctor has once again summarized the disposal*]
      F: No. I think, I think with what you've explained and the and the,
            you know, the risk to her later in life, you know, we ought to do
            something you know, (   ).

The two other pre-catheter consultations involving patent ductus
both concern symptomatic children and take a doctor's decision-
making form, although there is some negotiation in one about the exact
date of admission. The one post-operative case takes a form that we will
find common after successful surgery. The consultation is very brief,
there are congratulations all round about how well the child is doing
and the parents are assured that the child will be able to have a normal
life ('become a professional footballer' is this particular doctor's
favourite phrase).

We can now move on to the second category of conditions which tend
to be self-correcting or correctable. We will examine the ten cases in the
sample with the most common form of hole-in-the-heart (VSD). This
condition covers a wide range, varying from a small self-closing hole to
a large hole with complications. Seven out of the ten here are non-
problematic. In five cases, it seems that the hole is small and will close
while, in the other two cases, a larger hole has already been successfully
closed. All involve asymptomatic patients and the disposal, in every
case, is a routine follow-up.

As we might expect with asymptomatic children, the disposal of
routine follow-up is non-contentious and fits the medical decision-
making form. This is illustrated by the disposal statement at a child's
first out-patient visit:

(NB 12/11/80)
[*The doctor has already said that the child has a hole*]
      D: He's obviously very well and there is no need to do anything at
            present. I'm fairly certain that no surgery will be needed.

This patient-management form works non-problematically while the
child remains asymptomatic and no invasive tests or treatments are

being proposed. Parents do not need to be persuaded about this kind of disposal. Their main concern is to confirm the present course of inaction:

(NB 19/11/80)
1. M: You're not going to operate then?
2. D: No. I don't think there's any need for an operation
3. M: Oh good

In this situation of inaction, parents use the length of time between follow-up appointments as a means of charting their child's progress:

(NB 26/11/80)
1. D: See him in a year.
2. M: [*to child*] Hear that. That's good.

As Roth (1963) has noted, these 'bench-marks' serve to routinize the situation and to contain parents' fears. Moreover, after several such non-problematic follow-ups, used to document exactly when the hole has closed, the atmosphere becomes relaxed and even jokey. For instance, in the consultation above, the doctor had previously feigned upset because the mother didn't remember having seen him previously. When the child turns to face his mother prior to the examination, he adds in a spirit of mock affront:

D: He's turning his back on me, giving me the cold shoulder

Such light-hearted banter contrasts strongly with the lowered voices and serious atmosphere that are generated at the other end of the disease-spectrum. By the time the children are five or more, follow-ups are usually spaced three years apart and are typically very brief and jokey. For instance:

(Transcript 15d:16)
[*Child is being undressed for examination when a bleep is heard on a doctor's call device*]
1. D: [*to child*] That wasn't you was it? You weren't squeaking were you? eh?
2. Child: (   )
3. D: Is that your brother over there, making all that noise? Is it? Mm. (35.00)
4. D: That's very good. [*To doctors*] Almost as advertised really (*laughter*)

In cases like these, consultations become entirely non-problematic. Parents are reassured that all is well and doctors go through the motions, dealing with routine or 'bread-and-butter' conditions. They joke with parents and sometimes, as above (Utterance 4), with each other. Later on between consultations, the consultant is heard to complain jokingly about the number of routine cases seen at this particular clinic. Once again, the contextual sense of doctor's decision-making is never in doubt.

In the two cases where the child has recently undergone successful surgery (obviously for a larger hole than in the earlier cases), the light-heartedness (sorry about the pun) continues. This time, however, it is expressed less in open jokiness than in the mood of mutual congratulation that pervades the consultation. Atypically, doctors make comments to parents during the examination sequence. For instance after technical talk between the doctors about the X-ray:

> (NB 26/11/80 Case 2)
> D: [*to mother*] Very good.
>   [*Again, during the examination itself*]
> D: [*to child*] Gosh your scar's healing up nicely.

It is almost as if the good news, after the trauma of surgery, cannot wait to come out. Coupled with an emphasis on the child's wellness after the examination ('You're looking very well' and later, to the mother, 'she's very well') and the use of bench-marks like the stopping of medicines and of prophylactic dental-cover, both sides can be content. The successful result relieves parental anxieties and pays tribute to the skills of the medical team. All that is left is congratulation and normalization:

> (NB 26/11/80 Case 4)
> C 2.1, SC 4, P 1, E 1, P 1, FC 1
> 1.   D: How's he?
> 2.   M: Fi-ine
> 3.   D: (   ) activity, running around. Eating well?
> 4.   M: Mm. Oh *yes*, eating like a pig.
>   (5.0)
> 5.   D: Good X-ray
> [*post-examination*]
> 6.   D: Ve-ery good
> [*medicines are reduced*]
> 7.   D: Everything looks fine. There's no reason why he shouldn't be an olympic athlete.
> 8.   M: [*to child*] D'you hear that?

As already noted, the three remaining cases of VSD are, for varying reasons, more problematic. We have already encountered the first in Part One of the paper. It involves the mother who seeks to broaden the consultation out into areas like 'feeding' and 'normality'. Her case is interesting because it reveals the centrality of the patency of the condition to the doctor's decision to intervene by means of catheterization. We will consider four out-patients, over almost a year, in each of which the patency of the condition to the mother varies from the previous consultations.

At the first out-patients, the new-born baby is referred from another hospital. The condition is patent because the mother notices that he is 'breathless'. However, she has not noticed him going 'blue'. Given the disjunction between the mother's presumed assessment of the situation and the doctor's decision not to intervene, the consultation takes a 'persuasion' format. The doctor stresses that the hole, although 'not tiny' is probably quite small and so 'we don't have to do anything about it'. The mother's fears about normality are calmed and she is assured that 'we can close the hole' should it become necessary. The main emphasis is on a step-by-step approach, couched in a persuasive mode using the 'I' and 'We' voices:

(Transcript 20:3)
C 2.1, SC 1, P 3, E 1, PR 1, FC 2
1.   D: So I think what we should do at this stage is for your baby to go home [Baby wails]
2.   D: And er we will then re-assess. It's possible that um when we see him again that er we'd say well look (   ) so we might put his name down for further tests
              (. . .)
              It doesn't necessarily mean that we would have to operate, but we'd know the information rather than be guessing it.
3.   M: Yes.
4.   D: However, at this stage, a relatively well baby

The persuasion involves a stress on 'stages', the Unit's ability to cope with any eventuality and the appeal of the baby's going 'home'. When the mother seems to assent at Utterance 3, the doctor is free to abandon his persuasive voices and in the passive voice of patient-management to reconstitute the baby as 'relatively well'.

One month later mother and baby return and are seen by another doctor at the Unit. Now the mother reports the child as asymptomatic. He is not breathless, he is 'thriving' and the referring hospital is 'very happy' with him. She is informed that the hole is 'of moderate size' and that his lack of breathlessness without the use of many drugs is 'a good sign'. The hole has a good chance of 'closing on its own'. A three-month follow-up is arranged.

However, only eight weeks later, the baby is back at out-patients. The mother, this time accompanied by her husband to stress the seriousness of the situation, has brought forward the appointment. As a result, the first elicitation question generates a need for her to ground her presence and produces a 'long story':

(Transcript 73:1)
C 2.1, SC 2, P 3, E 1, PR 2, FC 1 → 2
1.   D: How is he?
2.   M: Well um it's a long story basically

The baby has been unwell since the last consultation and has been admitted to the referring hospital because 'his heart was very enlarged'. Medicines have made him much better but feeding problems have persisted and he is now breathless.

After examination, the doctor reports that it is possible that the baby has a 'moderate to large' hole but that he 'looks very well' although he is 'a little bit breathless'. In this kind of situation, clinical and parental realities converge. The size of the hole should probably be investigated and this will satisfy the mother's anxieties. Notice, then, how the disposal statement begins in the impersonal voice of the doctor's decision-making:

(Transcript 73:3)
1. D: Um then we come to the question of management. What is the right thing to do? Continue with treatment or do we need to operate on him? Quite honestly I think that we will be able to hold him with medical treatment but I think it's reached the stage now where probably we should be certain and we should investigate further. Um
2. M: My worry was that at the moment I'm feeding him ten times a day in very small amounts

The transcript shows how the doctor eventually moves out of the impersonal voice of 'management' into the 'persuasion' mode of 'I' and 'We'. However, the mother's response indicates that, faced with a breathless child that is feeding poorly, she hardly needs persuading. It is possible that the move into the more extended 'persuasion' format is an attempt to cope with what seems to be a highly anxious mother who might respond badly to a truncated medical decision-making format. Certainly, the referral letter mentions a mother who 'has obviously . . . become extremely *anxious* about the baby'.

The child is cathetered shortly after and the VSD is revealed to be small enough to be self-closing. At the follow-up clinic some months later, the child is now reported once again to be asymptomatic. The mother does briefly refer to his 'wheeziness'. However, the doctor locates this as 'normal in children'. The mother shows the increased competence that we would expect from experienced parents by asking about the 'black shadow' on an earlier X-ray and discussing her child's heart size.

Predictably, in an asymptomatic child offered a routine follow-up, where medical and parental expectations are congruent, the disposal can be entirely doctor-imposed:

(NB 8/10/80 Case 11)
1. D: We need to keep him under review. So how about coming to see us in 1 year?
2. M: Great!

Note the bench-mark constituted by the increase in time between consultations to one year. The apparent offer of choice at Utterance 1, however, has only the appearance of a democratic decision-making form. Since it conforms with and even exceeds everything the mother can hope for, she can hardly be expected to reject the offer. At most, she can offer the Royal Assent to a duly processed Act of Parliament. In fact, she simply expresses her enthusiasm for the decision.

In a situation like this, the catheter decision is strongly related to the patency of the condition. Even when the catheter reveals a fairly large hole, the decision to operate may hang largely on the parents' sense of how well the child is coping. For instance:

(NB 22/10/80 Case 8)
1. D: As you know he has a hole and the question is do we do anything?
[The parents stress how well their baby is coping]
2. D: It sounds like you're winning
[A routine follow-up appointment is given]
3. D: The evidence is that he's holding his own

In conditions where intervention depends upon the presence of troubling symptoms, parental opinions may exert considerable influence on decisions.

The two remaining children involve more complicated situations. Let us briefly watch them unwind through the longitudinal data available. The first involves a baby initially seen at seven months. Her cardiac condition was observed after she was admitted at another hospital with a chest infection. At this first out-patients, held at a joint clinic at the other hospital, the baby's condition is patent to the mother. Although not 'blue', the mother comments on her fast breathing and heart-beat. The doctor decides to admit the child for catheterization and mentions the likely prospect of surgery. Given the congruence between patency and disposal, the reference to parental agreement is purely formal and requires no direct statement of consent:

(Transcript 15h:36)
C 2.1., SC 1, P 3, E 1, PR 1, FC 1
1.D: What I think she's got is a hole ... Um what we will do *if you agree* [*baby crying*]
2.M: Sally stop it.
3.D: Sshh. We'll do the tests at the X Hospital. I think she's got a hole and quite a high pressure in the artery to the lungs. We ought to do special tests to find out exactly and I think she will need something done about it in the way of an operation. What we'd like her to do, *if you agree*, is to put her name down on the very early waiting list ... [*further details*]
We could, we would then know what was the best thing to do to help her and I would have thought we'd get her in within two or three weeks, *if you agree*
4. M: Where is this hospital? [my emphasis]

The thrice-repeated 'if you agree(s)' serve the purpose of inviting the Royal Assent. Given the early stage of her child's career and the patency of the condition, the only hold that the mother can get on the conversation is to ask about the location of the hospital. Her formal approval is assumed to take place simply by the silence that follows this closing statement:

> D: OK. Well we'll write to you and try to get you in, as I say, within three weeks. I'd have thought two to three weeks. OK?

Our notes do not record if the mother nods after this final 'OK?' However, the medical decision-making frame is so well-established by now that it is not clear that such assent would need to be given, nor even that the 'OK?' is to be heard as inviting assent to the disposal rather than simply closing the consultation.

The child is catheterized within a month and, two months later, an operation is performed to close the VSD. Six weeks after, she has her first post-operative out-patients appointment with a second doctor. However, the mutual congratulations that we found in similar appointments does not occur here. It is true that the mother reports that her baby is 'feeding well' and is 'not getting breathless'. The doctor, however, notes that 'she looks a little breathless to me now', that she is 'panting' and 'coughing'. His diagnosis is also relatively guarded compared to earlier post-operative consultations: It 'sounds like quite a good result from her operation', he says.

Congruent with the diagnosis, the child is given a fairly quick follow-up out-patients after six weeks. Although the avoidance of immediate intervention fits the lack of patency of the condition as perceived by the mother, the relatively unenthusiastic tone of the encounter together with the possibility of further interventions, means that the disposal is structured in the 'persuasion' format of 'I' and 'We':

(Transcript 30:3)
C 2.1., SC 5, P 1, E 2, PR 2, FC 2
> 1.D: So I think *we*'d like to see her again in two weeks. (1.0) I'm sorry six weeks. If she still has a cough and is still a little bit breathless like this *we* might want to repeat her cardiac catheterization, the test she had before the operation, just to check that everything was done properly at the operation and everything's pumping as we would expect. But I think she's going to be alright because (0.5)
> 2.M: Another operation needed?
> 3.D: No. I think it's very unlikely. Because her operation really seemed to go very smoothly and *we* were very pleased at the way it had gone. But I think it's mainly her chest [my emphasis]

Notice how the doctor draws upon his collegial authority ('We') in suggesting a quick follow-up and mentioning the possibility of a repeat catheterization. As a registrar, unlike a consultant, he may want to call upon the authority of the whole medical 'team' to bolster his decision-making, especially where it involves the prospect of unwelcome developments like a repeat catheterization. Again we can observe how the mother, now more experienced because of two in-patient stays, quickly sizes up the implications of a further 'check' at Utterance 2. However, faced with the medical version of her child and a further follow-up it would be irrational not to be persuaded by the proposed disposal.

There matters would end were it not for the fact that the registrar, aware that he is dealing with a single-parent, uses the indirect method of eliciting home circumstances that we noted much earlier:

    1.D: Are you managing alright at home?
    2.M: Er not really
    3.D: Not really. What's the problem?
    4.M: Well, I want to go to work
    5.D: You want to go back to work. Is there anyone to look after Sally?
    6.M: Well I'll probably get her into a nursery, get her into a nice
           nursery, or a child minder.
    7.D: That's what you'll do. Right

This broadening-out of the scope of the consultation nicely allows the mother to seek reassurance about her own behaviour. In a completely non-directive manner, the doctor offers just that. Once again, as in earlier examples, it is often not the disposal itself but care at home which parents want to discuss.

Six weeks later, Sally and her mother attend their third out-patient clinic when they are seen by a second registrar. Once more the mother reports no symptoms and here the doctor largely concurs ('super', 'fantastic', he comments). His only cautionary note is that 'the heart's still a little bit large on X-ray'.

The disposal this time is some medicine 'to help the heart get smaller' and a one-month follow-up. This uses the straight medical decision-making mode, while countering any anxiety about the heart-size and speedy follow-up by allowing the mother to repeat her earlier statements about Sally's progress:

(Transcript 37:3)
    1.D: OK. We'll see her in one month. I should think you're quite
           pleased with her, aren't you?
    2.M: Yes, she's doing quite well (   ).

Three weeks later, Sally is seen by the consultant. Now, although her mother still reports that 'she's doing well', she concedes that she still gets 'just slightly' breathless. Following his examination, the doctor goes through an elaborate 'selling' exercise to obtain agreement for a repeat catheterization. Bearing in mind that the mother could reasonably expect that the surgery would have satisfactorily resolved matters, he must now set her out once again on the path through catheterization to possible repeat surgery. He proceeds cautiously by playing down any doubts about the efficiency of the previous operation and stressing that he is not, at this stage at least, proposing further surgery:

(Transcript 38:2)
C2.1., SC 5, P 3, E 1, PR 1, FC 2
1. D: Um as far as Sally's heart is concerned, she's obviously miles better than she was before the operation. I'm still a little bit concerned that she's still slightly breathless. And when we listen there are still some noises in the heart. On the other hand, she's also had a lot of chest problems. What I think we should do is to put her name down just to repeat the heart test, not for an operation. Do you remember the catheter that she had to start with?
2. M: Yes.

The classical 'I-We' persuasion format is used here. The 'selling' continues with appeals to the rational good sense of 'finding out' in the context of a concern 'with the long-term future'. The statement concludes with a request for the Royal Assent which is duly granted:

3.D: What I'd like to do is to put her name down for that and in the next two or three months we'll get her in just for a couple of days, *if you agree*, to repeat the heart catheter to find out what the pressures are, and to see if there is a small residual hole. I don't think it's very big and it could be that we don't need to do anything else, but I think we ought to find out what's going on inside. Not cos she's not too bad now, we're worried not only about her progress now, we're most concerned with the long-term future. So *is that alright*? We'll put her name down to repeat the catheter and, er, as I say, try to get her in within probably six to eight weeks. *OK*?
4.M: Yes. [my emphasis][3]

Three months later, Sally is re-catheterized. A further year later, she undergoes surgery to close the residual VSD. It is only worth noting that the final decision to redo the surgery is not stated at a consultation. At a follow-up appointment six months after the catheter, the doctor simply undertakes 'to review the data' (i.e. to look again at the catheter films) but stresses that the 'situation' cannot be left 'indefinitely'. When the mother arrives for a further follow-up four months after this, the doctor announces that he has written to the surgeon who has confirmed that he will do the operation. Although clearly Sally's life is not at stake, the delay and the step-by-step approach seems to express a potentially embarrassing and difficult situation for the doctors — the polar opposite of the much more common mutual congratulation after successful closure of a VSD.

Holes in the heart generally rank relatively low in the order of seriousness of cardiac conditions. It is now time to look at an instance of a more serious but correctable condition. The example I will take is called Fallot's Tetralogy. It involves a combination of four lesions, the two most significant being a VSD and narrowing between the heart and the pulmonary artery. Depending on the severity of the condition and any associated abnormalities, correction can take place in either one or two stages. However, early catheterization seems to be very dependent upon the patency of the condition. Until the age of two at least, it appears that tetralogies will be investigated where the condition is patent and there is a threat to life.

The sample contains four cases of Tetralogy of Fallot: one case (with complications) followed through from first out-patients to post-first-stage correction, one at the post-first-stage correction stage only and two post-total-correction.

Let us begin with the case involving complications. We have longitudinal material on three out-patients with around one year between each visit. At the first out-patients, the baby is sixteen days old. She has come, together with a nurse and parents, directly from the Maternity Hospital where she was born. Her condition is clearly patent as the beginning of the elicitation sequence reveals:

(Transcript 3:1)
C 3.1., SC 1, P 3, E 1, PR 2, FC 1
 1. D: First baby?
 2. M: No.
 3. D: Other children?
 4. M: Two girls
 5. D: Have you noticed anything different about your baby?
 6. M: (   )
 7. D: Do you think she goes a bit blue?
 8. M: Yerr I think she does really.
 9. D: [*To Nurse*] Do you?
10. N: She does, yes
11. D: [*To Nurse*] When do you think she first went blue?
12. N: Well ... at birth emm ... quite a long time before (   ) and emm she didn't respond very quickly to oxygen. But ever since then ... I mean ... she's never been pink colour she's been a grey colour

The elicitation sequence is rapid and conducted in quiet, serious tones. There is no social byplay. The gravity of the talk contrasts strongly with the lightheartedness noted earlier at routine follow-ups. The child's blueness has been recognized by two observers classed as

competent-for-all-practical-observational-purposes.   The   mother's
assessment is based on comparison with her other children, while the
nurse can be expected to recognize a blue baby when she sees one.

In circumstances where the condition is so patent, the catheter
decision requires no selling. The doctor can appear to his collegial
authority, using the voice of 'We', to invoke the need 'to do more tests'.

> (3:2)
> D: What I think your baby has (0.5) We can't be completely certain
> just by looking and we do need to do more tests and find out, is
> that she has a hole here (he is now drawing a diagram) . . . (and)
> the obstruction here . . .

In response to this expected statement of further investigation, the
parents can hardly be expected to disagree. After all, according to the
chauffeur's model, they have brought in a 'faulty car' to the 'garage'.
However, they can and do seek further information.

Initially, the baby's father asks: 'What is the obstruction?' This
elicits further details and a renewed stress on the need for more tests:

> D: [*has just explained about the likely anatomy of the obstruction*]
> But exactly how small and exactly what is the precise type of
> obstruction we'd have to need to find out by a heart
> catheterization. What we shall do, if you agree, is to take the baby
> in if we've a bed today or just as soon as we do and to do a test to
> confirm that, to see if there's anything else that is different from
> what we've just said [*continues with details of the catheter*]

Throughout the doctor here stays in the 'We' voice: 'We' have to find
out and 'We shall do it'. Once again, the use of 'if you agree' is purely
formal. The Royal Assent can be assumed in cases where the condition
is patent and further tests are being proposed.

Although he nowhere seeks to challenge the 'doctor's decision-
making' format, the father presses several times for more details,
particularly about the likely prognosis. Searching for meaning in this
sudden, catastrophic event, he asks a series of questions:

> (3:3–4)
> 1. F: Is it common (0.5) or what?
> 2. D: Yes
> 3. F: This is the *normal* type of thing that they do have with heart
> trouble (0.5) you know (0.5) well
> 4. D: Yes well this is a bit more complicated than some cos there's one
> then one thing wrong and this condition always carries a risk.
> Assuming that we're right. It's possible that we'd have to change
> our story (   ) of the heart test (0.5)
> 5. F: Is it good that she's eating alright?

6.D: Yes. It's to the good that she's eating well, it is to the good that she's been brought here before she's / deteriorated

7.F: / Too old

As home interviews with parents of children with serious illness show (Davis, 1963; Voysey, 1975; Baruch, 1981), the initial response is one of shock, followed by attempted normalization. Here the father seeks to do that normalizing work by appealing to reference groups at Utterances 1 and 3. Rather pathetically, he also tries to draw some comfort from one of the few observably normal features of his baby — her eating.

His questions also elicit information about the likely complicated course of surgical interventions on his daughter. Normally, this is postponed until an in-patient post-catheter interview. So, when the father's questions dry up, he is referred to later possibilities for discussion:

(3:5)

1.F: That's all I can think to ask really.

2.D: If you're (0.5) if the baby's coming in (0.5) there are lots of people around all the time and er (0.5) you'll have plenty more questions.

However, one crucial question remains to be asked. Even if the baby is 'normally sick' can she ever be expected to be 'normally well'. The consultation closes with this poignant exchange:

1.F: When she, if she, got through all this (0.5) will she be you know *normal* (0.5) well obviously not normal would she you know (0.5)?

2.D: If everything went really superbly well the answer to that is yes. If the diagnosis is right, if the catheter confirms what we thought is there, if the first short operation works extremely well, if the pulmonary arteries, the arteries to the lungs grow cos they've now got more blood coming through them, and if the anatomy is such that they can grow and the next operation goes very well with no problems or complications (0.5) there are lots of ifs and buts.

3.F: Of course

4.D: Yes is the answer, you could end up with an essentially healthy child. OK?

5.F: Fine doctor. Well thank you very much.

As the doctor himself notes, 'there are lots of ifs and buts' (seven actually). Nevertheless, the father's questioning has elicited a great deal of information which would not normally be forthcoming at a first out-patients prior to a long career trajectory. Without such extended questioning, the doctor would normally rely on a step-by-step information flow unwinding over several visits. Indeed, as we shall see later in still more complex anomalies, where there is no extended in-patient stay, the long-term prognosis may never actually be raised at out-patient consultations.

It would be easy to see this as a form of medical paternalism, giving only as much information as the parent needs at each stage. However, as this consultation shows, doctors at the Unit do respond in detail to questions that the parents raise. The position seems closer to a common decision-rule about terminal illnesses: 'tell if the patient asks'.

In any event, in terms of the disposal decision there is no suggestion that the father wants to contest the doctor's collegial authority. After an earlier statement of the prognosis, he makes the statement which was discussed in Chapter Two:

> (3:3)
> F: Well that's all we can do. I mean obviously we gotta leave it in your hands anyway.

The baby is, in fact, admitted immediately and catheterized. Shortly afterwards she receives her first-stage correction. The situation is complicated by her tiny pulmonary arteries. Normally, in this difficult situation, a 'shunt' operation would be performed to make the baby less blue by increasing the flow of blood to the lungs. However, the small pulmonary arteries might not then be able to cope. Despite its high risk, the operation is successful and, ten months later, the family return for their second out-patient consultation.

This largely takes the congratulatory form that we have observed elsewhere after successful surgery. In addition, the baby has become quite a celebrity, having sailed through a complicated operation with such tiny pulmonary arteries.

> (Transcript 49: 1−2)
> C 3.1, SC 5, P 1, E 1, PR 2, FC 1 → 2
> 1. D: How is she?
> 2. M: Fine, ain't she?
> 3. F: Terrific.
> 4. D: [*Writing notes*] Very well. Does she go blue?
> 5. M: No.
> 6. D: She's growing. She's one year?
> 7. M: Yes
> 8. D: Slip her top off please. This is a very special baby (2.0)
> 9. F: The scar's still rather nasty on her chest.
> 10. M: It's bound to be

The congratulatory mode is established by the father's 'terrific' and the baby's high status by 'this is a very special baby'. Successful surgery in such difficult circumstances gains status for the Unit and the family bask in the reflected glory. Even the side-effects of surgery are properly minimized. So the father's remark about the 'scar' will not do at all. 'It's bound to be (rather nasty)' his wife rebukes him.

The consultation continues:

> 11. D: There's going to be a lot more discussion about this approach that (   ) surgery is (   ). Other people are having some success with it as well.
> 12. F: Are they?
> 13. D: Oh yes. We're interested to see how she does. Hello, we'll listen first. Don't you want me to listen?
> 14. F: She's got a cold at the moment.
> 15.   [*Baby whimpers*]
> 16. D: You are a clever girl.

The baby is now constituted as an outstanding topic of medical interest — the possible topic of research papers. Even her whimpering is cause for congratulation. Any baby who withstands such surgery and brings credit to the Unit must be, by definition, 'a clever girl'!

After the examination, the doctor continues the 'congratulations' theme, helped by the father, before turning to the next stage of treatment. However, given the present lack of symptoms, he reverts to the 'persuasion' mode to obtain the desired disposal:

> (49:3)
> 1. D: I mean she's done really splendidly
> 2. F: Oh we've no complaints at all
> 3. D: We, we're very pleased with her. We ought to repeat the catheter to find out how these arteries have grown.
> 4. F: Mm.
> 5. D: And what the size is and to check the pressure in her lungs, and so on. There's no urgency to do that, but the plan is to correct her between eighteen months and two years probably. Um, I think what we should do is to get her in for repeat cardiac catheterization in the new year, OK? And then we will know exactly where we stand. You will also know where you stand.

We find here a mixture of 'doctor's decision-making' and 'persuasion'. Initially, the appeal is to the 'We' voice (of collegial authority) and total impersonality ('the plan is ... '). This is justified presumably by the plan of action laid down at the first out-patients and probably confirmed post-operatively. However, the present lack of patency of the condition, apparent in the parents' early remarks, means that the basis of the disposal may have to be re-negotiated. Ironically, the very success of the first stage correction removes some of the emotional force behind the logic of further hospitalization.

Consequently the doctor speedily reverts to the 'persuasion' format, using the voices of 'I' and 'We' ('I think what we should do'). He actively asks for consent ('OK?') and refers to the need of both of us to 'know where we stand'.

After the doctor has provided further details and the parents have agreed that the baby although 'a little bit small' is 'growing', 'getting stronger all the time' and 'catching up', the doctor confirms that the 'persuasion' has succeeded:

(49:3−4)
1. D: OK, well that alright with you? We'll put her name down on the waiting list, I mean we may get through a little bit before that, that's not because anything's wrong.
2. F: When they do that catheter will you possibly keep 'er in then or would you return (0.5)?
3. D: We would definitely send her out after. This is not for surgery, this is for the (0.5) catheter
4. F: Yes
5. D: So that we can plan what to do OK?
6. F: Lovely, thanks a lot.

At Utterance 1, the doctor makes a further reference to the parents' agreement to a further catheter. However, his use of the 'You' voice, here and earlier, should not be read as a move towards 'democratic' forms. Although the child is currently asymptomatic, the sense of recatheterization has already been provided by a statement almost a year before about the timetable. This is only a more elaborated form of the Royal Assent 'if you agree' form found elsewhere.

As in other cases of likely further surgery the doctor assures the parents that only a catheter is proposed at this admission. At the end, the medical decision-making and persuasion modes have become so mixed that it is difficult to tell if 'We can plan what to do' should be heard as referring to the medical team alone or the medical team plus parents. In any event, the final 'OK?' generates enthusiastic assent.

The second catheterization is carried out and reveals that the pulmonary arteries, although larger, are still small. Consequently, at a third out-patients one year later, the second stage correction is postponed. Since this fits one of the contingencies of the plan (i.e. delay until the arteries grow) and accords with the asymptomatic status of the child, a 'doctor's decision-making' form prevails. Although, the father once again intervenes extensively this is only to ask the doctor to rehearse once again the diagnosis and prognosis.

Above all, the tone of mutual congratulation, begun at the previous consultation, is continued and embellished:

(NB 1/10/80 Case 14)
[*after the examination has taken place*]
1. D: I think she's terrific
2. F: I can honestly say we don't mollycoddle her.

In other cases, without the complications present here, the timing of a second-stage correction seems to turn on the risk to life of delay. The second case in our sample leads to a disposal involving simply a further follow-up. The child is four and a half. Although moderately cyanosed (blue), the doctor explains to the parents that she is 'not at risk'. The consultation then continues:

(NB 12/11/80 Case 11)
C 3.1, SC 5, P 3, E 1, PR 1, FC 1 → 3
  1. D: There's nothing to be lost by waiting. The bigger she is the better [*a one-year follow-up appointment is arranged*]
  2. M: [*smiling*] in a year. We've never had one as long as that.
  3. D: Listen you know her as well as we do. You are a good judge of what she needs.

We can note, first, the bench-mark provided, once again, by an extension of the period between consultations. Second there is the curious reference to knowing 'her as well as we do'. Partly, this seems to reflect the increased competence granted to parents at later stages of a career-trajectory. Partly, it may reflect a preparedness, in this kind of condition, to relate the timing of surgery to the parents' observations about the child's performance. The consultation thus *seems* to switch from a doctor's decision-making mode directly into a form of 'democracy'.

This analysis, however, depends on the previous negotiation about the proper sense to be attached to the child's 'blueness'. Unfortunately, the child was examined in a side-room and there is no proper recording of the earlier stages of the consultation. It would be interesting to know how much weight the parents themselves attached to the 'blueness' of their child. Nonetheless, it is clear from other consultations that parents' perceptions of cyanosis can often be directly related to the form of the disposal.[4]

The remaining two sample members are immediate follow-ups after successful one-stage total corrections of Tetralogy. As we would predict, both take a congratulatory-mode. At the first (Random Sample: Case 9), the doctor says, at various points, 'excellent result', 'that's a nice, nice result', 'very good, you've got a normal boy', 'he's done very nicely, a nice result'. A further two-year follow-up appointment is given and the doctor adds 'smashing'.

In the second case, the mother seems rather more anxious. There is an initially non-problematic elicitation sequence:

(NB 8/10/80 Case 3)
  1. D: Very good. She's active?
  2. M: She's running round.

However, the mother later intervenes as the doctors discuss the ECG:

1. M: Is that bad?
2. D: No. It's normal. It's normal after this operation
    [*and later*]
3. M: The only thing that concerned us is that her colour hasn't been very good.
4. D: But there's no reason why she should go blue.

A little later, after further congratulations, one piece of further reassurance is required before the disposal of a further routine follow-up is arranged:

1. D: An excellent result
2. M: What chance is there that something could go wrong?
3. D: Five per cent
4. M: So we can really relax?
5. D: Forget about her [*begins to detail the encouraging research on long-term follow-ups of total corrections*]

Tetralogy of Fallot, although relatively serious, is usually correctable. More complex anomalies, like a heart with a single ventricle, are far less likely to be correctable. However, this does not mean that they are untreatable. The normal procedure is to catheter to confirm the diagnosis and then later, when needed, to carry out a palliative operation either to increase the flow of blood through the lungs (a shunt) or to decrease it (pulmonary artery banding) depending on the character of the anomaly.

Not all such children will require a palliative operation. In some, the condition will be relatively self-compensating and, for a long while, they will not be blue or breathless. At the other extreme, some children will require a series of such operations.

I will consider four cases of complicated anomalies which cover a range of possibilities extending from no shunt/later corrective surgery through the negotiation of a shunt to the case of a child who has had already a series of palliative operations. The last case involves some cheating since it is drawn from outside the sample but I thought it would be instructive to examine an encounter with the parents of a child almost at the end of the road for possible surgical interventions.

The first case involves a girl of four who had been cathetered after a few days of life but has subsequently not needed recatheterization or palliative surgery. The opening exchanges follow a pattern noted earlier when the child arrives with only the father in attendance:

(Random Sample Case 15)
C 4.1., SC 3, P 1, E 1, PR 1, FC 1
1. D: Did you come with her on your own?
2. F: Yes (0.5) today (1.0). The other one's not well
3. D: Aah.

These few words clearly telescope a host of culturally available assumptions. Note how the question is not heard as surprising when addressed to a father on his own. Moreover, he feels obliged to offer two accounts in response. First, that his sole presence is not necessarily routine ('today'). Second, that there is a good reason explaining the mother's absence today. Again, consider how an absent father would be unremarkable and that an account in terms of looking after a sick child being part of the assumed 'mother's role' gives an immediate excuse for her absence which is at once acceptable to the doctor ('Aah').

The elicitation sequence then commences:

4. D: How is she in herself?
5. F: Alright

I note later (Chapter Six) that Down's Syndrome children tend not to get formulated as well in the elicitation sequence. This serves to remind parents that their children should be seen as 'damaged' and that corrective surgery, which normally can transform a state of 'unwellness' to 'wellness' may not be possible. It could be that a fuller analysis of the data involving children with complex heart anomalies, which also may be non-correctable, would reveal a similar avoidance of the use of 'well' in the doctor's initial question.

In this case, however, the doctor follows this up in the normal way:

[*the child is vigorously running round*]
6. D: She's / well?
7. F: / As you can see
8. D: Does she go blue?
9. F: Occasionally after eight hours of continuous [*general laughter*]
10. D: [*laughs*] I get the message [*more general laughter*]

The asymptomatic status of the child is reinforced after the examination. It concludes with a reference to the possibility of corrective surgery.

1. D: She's very good
        . . .
2. D: [*to other doctor*] She's very well-compensated
3. D: [*to father*] She's fine. In *due course* when she's older she will be suitable for an operation to make the blood go round the right way but the bigger she is the better. And she's obviously thriving and growing beautifully. And no indication to do anything. May we see her in a year please?

The follow-up disposal in terms of the 'We' voice of doctor's decision-making is clearly non-problematic for an asymptomatic child. One year later, at the next out-patients, the mother is present and the prospect of surgery closer. Once again, the elicitation sequence avoids an initial reference to 'wellness'.

(NB 19/11/80 Case 6)
C 4.1, SC 3, P 1, E 1, PR 2, FC 1
1. D: She's a good colour. Is she leading a normal life?
2. M: Ye-es. When she started school she was shattered

The mother continues, implying that, despite her daughter's tiredness, she is generally well. Before the doctor commences his examination, he mentions the possibility of partially corrective surgery and this meets a little resistance from the mother. After all, she maintains, her daughter is well. The doctor responds in terms of the need 'to think of the long-term future'.[5]

The mother's doubts are handled by delay rather than frontal assault. The disposal involves a further echo-cardiogram and a repeat catheter. Later on, the mother is assured, 'we'll discuss her case ' (the 'collegiate' We or the 'democratic' We?). She then tries to open up the discussion:

1. M: What does surgery involve?
2. D: [*Goes through the details of Fontane's procedure for tricuspid atresia; stresses that the child is particularly suited for corrective surgery* because *she is well and has not been already shunted*]
3. D: There's no rush. She's well. But *we* have to think of the long-term
4. M: How long are you thinking of?
5. D: It might be three to five years. *We*'ll decide when (my emphasis)

The mother's dilemma is that the asymptomatic status of her child, the very factor that recommends surgery to the doctors, given the underlying condition, makes her want to resist radical interventions. Nonetheless, the doctor here stays in the doctor's decision-making format using the voice of 'We' (now clearly the voice of collegial authority). This lack of congruence between an anxious mother and an imposed decision may be storing up later troubles. However, it has to be borne in mind that the 'planning' of the child's career trajectory has been mutually agreed much earlier and that the mother is slightly resistant now, quite understandably, because her child has developed so well in the interim. It is also likely that after catheterization, the options will be discussed in a much more open way.

This is an unusual case clinically, apart from the social lack of congruence. Most children with this kind of complex condition do experience symptoms and decisions about palliative operations have to be made. Sometimes, parents are actively involved in decision-making. For instance, in the case of a fifteen month old baby with A-V canal defect and patent-ductus, even though the child is rather blue and breathless, the doctor does not decide by himself. He suggests a shunt to the parents as an 'option' which 'could make him less blue'. This leads to the following exchange:

(NB 22/10/80 Case 6)
C 4.2, SC 3, P 3, E 1, PR 1, FC 3
  1.　F:　He's not restricted at all
  2.　D:　That's what I was fishing for

Here the parents are accorded great weight in the decision-making. Given the competence they will have accumulated in nursing the child, their sense of his degree of 'restriction' can be taken very seriously. Equally, however, shunting is only sensible where the clinical evidence points to a possible risk to life. Where such evidence is absent, the parents' account that a child is coping with his symptoms settles the matter.

From one side, then, this looks like a 'democratic' format. From another side, the parents' lack of concern makes it easier for the doctor to make the disposal that he already favoured.

In the case of the third child I will consider, with a univentricular heart, the clinical evidence seems to point much more directly towards intervention. The format eventually turns out to be straight 'doctor's decision-making' but only after considerable persuasive work in establishing the patency of the condition.

(Random Sample Case 17)
C 4.1., SC 3, P2 → 3, E 1, PR 1, FC 2 → 1
  1.　D:　Right. So how are things *at the moment*?
  2.　M:　Well fine *at the moment* (my emphasis)

Again note the avoidance of 'wellness' in the initial elicitation question. As both doctor and mother acknowledge with such a child 'things' have to be judged on a day-by-day basis ('fine at the moment'). Nonetheless, the mother goes on to emphasize that apart from her 'teething' and 'snuffles' her development is going well. However, the doctor, at this point, introduces the child's past breathlessness:

  1.　D:　Now. She got very breathless when you were in Australia. Is that right?
  2.　M:　Well she had pneumonia before we left
  3.　D:　So it may have been the chest problems she had
  4.　M:　(　　　　　　　　)
  5.　D:　Thing is when you were in Australia, the cardiologist thought she was in heart failure
  6.　M:　Any chest problems she has goes to the lungs. The lungs flood with blood apparently. But she has been doing fine except for the teeth as I say [*child begins to cry*]
  7.　D:　She's quite quite blue, a little bit blue when she cries
  8.　M:　A little bit

Confronted with evidence of her child's problems, the mother retreats, first to her 'chest problems' and then to her 'doing fine'. Only at the end does she concede that the child is after all 'a little bit blue'. At this point, after considerable effort, the doctor has established the patency of the condition. Subsequently, after the examination, the doctor simply states the management plan, relying largely on the voice of 'We'.

1. D: Well it seems to me that her catheter needs to be repeated. (   ) Well really she's in a bit of heart failure actually. Her liver's quite big, heart's big, you know, she's really (   ) small, she's not growing up OK. (   )

2. D: So what *we*'ll do is to review the film. It looks as if she should have something done. *We* don't want to risk any damage being done to her lungs/really

3. M: /No no

4. D: It's a rather complex situation though. It's not easy to decide what to do. She's a little bit blue isn't she? / If we

5. M: / On and off

6. D: On and off. And if *we* (0.5) try and put a band on her pulmonary artery, its effect will be to make her more blue

7. M: Mmmm.

8. D: Anyway (1.0) *We*'ll have a talk and see what we think is the best thing to do

9. M: Mm.

10. D: And I'll write to you. But I think she'll have to have a catheter test

Given a child that has been negotiated as symptomatic, the management team are free to work on the possible solutions. However, the situation is complicated by the few remaining options and by the mother's continuing attempts to redefine her child as relatively well. For instance, she will only concede that her child is blue 'on and off' (Utterance 5).

Recognizing the sombre character of his disposal statement and the mother's obvious anxieties (expressed in her long drawn out 'mmmms'), the doctor closes the consultation with an attempt to lighten the gloom:

1. D: So we'll be in touch (2.0) She looks reasonably well. Anyway we'll just want to make sure she doesn't get /any worse

2. M: / She's fi-ine, you know, I hope (   ) having to have anything but you know it's just one of /those things

3. D: /Mm

4. M: She's up and down you might say / you know

5. D: / Mm

6. M: She'll be *really* fine and then a few days later she's not quite so happy

7. D: No, no

8. M: With herself. But I do feel it's her teeth and I'm hoping when her teeth are through that it will be easier for her, anyway
9. D: Yes
10. M: It probably won't change / any situation in her body really
11. D: It will make it
12. M: It will make it easier for her
13. D: OK (1.0) See you soon

The doctor's comment about 'reasonably well' allows all the mother's hopes and anxieties to come flooding out. She transforms her child's symptoms into a varying presence ('up and down') perhaps due to her teeth, although, at Utterance 10, she recognizes the importance of the underlying situation. This example shows clearly how professional dominance depends on the negotiation of 'patency' and, even then, need not preclude opportunities being created for the expression of parental anxieties.

The three cases so far examined all suggest that very complex conditions are associated with a 'doctor's decision-making' format. There are exceptions, however, and I will briefly look at a couple of instances, where the framework is much more open. To do so, I will have to go beyond the data contained in the sample.

The first instance arises in a discussion between a consultant and a doctor about an in-patient interview with the parents of a child who has recently been catheterized to investigate a complex anomaly which is probably not correctable:

(Transcript 112:1)
1. D: I've just had a long chat with (   ). Um well my my feeling, having spoken to them which is different from my own feeling (   ) as it's quite significant the feeling that I've come out with
2. C: Hm
3. D: Having spoken to them at length is that um, I think they would like the baby to be shunted
4. C: Hm
5. D: And um (1.0) I think that that being (   ) I mean that's the conclusion I came out from having spoken to them, though I do /
6. C: / which is against what you actually thought until now?
7. D: It was against my personal/
8. C: / Right
9. D: um feelings about it . . .

Here clearly parental decision-making is being given a large part to play even though their opinions seem to go against that of the doctors. Later on the doctor says that, although the parents realize that total correction is impossible, they still want a palliative operation:

1. D: I don't know they they think it's their baby (   ) could um enjoy some sort of reasonable life if if there was a big result from the shunting that (2.00) that um (2.00) I mean it's possible that that that with a shunt the baby might, um develop and grow. Um and it wouldn't preclude anything being done later. It wouldn't force them into a particular position (   )
2. C: Hm
3. D: I said that maybe that as the (   ) wasn't technically feasible. And I spoke to them for about an hour. And I think they would like something to be done at the moment. I don't think, I think, they feel very um unhappy if things are just left and (   ) . . .

Using the powerful symbol of parents' ultimate rights to decide ('it's their baby'), the doctor is clearly attaching considerable weight to their views.

The doctor's apparent preference for having things 'just left' is underlined in a final case of a ten-year-old boy who has already had three shunts but whose pulmonary arteries remain very small. After the parents leave, the consultant writes in his referral letter:

(Transcript 91:13)
> D: I think we have probably reached the end of the road in terms of surgery on this boy.

In a discussion with a doctor just before about the child's poor prognosis, he has already commented:

(91:12)
> D: I mean (2.0) We are intensely aware of the fact that palliative surgery may be stirring up disaster

The 'disaster' probably concerns losing a teenage child in tragic circumstances. The clear medical preference is for non-intervention and the likelihood of an early death before the parents have had much chance to build up expectations about the child's future. Nevertheless, as the previous case suggests, and this case illustrates, parental feelings in favour of palliative surgery do have an effect.[6]

Given the situation that has been created, the consultation largely concerns itself with the child's drug-regime and a stitch-infection arising from his last operation. All that can be offered, despite reported episodes of unconsciousness, is an oxygen supply for home use.

Unusually, after the examination, the child is asked to leave.

(91:7)
1. D: Come on, off you go. I'm going to have a quick word with your mum and dad and er [*next 40 seconds, boy leaves room, father mumbles inaudible comments*]

   2. D: I don't, I think basically there isn't really very much more we can
       do surgically. Quite a big risk
   3. M: Hmm
   4. D: Because of the size of the pulmonary arteries, they seem to be
       limiting what (0.5) what we've done, um (0.5) Quite a battle this
       time. He was quite sick after it.

Faced with 'the end of the road', there is no point in using persuasion
and no basic medical decisions to be imposed. Even the sense of past
operations is seen not to reside as much in producing health but in
improving morale:

   1. D: It has made him pinker
   2. F: Hmm
   3. M: Yeah that (   ) do that [*laughing-utterance inaudible*]
   4. F: This is one, this is one thing he was pleased about because it's a
       thing that has been upsetting him.
   5. M: Yeah.

Later on, the child returns and a disposal of a six-week follow-up is
arranged. His father tries to explore the possibility of further action and
hears the unvarnished truth in response. He begins by seeking to
confirm that the only thing that can be done at home is to provide
oxygen:

   (91:10)
    1. F: There's little more we can do?
    2. D: I'm afraid so
    3. F: (   ) is there no more you can do?
    4. D: I think that
    5. M: [*to child*] Sit up!
    6. D: I think oxygen is all we can (0.5) give him
    7. F: Mmm.
    8. D: I don't think there's any magical operation that's going to (0.5) in
        fact I don't think he would survive anything else quite honestly
    9. F: Hmm.
  10. D: Each time he's felt a bit grim for a day or two and we get quite
       worried and concerned that we may have done the wrong thing by
       putting him up for surgery
       (3.0)
  11. M: Alright, so I see Dr X in six weeks.

Where further medical action is ruled out, parents and doctors take
on a discursive equality. There are no more battles to be fought or even
arguments to be won — for what point is there in a verbal triumph
which cannot change the gloomy prognosis? Only the truth will do and
the truth reveals the end of the clinical road.

This is reflected here in the inability of the doctor to organize his own
ending of the consultation after such a grave statement. A reiteration of
the disposal *from a parent* terminates the embarrassed silence.

Conclusion

The hypotheses suggested in Part One of this paper have been supported and deepened by the analysis of the data. In addition, the analysis has revealed regular patterns like the use of a congratulatory form after successful surgery and the appeal by parents to bench-marks and occasional features like the 'consumerist' and 'collegial' forms. It has also shown how particular combinations of pronouns (or 'voices') serve to constitute the different discursive forms.

Above all, the analysis has suggested how the form of consultation varies both *between* successive consultations, largely due to the patency of the condition, and *within* consultations as parental questioning or responses change the context of the encounter. In particular, the continuing negotiation, according to varying criteria, of 'wellness' and 'unwellness' points to a central feature of the social organization of illness.

Notes

1. This reconstitution is revealed most clearly in a summary disposal statement offered by the doctor towards the end of the consultation (I have removed the parent's mutters of agreement)

117:9

> D: So what I think we should do is to put her name on the non-urgent waiting list for the heart test . . . And that'll probably be in the New Year. Cause there's no rush. She's a well child . . . She's not in any danger or anything.

2. A degree of patient control over the agenda seems to distinguish private practice from NHS consultations — see Chapter Five.

3. After the mother has departed, the doctor explains that the delay over repeat catheterization was in order to see whether the residual VSD would close. He explains his strategy to another doctor:

(Transcript 38:3)

> D: So she requires repeat catheter. I'm not too happy about, OK? I didn't really want to get into all that talking to her, I thought we'd take it step-wise, but she requires repeat study. I'm sure Mrs B appreciates that might mean we need to do more.

4. In another case of Fallot's Tetralogy, not in the sample, a catheter is postponed because the mother does not perceive the condition as patent in any way. (Transcript 28) However, at a second out-patients, three months later, after starting off by denying that her child goes blue, she suddenly admits it as follows:

(Transcript 27:2)

C 3.1., SC 2, P 1 → 3, E 1, PR 1, FC 2

1. D: I think you may find over the next few months that he does go a little blue. It doesn't matter

2. M: Well he does when I bath him

3. D: Does he? He goes blue does he? Very blue?
4. M: No, only now and again
5. D: His lips
6. M: Mm.

The disposal now speedily becomes catheterization via a 'persuasion' format ('I' and 'We' voices, 'if you agree' plus stress on the child's current 'wellness' but 'future' problems).

5. Unfortunately, I am relying on notes made at the time here and so cannot offer a full transcript.

6. Only in the case of Down's Syndrome children is there any evidence of the use of passive euthanasia sometimes by employing delaying tactics in response to parental requests for intervention.

4

A Policy Intervention:
The Pre-Admission Clinic

Introduction

In the preceding two chapters, I have sought to demonstrate how the trajectory of treatment for different heart conditions constitutes a 'site' around which the parties orient themselves. As promised, I now want to broaden out the analysis, methodologically and practically. Two questions are central to this discussion:

1. To what extent can the qualitative analysis of data in Chapter Three be supported by quantitative measures, however crude?

2. What practical relevance, particularly in relation to parental concerns, do these findings have?

Shortly, I will present such quantitative measures and discuss the practical intervention where the analysis was applied. It is first necessary, however, to consider the character of the 'parental concerns' to which I have just referred.

When neonates or young infants are admitted to paediatric cardiology units as emergencies, events occur so rapidly that problems of adaptation for parents may be magnified (Sheridan and Johnson, 1976). Even when a child is admitted via the more leisurely route of an out-patient clinic consultation (some months or years after birth), these difficulties do not dissipate.

At a first out-patient consultation, parents interpret the physician's comments in terms of an assumed sentence of death which they associate with any malfunction of the heart. Most parents do not distinguish between different kinds of cardiac anomaly: thus the response of a parent who learns that her child has a ventricular septal defect may be a little different from one who learns that the child has a univentricular heart. In our home interviews with a sample of twenty families, sixteen felt they should have asked more questions, six said they were inhibited by the number of staff attending the consultation and seven referred to finding the process a 'rush'. Two other studies (Apley et al., 1967; Sheridan et al., 1976) produced similar findings, stressing parental dissatisfaction with the doctor's preoccupation with the physical aspects of the condition and the lack of opportunity for parents to ask questions.

These data have to be viewed with care. First, most studies lack a longitudinal element and consequently fail to compare consultations at different stages of the child's medical career. Second, few studies present detailed objective data on out-patient consultations as opposed to parents' own subsequent responses.

Counting Questions

In Chapter Three, I tried to demonstrate the salience of the clinic site for shaping the form of out-patient consultations. This accounted for the increasing competence attributed to parents as their child's hospital career unfolded. It also highlighted parents' limited basis for intervention at their first clinic visit — provided that their perception of symptoms and the medical disposal were congruent.

This qualitative analysis received additional support in a simple quantitative analysis of the clinic data. From the 1200 recorded consultations, a further sample of 102 consultations was drawn from 20 clinic sessions selected at random. Only consultations recorded on the second side of the first C90 cassette were included in order to minimize the impact of extraneous factors associated with the beginning and end of the clinic. Nearly all the consultations involved the same paediatric cardiologist, although in a small minority of cases another doctor conducted the consultation.

As an attempt to obtain an objective measure of parental participation in the consultation, the numbers of questions asked, uses of technical terminology and introduction of non-cardiac topics were counted. Inevitably, when coding natural language difficulties arise. For instance, it was decided to count as a question those utterances which asked for a substantive piece of information and to exclude utterances which simply asked for repetition (e.g. 'Can you repeat that please?'). Thus not all interrogatives were coded as questions (e.g. 'Hm?', 'I beg your pardon?'), while some utterances which are not interrogatives were counted as questions (e.g. 'We wondered whether he could have his injections.') (For a more sophisticated approach to counting questions in medical interviews see West, 1984, and Fisher, 1984).

These measures of parental participation were then related to factors associated with the treatment situation, particularly the stage of treatment, seriousness of condition and the outcome of the consultation, as well as particular contingencies such as physicians' statements of change or difference in the medical opinion or of uncertainty in the diagnosis or treatment of the condition. Chi-squared tests for goodness of fit were used, based on the null hypothesis that there was no difference in the frequencies for each group (controlling for n).

Stage of treatment was based on the three most crucial career contingencies of the child with congenital heart disease: initial consultation, cardiac catheterization and surgery. Seriousness of condition was assessed according to three diagnosis groups based on the prognosis as follows:

Group I: Innocent murmurs, paroxysmal supraventricular tachycardia, small or medium sized ventricular septal defect, persistent ductus arteriosus, pulmonary stenosis, mild aortic stenosis, ostium secundum atrial septal defect.

Group II: Tetralogy of Fallot, complete transposition of the great arteries, large ventricular septal defect, ostium primum atrial septal defect.

Group III: Hearts with double inlet or absent right atrioventricular connexion or other complex abnormalities.

Finally, outcome of consultation was determined by whether the child was referred for in-patient treatment or investigation (normally cardiac catheterization), surgery, or was given a further out-patient appointment or discharged.

Results

For the sake of brevity, only data on parental questions are reported here. Other measures of parental participation in the consultation do, however, broadly follow the same pattern.

TABLE 1
Questions and Stage of Treatment

	Patients ($n = 102$)	Total questions asked (q)	Mean questions asked ($\overline{q}$)
Pre-inpatient	30	64	2.13
Post-catheter	32	124	3.87
Post-operation	40	130	3.25

$\chi^2 = 15.372$ (2d.f.) significant at < 0.01.

TABLE 2
Questions and Diagnosis Group

Group	Patients ($n = 102$)	Total questions asked (q)	Mean questions asked ($\overline{q}$)
I	29	33	1.14
II	53	227	4.28
III	20	58	2.9

$\chi^2 = 59.84$ (2 d.f.) significant at < 0.01.

In the sample of 102 consultations, the mean number of questions asked by parents was 3.2 ($n = 318$). However, as Table 1 shows, there was considerable variation according to stage of treatment with the first two stages of treatment differing most from the expected figure. In the pre-inpatient stage, parents ask considerably fewer questions than the sample mean, while after cardiac catheterization more are asked. This pattern is continued when we introduce other independent variables.

In Table 2, we see that in the least serious cases (Group I), the number of questions asked are considerably less than the sample mean, and in the most serious cases (Group III) quite close to the mean. Only in the case of medium severity (Group II) were significantly more questions asked.

The outcome of the consultation also produces a statistically significant association with the number of questions asked (Table 3). Thus parents whose child is being recommended for hospital admission ask more questions than parents whose child is not to be brought into hospital. Another factor that seems to affect parental participation is the mention by a physician of a change in the opinion about the diagnosis, prognosis or treatment of their child (Table 4), there being a highly significant relationship between a stated medical change of opinion and the number of questions asked.

TABLE 3
Questions and Outcome of Consultation

	($n = 102$)	(q)	($\bar{q}$)
Not for CC or surgery	62	158	2.55
For CC or surgery	40	160	4.0

$\chi^2 = 16.43$ (1 d.f.) significant at < 0.01; CC = cardiac catheterization.

TABLE 4
Questions and Change or Difference in Medical Opinion

	($n = 102$)	(q)	($\bar{q}$)
Change	22	115	5.23
No change	80	203	2.54

$\chi^2 = 40.04$ (1 d.f.) significant at < 0.01.

It would appear that a physician's statement of uncertainty is analogous to a change in his opinion. However, Table 5 suggests that uncertainty, unlike change, is not associated with parental questioning. Here we are not able to reject the null hypothesis. The statement of medical uncertainty does not, in itself, generate more questions. One possible explanation is that, where uncertainty exists, the physician is often likely to suggest the need for more investigations to be conducted and parents postpone their questions until a later consultation.

TABLE 5
Questions and Uncertainty of Diagnosis or Treatment
Expressed by Physician

	$(n = 102)$	(q)	$(\bar{q})$
Uncertainty	36	99	2.75
None	66	219	3.32

$\chi^2 = 2.406$ (1 d.f.) *not* significant at < 0.05.

One possibility, suggested by parents in home interviews is that their low participation in initial out-patient consultations is related to the 'rush' they experience. However, our data suggest that pre-inpatient consultations are on average considerably longer than post-operation consultations and almost as long as that held after cardiac catheterization.

Table 6 suggests that the link between stage of treatment and parental participation (outlined in Table 1) is not related to the length of the consultation, contrary to parents' own reported feelings about early consultations.

TABLE 6
Length of Consultations by Stage of Treatment

	Proportion of consultations > 10 min (%)
Pre-inpatient	56
Post-catheter	62
Post-operation	26

One further parental assumption is that the presence of many people limits their own participation in the consultation.

The results of forty consultations for which such data were available are shown in Table 7. There was indeed a significant relationship between the presence of five or more non-family (e.g. students, nurses, researchers) and number of questions asked, but parents ask more questions where there are more professional staff present.

TABLE 7
Questions Asked and Non-Family Present

	n (40)	q	$\bar{q}$
> 5	23	99	4.30
< 5	17	48	2.82

$\chi^2 = 5.83$ (1 d.f.) significant at < 0.05.

Parents' Accounts and the Clinic Data

The lack of congruence between parents' perceptions of the consultations and the tape-recorded data is of interest. One explanation is that parental accounts of medical encounters may be a means by which parents re-establish their claims to responsible parenthood in a guilt-laden situation when they have produced a child with an abnormality. By remarking on 'rush' and 'being crowded out' of the consultation, they accommodate their own feelings of inadequacy. If 'rush' is indeed a problem it may principally arise not through the overall length of the consultation but because of how that time is organized. Parents may find it difficult to 'collect their thoughts' at a first consultation, especially when they are confronted by a sudden statement of their child's condition and need to generate some sort of immediate response in a one-to-one situation. Conversely, where discussion between many doctors occurs after the initial diagnosis statements, parents have time to reflect upon what they have been told and, perhaps, to hear it formulated in different ways by a number of doctors. Using consultations for professional purposes (discussions, teaching, etc.) may thus serve a latent function for parents and patients, encouraging them to participate rather than silencing them.

Overall, the data suggest that there is not a direct relationship between parental participation in the consultation and length of contact with the hospital or degree of seriousness of the child's condition. The most experienced parents (post-operation) do not ask the most questions (Table 1), nor do the parents of children with the most serious diagnoses (Table 2). Parents ask most questions when:

1. the child has just undergone cardiac catheterization (Table 1);

2. the child's suspected condition is serious but treatable (Table 2);
3. following the consultation, the child is to be admitted into hospital (Table 3);
4. the physician states a change in the medical opinion (Table 4);
5. five or more staff are present (Table 7).

This suggests that parental demand for information is greatest in situations where soundly-based knowledge is available (e.g. after cardiac catheterization) or where active intervention is contemplated (e.g. surgery for tetralogy of Fallot).

This study has demonstrated considerable variance in the amount of parental involvement in out-patient appointments. While we have no direct data to support it, our experience is that this variance bears little relation to traditional social science explanations such as parents' social class or education, or the consulting style of the doctor. Rather, the variance may be explained in terms of factors internal to the treatment situation such as precise diagnosis (excluding the first out-patient appointment) stage of treatment and disposal.

The Sense of Parents' Accounts
It is tempting to treat what parents said in interview as 'subjective' misunderstanding of the 'objective' facts revealed by the clinic data. Such an approach to commonsense knowledge is quite prevalent in the social sciences. I vividly recall attending an Introductory Sociology course over twenty years ago in which the lecturer claimed that social research could once and for all cut through the 'inadequacies' of commonsense thought. Such research, we were told, could conclusively determine whether 'too many cooks spoil the broth' or 'many hands make light work'!

However, such sharp distinction between scientific fact and commonsense knowledge fails to attend to the power of everyday conceptions of reality. Since Durkheim's day, many sociologists have pointed out the moral structures present in such conceptions and their link to the social order itself. We cannot, then, dismiss parents' accounts as inaccurate expressions of reality for such accounts constitute a powerful reality in themselves. This is what we tried to demonstrate using our interview data.

In Chapters Two and Three, I have discussed field data based on transcripts of clinic encounters. This, however, was only a part of the research at the PCU. A sample of twenty families also consented to give a series of interviews in their homes over a two-year period. This research was largely carried out by Geoffrey Baruch and is extensively reported elsewhere (Baruch, 1981; 1982). Baruch's approach to interview data followed Voysey's (1975) interest in the moral structures present in parents' formulations of their child's condition.

Using qualitative and quantitative data, Baruch demonstrates how the same parents can variously appeal to depictions of their child as an 'innocent', requiring protection, and as a partially rational actor who can be reasoned with. Generally, however, the child was presented as a dependent requiring care. Mothers particularly produced 'moral tales' which showed that their child depended upon them. These could take the form of 'atrocity stories' describing how, despite the mother's suspicions, health-care professions had failed to detect early signs of the condition. Additionally, a dramatic incident that had occurred during the child's stay in hospital would often be reported. Usually this involved a separation from the mother which was reported to have caused the child great emotional stress.

In such ways, mothers appealed to the salience of their parenting skills even in the context of potentially mystifying high technology medicine. Dissatisfied with the quality of the information they had obtained at the first out-patients consultation, parents often sought the help of their GP. Where the GP referred them back to the hospital doctors, they turned to encyclopaedias and popular medical texts or sought the advice of researchers conducting home interviews.

Central to these activities were conceptions of being a 'normal' parent and practices which invoked a parent's moral responsibility towards her child. This seems to be overlooked by approaches which treat parents' interview responses as displays of 'anxieties' which are best handled by professional interventions.

Take the case of 'puppet therapy' as recommended by some psychologists (Friedberg and Caldert, 1975). This has the laudable aim of preparing the child for cardiac catheterization and surgery by getting nurse educators and, sometimes, child psychiatrists to 'act out' what will happen to the child, using glove puppets.

Two principal problems arise with this approach. First, it overlooks the ways in which parents already prepare their children using their own improvised techniques. So professionally-administered puppet-therapy may threaten parents' moral sense of their own responsibilities by passing on some of their perceived functions to 'experts'. Second, such psychiatrically-oriented initiatives may cast doubt on the mental health of members of the family, assuming that the hospital experience tends to disrupt family life rather than offering an opportunity to re-assert it.

If we focus on the clinic encounter alone, however, it is not at all clear that the most effective way forward is for better training of doctors in techniques of 'effective communication'. This may under-estimate the need for balance between attention to the patient's perspective and practical requirements of clinic work as well as different parental needs at various stages of their child's career.

Moreover, apparently 'poor' communication techniques, such as breaking off from the consultation to engage in teaching, may actually encourage parental involvement (Table 7 above).

Trying to improve the communication skills of medical staff (e.g. Byrne and Long, 1976) has parallels to policies encouraging patient or parent 'adjustment'. Both approaches seek to promote a more appropriate response to the setting on the part of its participants. Such a prescribed orientation might be, on the part of the families, a 'healthy' or 'positive' response to the child's illness or, on the part of doctors, a 'patient-centred' approach. This kind of approach seems unlikely to meet with any real success because

1. We have no way of legislating for the behaviour of future generations of participants, uninstructed by us.

2. It tends to offer a critique of the strategies adopted by participants, by comparison with an ideal model of medical encounters, while ignoring the probability that the strategies adopted are well grounded in the contingencies in which the participants find themselves. These strategies cannot be simply wished away. As Freidson (1970) has noted, the contingencies of practice are likely to be far more relevant to medical staff than professional or in-service training.

3. Ultimately, can sociological observers be confident that they know more than parents facing the serious illness or death of a child, or doctors doing their work according to canons of which sociologists remain largely ignorant?

In formulating policy recommendations based on our research, we have tried to remain aware of the limits imposed by our particular position, but also of what it permits us. In the last two chapters, I used transcripts to formulate a working model of participants' decision-making rules. The quantitative data has supported my claim about the site-bound character of interaction. So we can observe the variability in medical encounters in the Unit. By analytic means unavailable to the participants to the setting, we can attempt to discover the conditions of these variations. Finally, by categories of 'success' and 'failure' derived from the participants themselves, we can suggest what conditions might promote more successful encounters, or deal with the problems the participants themselves encounter.

It would be impractical for us to construct for medical staff or families an appropriate attitude to the illness of technique for dealing with the other participants, and then suggest that those concerned adopt the form we have proposed. What we can do, however, is to look at cases where things in practice work well within the setting, and attempt to discover the conditions which in practice promote these forms. We can hope to turn what happens already but haphazardly into something which happens routinely.

We cannot attempt to offer doctors a technique for dealing with families, and would not wish to. We cannot ourselves tell families what they want to know. We have tried to discover the variability of the conditions upon which dialogue takes place. On the basis of this, we have tried to construct situations in which these conditions are as favourable as possible.

Practical Implications

The admittedly crude quantitative analysis of family questions confirmed the nature and direction of the influence of the clinic site on parent behaviour. What site-specific policy proposals should follow? We need to consider first the constraints created by the site of the first out-patient encounter. This reveals, I believe, that many of the problems that parents experience with it cannot be addressed by reforming the communication styles of doctors. However, this will allow us to take up some of the more positive implications of the analysis.

Prior to the admission of their child, the majority of families have contact with the Unit only during one or more out-patient consultations. At these consultations, parents' questions are invited and information about the probable diagnosis and proposed treatment, and the details of hospitalization are freely given. However, we felt that these consultations may be an inappropriate occasion for this kind of discussion.

1. At these out-patient consultations, the important matter for parents, understandably and inevitably, is the verdict that they are awaiting on how seriously ill their child is. Immediately after hearing that their child is to be admitted for cardiac catheterization or an operation, it is difficult for parents to know what further information to ask for, or to follow an explanation of a complicated illness.

2. Again unavoidably, much of the out-patient consultation involves the carrying out of 'doctors' business', or examination, diagnosis, discussion and teaching, with the family's help where appropriate. It seems that it is then difficult to alter the focus of the consultation, after these matters have been dealt with, to allow the family to raise their own concerns. However much doctors try to be, and are, helpful to the family, the main business of these consultations is for the family to be helpful in the doctor's work. Families we have interviewed regard the consultation in this way.

3. For good practical reasons, the conversational structure of the out-patient consultations is that of an interview. In interviews, typically, one 'side' opens and closes the encounter, selects the topics

for discussion, controls the rights of those present to speak, asks the questions (or decides when it is proper for somebody else to ask a question), and so on.

This similarity of the consultation to an interview tends to inhibit the behaviour of the parents, if not that of the children. Whatever the approach of the consultant or registrar, parents find difficulty in asking questions which they consider the doctor would regard as trivial or silly.

4. Families do not usually come to an out-patient appointment with prepared questions about their concerns. They are unprepared to respond to a new development in their child's condition or to a first decision to put the child on a waiting list for in-patient treatment. There is not time for family members to think or talk to each other about what they wish to ask.

5. There are problems for the families associated with any out-patient consultation. They are aware, for instance, that they are taking up the time of other patients waiting outside. Additionally, families seen towards the end of the out-patient session may find the consultation harder to cope with, having waited for a long period with tired and hungry children. These families may then have a shorter consultation, if the consultant or registrar's time is limited.

On such an occasion, therefore we may expect families to be relatively unprepared to discuss their concerns, inhibited from raising them, distracted by the more important issues and least able to understand the medical complexities they are introduced to.

There are, however, a number of more encouraging implications of the analysis. Parents do gradually participate more in the consultation during the child's hospital career and certain career contingencies are associated with greater questioning whatever the stage of treatment. Strangely, parents also participate more when there are many people present in the clinic, typically when 'teaching' is taking place. What can we learn from this finding?

On reflection, we came to think that the doctor breaking off the consultation to engage in teaching might have an unintended function. In this situation, parents are no longer in direct eye-contact with the doctor. They no longer need fear a possible death-sentence in every word. Nor do they need to spend time keeping their children in order so that the doctor can examine the child or speak without interruption. A space opens up in which parents can collect their thoughts, while reflecting on the different versions of their child's condition being offered in the teaching session.

Now, of course, it is easy, *after the fact*, to rationalize findings. However, this explanation is given weight by a further observation made at a regional PCU. Here no teaching took place but patients were seen by the doctor before having an ECG. This was unlike the London PCU where all patients had a prior ECG.

The regional PCU practice seemed an irrational waste of time. It meant that the family had to go away to have the ECG and then return. Yet, although we have inadequate data to provide comparative tabulations, we believed that new families on the whole participated more than at the London PCU. The gap between the two consultations seemed to serve the same purpose as the teaching sessions in London. A space was opened for reflection without the pressures of the normal medical interview.

Both the sites associated with greater parental participation unintentionally created space for parents. The question now became: how could we build on this experience to plan a less constraining setting?

The Pre-Admission Clinic
The thrust of our analysis had pointed to the limits of reforming the first out-patient consultation. Parental anxieties, coupled with the need to examine and diagnose the child, implied that any attempt to improve communication techniques was unlikely to be successful. We thus considered structural changes (changes of site) which would pose less constraints upon parental participation. We were guided by three considerations:

1. Rather than invent new strategies for medical staff or parents, we wanted to build on successful strategies already used in the setting. For instance, families who seemed most successful in coping with the strains of their child's hospitalization often achieved close contact with one member of the unit's staff. Could this contact be achieved in a less ad hoc way?

2. Many policy interventions are based on the introduction of additional professionals into health-care settings — for instance social workers, health visitors or psychologists. Conversely, we wanted the existing participants to apply their own competences and preferences to the encounter.

3. Relatedly, we wanted to avoid transforming these families into a group of 'problem' people with special needs. As a perceptive nurse at the PCU had pointed out to us at an early stage of the research, these were 'normal families'. Any intervention should lay the ground for that normality to be enacted. All these considerations led in the direction of keeping the present first clinic consultation in place but adding to it a later voluntary pre-admission visit. At this visit, the family would be able to discuss their child's illness and proposed treatment with a more junior member of the medical team. In this way, it was hoped that:

1. families would be better prepared for their child's admission

2. the family would establish closer contact with one member of the unit's staff.

3. the proposed consultations would be more adequate at a discursive level than out-patient consultations, through the removal of or alteration of the typical constraints upon and expectations of the latter. In particular, families would have had time to reflect on the information they had been given at the first out-patient visit and would not be so constrained by the fear of taking up the precious time of senior doctors.

This proposed intervention study also had a more theoretical intention. It was an opportunity for us to vary experimentally the conditions of the encounters we observe, their 'sites', while holding constant the stage of treatment. How would consultations differ if they involved a more junior doctor, if the family's 'business' was the matter at hand, and if the child was not examined?

A document setting out the proposal was then presented to the staff of the Paediatric Cardiology Unit. It was decided that a sample of families of children due for cardiac catheterization would be invited to attend an additional clinic, held by an SHO (junior hospital doctor), shortly before an admission. At this clinic, no examination of the child would take place and families would be invited to raise any concerns or questions they might have. The letter offering the sample of families this appointment was then drafted by the research team.

Such an additional clinic had the advantage of circumventing the usual admission procedure at the unit. Although admission to the ward was a stressful occasion it was often invoked, despite its unsuitability, as a primary occasion for the communication of information to the families.[1]

How the Clinic Worked

When parents arrived, those who brought young children were directed by the ward clerk to the playroom run by a member of staff while they waited for the SHO. Parents who brought babies were directed to one of the rooms in which babies slept and were attended to by a ward sister. In both these settings, we observed how parents requested and obtained a great deal of information to do with the practicalities of looking after their child which they would probably have considered too trivial to ask a doctor, even a junior doctor. Moreover, the children soon became involved in the activities of the playroom and so acquired an unfrightening impression of what they could expect when they were admitted. Often they stayed there for a part of the time while their parents saw the junior doctor.

Here parents confirmed that they would be able to stay at the Unit while their child was undergoing catheterization. This usually involved them making the request to the SHO who then went with them to the ward clerk who made the necessary administrative arrangements. In our previous study, we had documented how parents found the uncertain availability of overnight accommodation a great source of anxiety. Those who required assistance from social services took the initiative in obtaining help from the SHO in arranging this with one of the hospital's social workers. Usually they were seen by a social worker following the encounter with the doctor. Finally, the SHO showed the parents around the ward and the paediatric intensive care unit if it was known that the child would definitely require surgery.

The salient features of the experimental clinic may be summarized diagrammatically (see Figure 1).

FIGURE 1

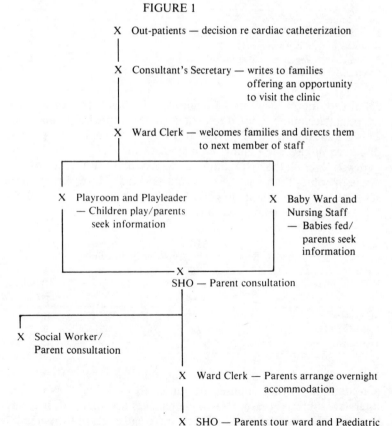

X   Out-patients — decision re cardiac catheterization

X   Consultant's Secretary — writes to families offering an opportunity to visit the clinic

X   Ward Clerk — welcomes families and directs them to next member of staff

X   Playroom and Playleader — Children play/parents seek information

X   Baby Ward and Nursing Staff — Babies fed/parents seek information

X   SHO — Parent consultation

X   Social Worker/ Parent consultation

X   Ward Clerk — Parents arrange overnight accommodation

X   SHO — Parents tour ward and Paediatric Intensive Care Unit

An Evaluation of the Clinic
In order to evaluate the effectiveness of the pre-admission SHO clinic, questionnaires were administered to thirty families after their consultation. The results were compared to the answers they had given to the same questions after their earlier first out-patient consultation. All consultations were tape-recorded and all families were asked to give open-ended home interviews after the second clinic consultation.

Table 8 gives parents' comments about topics discussed at each consultation.

TABLE 8
Parents' Comments After Each Clinic

Topic	Whether discussed at each clinic	
	Out-patients (%)	SHO Clinic (%)
Likely future developments	30	45
Your child's behaviour	23	28
Health or general development	17	38
Problems of coping with child at home	13	28
Practical aspects of attending hospital	17	62

As already noted, parents particularly liked being able to arrange overnight accommodation during their child's future hospitalization. This is indicated in the 62 percent of parents who said this topic was discussed at the SHO clinic, compared to only 17 percent at out-patients. Overall, the SHO clinic was perceived to cover a far broader range of topics than had arisen at out-patients. Moreover, twenty-seven out of thirty families reported that they found the second clinic 'very informative' compared to twenty after the first clinic.

TABLE 9
Parents' Reported Anxiety After Each Clinic

	After Out-patients (%)	After SHO Clinic (%)
More worried	23	10
Less worried	30	45
The same	47	45

We also asked parents how anxious they felt after each consultation. Their responses are tabulated in Table 9. When the interview subjects' reasons for these changes are analysed, it seems that these figures relate to the slightly different stages of the patients' medical careers. Respondents who were 'more worried' after out-patients consultation tended to be worried about the diagnosis of their child. For the first time, they had been told that the condition was serious enough to require catheterization and probable eventual operation. Respondents who were 'less worried' after SHO clinics tended to mention, more than the diagnosis, what was involved in treatment and the practicalities of attending the hospital.

We also asked parents how much they had understood of what they had been told. At 30 per cent of out-patient appointments, respondents mentioned that they had not understood something. The difficult question 'what was that?' was answered usually as 'the technical terms'. In two cases, details of treatment were mentioned. Details of the diagnosis were not mentioned. Conversely, only two of the respondents at SHO clinics (6.9 per cent) reported being unable to understand technical terms.

Data about respondents' reports of what they were told was limited by the need to avoid subjecting parents to long interviews. However, comparison of the two sets of questionnaires revealed (1) a tendency to give *names* of the condition (e.g. 'Pulmonary Stenosis' or 'a hole in the heart') at out-patients compared to a *description* of the condition at SHO clinics (e.g. 'a blockage in the artery to the lungs') and (2) more description of tests or treatment, versus diagnosis, at the SHO clinics.

The present project was in part an attempt to vary the circumstances of the consultation in order to promote a measurable increase in parental involvement. Three measures of parental involvement were employed, each derived from earlier qualitative analysis of the variance in consultation structure. These were: the number of questions parents asked; the proportion of consultations in which technical medical technology was used; and the number of discrete topics mentioned in the consultation.

According to each of these three measures the experimental SHO clinics promoted greater parental involvement. Parents asked an average of 6.07 questions, technical terminology was used in 93 per cent of the clinics and, of the list of nine possible topics on our coding form, an average of 5.96 were mentioned in the additional clinics. By comparison, in those circumstances found earlier to be associated with the greatest degree of parental involvement at out-patient clinics, i.e. the situation in which a child who had undergone cardiac catheterization was referred for an operation, the mean number of questions asked was 4.55, 85 per cent of consultations employed technical terminology and a mean of 3.35 topics were mentioned.

It was possible from the design of the coding form to analyse some of the circumstances associated with this increase in parental participation.

(1) The SHO clinics were of similar length to out-patient consultations, but did not include periods in which a history was taken.
(2) Doctors invited parents' questions in 89 per cent of SHO clinics. In out-patient consultations this invitation was found to be extremely rare.
(3) Families more readily presented some problem they had experienced with their child, or described some symptom they had observed. This, which I have elsewhere described as 'patency', occurred in 69 per cent of experimental clinics, and in only 30 per cent of out-patient clinics.
(4) 62 per cent of the experimental clinics displayed one or more of the criteria we have elsewhere labelled the 'democratic' form. Most commonly, in these clinics more than one possible diagnosis or potential disposal was mentioned by the doctor. This occurred in only 37 per cent of out-patient consultations.

Since I have concentrated entirely on family responses to the clinics, I must conclude by mentioning how medical staff responded. Initially, the junior doctors who were asked to carry out the pre-admission clinic were anxious about what was expected of them. Their anxiety was heightened when we refused to advise them about what they should do. However, they subsequently reported to us that they themselves had found the clinic useful as a way of getting to know families before the stressful admission interview.

Conclusion
Our reticence at offering instructions to medical staff about their behaviour arose from reasons which were partly ethical and partly analytical. Ethically, our research team was committed to a form of policy intervention opposed to social engineering. Instead we wanted to mobilize the talents and innovatory capacity of the participants themselves. Teaching techniques of 'better communication' would have no place in our intervention.

In addition, our analysis had emphasized the way in which the structural properties of the setting, embodied in what we have called the 'site' of the encounter, established a field of possibilities and limits for the participants. By varying the site, we set out to show that people could do more things that they perceived to be worthwhile. And so it proved!

This is, admittedly, only an initial attempt to deploy the concept of site. It is weakened by the use of illustrative material from transcripts supported by sketchy quantitative material. The strength of the analysis resides, I believe, in its grounding in longitudinal data and its theoretically derived attempts at innovation. This led to a decisive rejection of reforms which hinged on changing styles of communication without regard to site-specific factors.[2]

As I mentioned at the beginning of Chapter Three, the concept of site implies 'macro' factors related to the structure of health-care as well as the minutiae of career trajectories. I now turn to examine the impact on behaviour of just such a macro-factor — the method of payment for health care.

Notes

1. I must make it clear that the negotiation and conduct of the pre-catheter clinic was not all plain-sailing. SHOs usually only stay for a few months in any one hospital department. This meant that the new clinic had to be re-negotiated with successive cohorts of junior doctors. An additional problem arose in relation to the Social Work department of the hospital. Careful explaining was needed to make it clear that our policy intervention did not imply any criticism of their previous work with patients. On reflection, it would have been more sensible to liaise with social workers at an earlier stage.

2. This still suggests that 'reformism' of some kind can give parents or patients a greater voice in medical encounters. As implied in Parts Two and Three, this neglects the historical and cultural factors which give 'voices' to subjects and incites subjects to speak. If we follow Foucault and regard power as enabling as much as constraining then both forms of reformism, psychological (Byrne and Long) and sociological (changing sites), become problematic. This does not mean that the concept of site has no value but that a purely situational analysis cannot do full justice to the field of power and knowledge.

5

Going Private: Ceremonial Forms
in a Medical Oncology Clinic

For over three decades, health-care in the UK was identified with the National Health Service. Of course, everybody knew that Harley Street existed but its services were assumed to be the prerogative of oil-rich foreigners, Hollywood stars and a few very wealthy or aristocratic British people.

In the last few years, however, the picture has changed considerably. Aided by a Government committed to a critique of state institutions, private medicine has flourished. By 1982, 4.2 million people, rather more than 7 per cent of the total population, were covered by private health insurance (ranging from more than 10 per cent in the Home Counties to under 4 per cent in the north of England, Scotland and Wales) (Forman, 1983). Moreover, the growth rate of such insurance cover had been very rapid: 25.9 per cent in 1980 and 13.9 per cent in 1981. Private medicine now extended beyond the ranks of the well-off or high-born: business enterprises and some trade unions were broadening their fringe-benefits to include private medical cover. Only in 1982 was there very much slowdown in these high rates of growth. But this was easily explicable in terms of the recession affecting so much of the British economy (see Griffith and Rayner, 1985). It was also more than balanced by the influx of foreigners, particularly from the Middle East and Greece, flocking to British private medicine (*The Times*, 1983). By 1984 moreover, the trough in new subscribers to private health insurance seemed to have passed.

Only isolated critical responses greeted the onward march of private medicine. Encouraged by health-service trade unions, the Callaghan Government of 1976–9 legislated for the control of pay-beds within NHS hospitals. On the academic front, the data about private medicine's high administrative costs (estimated at 10–20 per cent of total costs, as compared to 5 per cent in the NHS) (Galbraith, 1983) and tendency to overtreat (Abel-Smith, 1976) evoked little popular response.

This is an extented version of a paper of a similar title that originally appeared in 1984 in *Sociology* 18 (2): 191–204. It is published here with the permission of the journal.

As we entered the 1980s, it was the expansion of private medicine to new patients and to new services that caught the eye. Britain's first comprehensive private primary care service opened in a London suburb in November 1982. For £97 per annum adults are covered for an initial health check, a 24-hour service throughout the year and all drugs. If under 65, they will also be able to obtain health insurance for private hospital care at a big discount. The clinic initially attracted 9000 patients and, using six GPs, this meant a considerably lower number of patients per doctor than the usual doctor/patient ratio within the NHS (*The Guardian*, 1981).

On the political front, it was reported in December 1981 that a joint committee of civil servants and representatives of private medicine was proposing to end the financing of the NHS by taxation and to switch towards a 'social insurance' system, common in the EEC. 'The proposal is expected', *The Guardian* reported, 'to lead to a two-tier health-care system, with a safety-net for the poor and old' (*The Guardian*, 1981). Only the leaking, one year later, of a Government sponsored report that critically assessed the costs of the NHS, led to an official denial that it was intended to 'abolish' the Health Service. Although these denials were repeated in the election campaign of June 1983, some form of 'two-tier' system of health-care is still in prospect.

The global effects of different types of health-care system have been revealed in a number of works (Abel-Smith, 1976; Elling, 1980; DHSS, 1980). As Strong remarks, however, the absence of studies of private consultations is striking both in the UK and, more surprisingly, given the dominance of the form, in the USA (Strong, 1982). Whether the reason lies in lack of interest or lack of access is not at all clear.

The lack of previous work makes it essential that any study of private consultations should have a sound historical and comparative perspective. The greater danger is that, like an inexperienced anthropologist studying a new tribe or a tourist on a day-trip, we dwell on what is strikingly different. We must ground our observations within our knowledge of doctor–patient routines, their present character and their historical emergence. Fortunately, in two papers, based on observation of hospital encounters within the NHS and within public and private medicine in the USA, Strong (1982; 1977) has provided a valuable comparative perspective. We may treat what he says as a set of hypotheses providing a point of orientation for our study of private consultations.

Variability in the Doctor–Patient Relation

To ask about the impact of method of payment on the form of the doctor–patient relationship means controlling for the impact of such variables as doctors' consulting styles and patients' social class.

Leaving out such traditional psychological and sociological factors, Strong notes that, by the mid-nineteenth century, the professionalization of medicine had meant that, within the consultation, clinical judgment reigned supreme. Doctors had many clients and used routinized practices based on their technical authority to assert their professional dominance.

The authority of doctors within the consultation was, however, matched by their inability to enforce their decisions. With certain limited exceptions, like mental illness, the state did not give any power of compulsion to the medical profession. Patients were thus free to decide when to visit the doctor and whether to comply with his advice.

Within what Strong calls this 'classical form' of the relation, competition between doctors had two interactional consequences. First, doctors tried to sell themselves. By being attentive to the personal wishes of their clientele, they offered a differentiated, personalized product. Second, doctors employed tacit idealizations of the character of their clientele. This 'politeness ethic' served two functions: it minimized 'upsetting' valuable clients and it fitted neatly with the medical predisposition to treat illness as a natural, rather than a social, phenomenon.

Strong's central argument is found in the title of his paper, 'Private Practice for the Masses'. According to him, the NHS simply transferred these interactional patterns from a private to a public setting. With one exception, 'the classical form survived and is now applied universally' (1977:7). The exception was the pattern of product differentiation. This is illustrated in Table 1.

TABLE 1
Classical and NHS Interactional Forms — Strong's Argument

	'Classical' Medicine	NHS
Professional dominance	yes	yes
No state enforcement	yes	yes
Politeness ethic	yes	yes
Product differentiation	yes	no

The absence of private competition has meant that the NHS consultation typically offers 'a standard, somewhat impersonal product with a minimum of choice' (Strong, 1977). This impersonality is based on an appeal to 'collegial' authority — the authority of the institution rather than of any individual practitioner. Doctors tend to be anonymous and to avoid differentiating between themselves, their colleagues or, indeed, doctors in other NHS institutions. Conversely, the individualization of service in private medicine means that doctors are more likely to seek to personalize their communication methods and, in return, to expect patients to act more like the clients of any fee-paid service, i.e. to question the competence of the practitioner, to evaluate services and to shop around.

Sample and Methods

A small-scale study of a private London oncology clinic carried out in 1982–3 provides the possibility of evaluating some of Strong's hypotheses. The study developed as an off-shoot of a comparative study of two oncology clinics at a London teaching hospital within the NHS (Silverman, 1982). One clinic dealt with patients with leukaemia, the other mainly with patients suffering from Hodgkin's Disease — a cancer of the lymph system which, of all the cancers, seems to respond best to treatment and to offer the most favourable diagnosis.

The consultant physician running the Hodgkin's Clinic offered access to his private practice. This allowed comparison of consultations, many of which involved the same doctor and the same condition, but with the distinguishing variable being the location and the method of payment. The number of consultations observed is noted in Table 2.

TABLE 2
Consultations Sample

	Consultations	Clinic Sessions	Doctors
Leukaemia Clinic (NHS)	55	6	4
Hodgkin's Clinic (NHS)	49	10	5
Oncology Clinic (Private)	42	9	1
Total	146	25	9*

*Doctor in private oncology clinic was also observed in the Hodgkin's Clinic.

The sample of private patients had broadly the same age and gender distribution as the NHS sample. Predictably, however, only one manual worker was a private patient (an Asian working in the garment industry). Two out of five of the NHS patients whose occupation was recorded were manual workers. Again, as expected, nine out of the forty two private patients were foreign nationals. Although the mean length of their consultations was one minute longer than those involving British subjects, they tended to participate far less. This may have been due to language problems. Finally, private patients were rather more likely to be accompanied by family, friends, or in the case of foreign nationals, interpreters. This is shown in Table 3.

TABLE 3
Accompanying Family

	Private Clinic ($n = 42$)	NHS Clinics ($n = 104$)
Family present	20	29
No family	22	75

(Difference not significant at 0.10.)

Data from the NHS clinics had shown a statistically significant relation between the presence of family and patient participation in the consultation (Silverman, 1983b). Here, however, although patients who are accompanied do participate slightly more than patients on their own, the difference is not significant ($\chi^2 = 2.1$, 1d.f; not significant at 0.10).

The study was preceded by two weeks spent observing ward-rounds, case-conferences and day wards and informal interviews with in-patients. It was not possible to secure agreement to tape-record out-patient consultations. Normal methods of note-taking were therefore used but efforts were made to record 'routine' as well as deviant patterns and to establish any special forms that might arise in particular situations e.g. 'new' or medically qualified patients.

The researcher identified himself in the NHS clinics by a name badge that was commonly worn by doctors there. No such identification was used at the private clinic. In the NHS clinics, doctors varied as to whether they informed patients and asked consent for my presence. In the private clinic, the doctor usually asked for consent. Patient response to my presence is discussed below.

A simple coding form was developed and pre-tested in fourteen consultations drawn from a Hodgkin's and a non-Hodgkin's Lymphoma clinic, observed prior to the collection of the main sample. This allowed the generation of comparative, quantitative data across a number of variables (e.g. the length of the consultation, the number of questions asked or unsolicited statements made by the patient or patient's family, the extent of small talk between doctor and patient). In all, ten independent variables and fourteen dependent variables were counted and then related through chi-square tests. The comparison of the two NHS clinics is discussed in Silverman, 1982.

Observational methods necessarily concentrate on particulars deemed 'interesting' according to certain theoretical or practical frames of references. This study followed Strong in focusing on what he calls the 'ceremonial order of the clinic'. Closely tied to Goffman's model of the encounter (Goffman, 1961), this attends to the display of identities within rules of etiquette. It is particularly concerned with 'who is to be what ... and what sorts of rights and duties they may expect, exert and suffer' (Strong, 1982: 3).

These interactionist concerns understandably are not representative of the majority of work concerned with the social and psychological aspects of health and illness. For instance, a review of the literature on social aspects of cancer care, carried out by the author, reveals a huge concentration of work on accounts offered by patients outside medical settings (e.g. in home interviews), an attention to dramatic medicine (e.g. childhood leukaemia, breast cancer) and a concern with medically-defined issues (e.g. how to improve information-flow from doctor to patient).

Interactionism is used here as a means of gathering basic data on social process in an unexplored area. Although it offers its own 'blinkers', it nonetheless frees the researcher from the varying forms of reductionism offered by purely structural sociologies or by adopting medically-defined problematics. When wedded, as here, to simple methods of quantification, it seeks to combine theoretical insight with methodological rigour, while being sensitive to policy issues see Silverman (in press).

Similar Forms

Some of the quantitative data discussed elsewhere (Silverman, 1982) has revealed that the private clinic offers important instances of continuity with the NHS clinic. This should not be so surprising if we remember Strong's argument that the NHS provides 'private practice for the masses'. Each of the three features of 'classical medicine' which he claims are reproduced today can be found in equal measure in both the private and NHS clinics.

1. Professional dominance

Private patients, like NHS patients, generally take the role of laypersons confronted by an expert. In a clinic which treats life-threatening diseases, the relief and satisfaction that greets the doctor's judgment that all is well at the moment is universal. However, even where the medical verdict is unfavourable and out of line with the patient's own feelings of wellness, it is generally accepted stoically. Take the case of Mrs A, a lady in her sixties, with a diagnosis of hypoblastic anaemia — potentially an early stage of leukaemia. The doctor has just suggested that further extensive treatment is necessary and Mrs A (A) questions him closely about the outlook:

(P:7)
1. A: Don't you think this rights itself?
2. D: It's going to continue to be a nuisance

3. A: So what's the point of feeling well if you're going to feel bad again?
4. D: (explains that the blood count will go very low unless Mrs A is transfused and takes a cytotoxic drug)*
5. A: I thought I wouldn't need more treatment. I've been feeling so much better ... Oh well, there's always miracles. I'm a great believer in miracles.

The professional's judgment reigns supreme here as elsewhere in the private clinic. Despite the lack of fit between the patient's perceptions of feeling 'well' and 'better' and the proposed treatment, the doctor's version of the situation takes precedence. Notice, moreover, that the doctor dwells in the discursive space of clinical definitions at Utterance 4. Despite Mrs A's attempt at 3 to raise broader practical or everyday issues, the doctor stays firmly in the clinical realm, leaving homespun philosophy to the patient (as at 5).

It must be borne in mind that this is an example of specialist private medicine. Although they can always seek 'another opinion', these patients are much closer to 'the end of the line' than those receiving primary care. Specialist medicine, dealing with life-threatening, complex processes, may encourage simpler patterns of professional dominance in both NHS and private settings.

In specialist medicine, private as well as NHS, the patient may even come to doubt his own experience of 'wellness'. This possibility is raised in another male patient's (A) response to the elecitation question:

(P:8)
1. D: How are you?
2. A: Pretty well I think

While too much weight should not be attached to the patient's 'I think', it is rarely found in answer to elicitation questions. After all, we can all be presumed to know how we feel and to know with reasonable certainty. Yet Mr A, with leukaemia, seems to have learned, like Mrs A, that his own experience of wellness gives no certain guide to his state of health. Like many patients with his diagnosis, the blood-count rather than how he feels has become his own basis for assessing his wellness.

This form of specialist private medicine, then, is not salient in relation to many of the features of the 'normal' lay–professional encounter. This is well illustrated by a comparison with an NHS consultation involving a patient with some medical background — she

*Brackets are used in these transcripts to summarize what was said where the words were not noted at the time or for reasons of space.

works as a pharmacist. This generated this grossly atypical elicitation question:

(H:5)
> D: Clinically, how are you?

The use of the term 'clinically' underlines how the medically qualified patient is granted the ability to judge the significance of her own symptoms. Such a right even extends to medically qualified spouses of patients. As Strong (1979b) has noted, nurses are treated as good informants. Thus, at the private clinic, the doctor breaks into the elicitation sequence to turn to the patient's wife — a nurse:

(P:4)
> D: How breathless did he seem to you? Did he go blue?

For most patients, NHS or private, subjective perceptions of 'wellness' are recognized to be merely one fact among many that only the doctor is in a position to weigh and assess.

However, we should not assume that this technical dominance of the doctor always carries over into all the forms of *social* control of the consultation that are usually associated with professional dominance. As we shall see later, although these private patients do not challenge the clinical judgments of the doctor, many claim the kind of extensive rights over the agenda of the consultation which are rarely claimed or granted in the NHS clinics observed in this study.

2. No enforcement of decisions

In none of the clinics do the doctors seek to enforce their decisions. They present their conclusions as 'advice' which patients are free to reject, at their own risk. However, this does not mean that doctors are constrained from expressing their displeasure when patients seem like taking a contrary line. When, for instance, the pharmacist (B) shows concern at the possible effect of cytotoxic drugs on her ovaries (and hence her fertility), she is firmly put in her place:

(H:7)
1. B: Will it affect my ovary?
2. D: I think that's neither here nor there. We're dealing with a question of life and death. It actually doesn't affect the ovaries but the important thing is that (you should be in the right shape for looking after children).

While the issue of cancer treatment and fertility questions is discussed elsewhere (Silverman, 1982), we are here concerned with the aggressive response generated by patient questioning of medical advice over matters of 'life and death'.

In this case, the patient accepts the treatment. At the private clinic, where another patient (Mrs B) had rejected treatment for her cancer of the colon and had now developed lung secondaries, the doctor once again made his displeasure clear. The patient makes extensive displays of deference to professional dominance:

(P:8)
1. B: You're the doctor ... (further discussion of the blood transfusions she is to have as a palliative measure)
2. B: Forgive me ... to my lay mind ... can I have it (the blood) over separate days?

Despite these statements acknowledging her lay status, Mrs B will not budge from her refusal to accept active treatment of her cancer. The doctor makes his displeasure clear, avoiding eye contact throughout and sternly remaining in his professional role.

3. Politeness ethic

At all clinics, patient's moral worth is never directly questioned. As Strong found, in a paediatric clinic, even potentially disturbing social information elicited from a parent rarely led to further questioning (Strong, 1979b). An indirect example of this is to be found in the private clinic. Following a form of social elicitation much more commonly found here than in the NHS, as we shall show later, disquieting news is allowed to drop:

(P:4)
1. D: Wife well?
2. B: No. She's got a problem at the moment

Despite Mr B's statement, the doctor changes the topic. It seems that, in the clinic, the doctor's question is to be seen as a polite enquiry, which is not intended to maintain its topical status whatever reply is elicited.

The only departure from the normal avoidance of 'personal' issues arises in the discussion of diet and alcohol. Nevertheless, the doctor's advice in both clinics is always presented in a light-hearted, bantering manner. The first two extracts below are taken from the private clinic, the third from the NHS Hodgkin's Clinic.

(P:4)
[After discussion of patient's alcohol intake]
1. D: I'm not giving you any moral homilies but I think it's a message you're getting
2. C: Sounds like a dry Christmas, doesn't it?
3. D: No, the last thing I'm trying to say is to change your life. Don't ruin your Christmas.
   D: You've lost a stone you say; you could do with losing another

(H:6)
    D: You'll have to lose some weight won't you?

We may add to these similarities between the clinics certain other forms, some of which seem specific to oncology clinics. As so much popular and academic attention has focused on how much to tell the cancer patient, we should not be surprised that this is a common thread at both NHS and private clinics. Sometimes this is taken up by the family:

(P:3)
[Patient is in the examination room getting dressed]
Daughter: [*to doctor*] He doesn't know it's a malignant tumor, he thinks it's benign.

Sometimes the patient wants to avoid letting the family know. Mrs B, for instance, asks the doctor, not to 'let on' to her children while she is an in-patient; because 'they can't do anything' she does not want them troubled.

In all cases, doctors are very sensitive about informing the newly presenting cancer patient. Invariably the first question that is asked, prior to any diagnosis statement, is some form of: 'What have they told you so far?' In the light of that information, the news is broken to the patient: the term 'cancer' appearing rapidly or slowly according to the patient's present state of awareness. At subsequent consultations, the usual preferred term is 'the disease', while, in the course of the elicitation sequence, all doctors have a preferred form of euphemism about the spread of the condition:

(P:8)
    D: Any lumps or bumps?

I have heard this phrase used by nearly all the nine doctors I have observed.

Different Forms
So far, we have found evidence to support Strong's hypothesis about the common existence of forms of professional dominance, non-enforceable decisions and the politeness ethic in both NHS and private clinics. It will be recalled that he also suggests that the main areas of difference in the private clinic will be in terms of product differentiation based on individual rather than collegial claims to authority and on patients' willingness to evaluate and challenge the medical services they are receiving (a legitimated form of 'shopping around'). We will find these and other, unpredicted ceremonial forms, in our private clinic. First, however, it is necessary to describe

the setting in order to define the context in which these forms operate. We will then discuss, in turn, doctors' and patients' practices.

1. The Setting

a) *Territory*. Both NHS clinics are held in functional rooms, with unadorned white walls, no carpets, simple furniture (a small desk, one substantial chair for the doctor and a number of stacking chairs for patients, families and students). Like most NHS hospitals, heating pipes and radiators are very obtrusive. The only exception to the uniform functionality are the jolly 'Paddington Bear' curtains which separate the examination couch from view in the leukaemia clinic. This incongruity, together with the toys in one corner of the room, is explained by the use of the rooms for a paediatric clinic at other times of the week.

To enter the consulting rooms of the private clinic is to enter a different world. The main room has the air of an elegant study, perhaps not unlike the kind of room in a private house where a wealthy patient might be visited by an eighteenth-century doctor. The walls are tastefully painted and adorned with prints and paintings. The floor has a fine carpet. The furniture is reproduction antique and includes, as well as a large leather-topped desk, several comfortable chairs, a sofa, a bookcase which holds ivory figures as well as medical texts, and a low table, covered with coffee-table books and magazines. Plants are placed on several surfaces and the room is lit by an elegant central light fitting and a table lamp. To add an executive touch, there are three phones on the desk, as well as a pen in a holder.

The room establishes an air of privacy as well as luxury. At the NHS clinics, with one exception, all the patients are examined in curtained-off sections of a room. As the door may open at any time, it is always important to make sure that these curtains are fully drawn during an examination. Here, however, the examination couch is in a separate room which can only be entered via the consulting room. Although more functional than the latter, it nonetheless is carpeted and has a radiator set to a high temperature to keep the patient warm.

Above all, the private rooms offer privacy. When the outside door closes, doctor and patient are alone, cut off from the outside world except by telephone. At the NHS clinics, any member of staff may enter at any moment, announcing their arrival by merely a formal knock. So the patient may face a shifting population of students, colleagues entering for advice, a nurse arriving to change the paper sheets on the couch or a bookings clerk entering to sort out appointments. Here even the doctor may knock before entering the examination room while a patient is dressing.

This emphasis on privacy creates a special problem for the

researcher. At the NHS clinics, hidden behind my name badge (complete with the misleading title of doctor), I felt secure in a role as a disinterested observer. I was rarely introduced to the patients but they seemed untroubled by the presence of yet another professional (student? doctor?) among the assembled throng.

At the private clinic, my presence was nearly always explained, if ambiguously: 'Dr Silverman is sitting in with me today if that's alright.' Although identified and accepted by the patient, I remained uncomfortable in my role. The physical setting, with its air of quiet seclusion, made me feel like an intruder. Like the doctor, I found myself standing up when patients arrived and left, adopting a smile of greeting and shaking hands. I could no longer merge into the background as at the NHS clinics. There I was not troubled by the incongruity of a person identified as a student or doctor not observing the examination at the couch. Here, I felt awkward when the patients and their families saw that I did not accompany the doctor to the examination room and was not shown blood counts or referral letters. I occasionally tried to affect a learned glance at X-rays or scans but this barely limited my sense of embarrassment. Here, but not elsewhere, I experienced a sense of intruding on a private ceremony.

b) *Organization of care.* Within the NHS, referrals to a hospital clinic invariably come via the patient's GP or via another specialist. At this clinic this is only one of many referral routes. Four other sources of referral were noted in this sample: (1) via foreign embassies and/or foreign medical entrepreneurs; (2) via an annual private check-up; (3) via relatives or friends who are also private patients of the doctor and (4) via relatives or friends who are also NHS patients of the doctor.

At the private clinic, appointments are arranged at half-hourly intervals; at the NHS clinic at fifteen-minute intervals. (Although, at the more informal leukaemia clinics, patients arrived at any time between 9 a.m. and 11 a.m. at their convenience). The practical effect was marginal: private patients rarely waited more than fifteen minutes. If there was such a delay, the doctor would apologize. They would always be seen by the same doctor. Conversely, NHS patients might wait more than an hour — their appointment was simply an indication of when they would be available to be seen, not a guarantee of their consultation time — and would be seen by whichever doctor happened to be free. The only exception was new patients who would always be seen by the consultant. On the one occasion when a new patient was booked in on a day when the consultant was absent, the registrar who saw him evidently felt this to be remarkable, announcing, at coffee break, 'I've just seen a new patient'.

Being seen by the same doctor provided a context for personalized care. The doctor would build up a familiarity with the patient which,

as we shall see, offered a basis for extended social elicitation. Instead
of needing to read through extensive case-notes to 'bone up' on a
patient, he could quickly remember the patient's details.

This personalized service was reflected in the case-notes. Instead of
the bulky, official NHS bundle of records emblazoned with the
patient's name and number, in the private clinic, the doctor made
notes on individual sheets of paper which were then inserted into a
slim wallet-folder. Rather than assembling official records, he was
simply keeping notes for himself. In turn, the status of the
patient–doctor relationship was confirmed as that of a private
contract rather than as public and hence as anybody's business.

In the NHS clinics the patient only has a relation to a medical *team*.
Moreover, this team is interested in a large number of patients. So
doctors may leave the room to discuss another case or keep patients
waiting while they discuss the morning's work at a coffee-break
announced by the code words: 'Dr Brown is waiting to see you next
door'!

There is nothing sinister in such arrangements. Discussion between
colleagues is, indeed a positive gain compared to the one-to-one
situation in the private clinic. Nonetheless it emphasizes that the NHS
patient is always confronted by a bloc of interchangeable medical
staff.

The public, bureaucratic nature of the relationship at the NHS
clinics is made visible by the ever-present authority hierarchy. Patients
will encounter junior doctors and consultants, nurses, receptionists
and appointments clerks. They will sit with large numbers of patients
all attending the same clinic. Conversely, at the private clinic, apart
from their doctor they will only see his secretary, while, if they use the
waiting room, they are unlikely to encounter another patient waiting
to see the same doctor. Apart from the rare (and uncomfortable)
presence of a researcher, the only outsiders who intruded on the
doctor–private patient relationship, unlike the NHS clinics, counted
as the patient's helpers. These fell into two distinct categories:
translators for foreign patients and GPs for some local patients.

Most foreign patients seen at the clinic are Arab or Greek. Many will
have been counselled by their Embassy to contact a medical adviser in
London. Part translators/part entrepreneurs, these people have
extensive knowledge of the names and reputations of private doctors.
They will make the appointment for patients and accompany them to
the consultation. Here, they translate where necessary and perform
other services. For instance, one such man (D), accompanying two
sisters to the consultation, managed to secure an examination for a
patient's sister who was supposed merely to be in the role of
accompanying relative:

(P:2)
  E: They can't take much money out of Greece. I wonder if you
     could have a look at the other lady?

The doctor acceded to this request. Where there is mutual benefit
from the referral, 'two for the price of one' is a small price to pay!
Hence the relationship between entrepreneur and doctor is always
friendly and often provides displays of mutual goodwill:

(P:6)
  D: Thank you for your expert help.
  E: It was a pleasure to increase my knowledge.

I have been told that, some time ago, it was not unusual for a GP to
accompany his private patient to a consultation with a specialist. In a
pilot study of five private consultations one year earlier, I had indeed
observed such an encounter. The patient was a young man who had
not yet been informed that it was very likely that he had Hodgkin's
Disease. The GP saw the specialist before the consultation and
apprised him of this and of the patient's family and work
circumstances. He attended the consultation, provided information
and support as needed and accompanied the young man home.

Only one instance of a GP in attendance was observed in the main
study. The patient was a much older man and, it transpired, the GP
was a close family friend. The latter was invited to sit at the specialist's
side (behind the desk) and was asked to go through the history. He
discussed the diagnosis, the treatment so far and what the patient and
his wife had been told along the way. Where there were matters that
apparently he wanted concealed from the patient, the GP would
merely point at a line on the papers before both doctors.

But the GP's role was not limited to strictly medical territory.
When the patient intervened to talk about his possible retirement and
his wife patted his leg (as if to indicate that he was talking out of turn)
the GP encouraged him to continue:

(P:5)
  GP: Yes it's all relevant, go on

Again, while the patient was out of the room, the GP commented that
he 'has his wits about him' and offered more personal information.
Finally, before the specialist recommended a disposal, he asked the
GP how he wanted the patient treated.

So, if the territorial setting encourages an atmosphere of privacy,
the presence of advocates and representatives (in addition to family
members) gives added support to patients and emphasizes the unique
character of their needs.

c) *The cash-nexus*

(P:14)
[*Patient has just entered the room*]
F: I've got something for you, apart from a cheque book
[*hands over his blood test results*]

Viewed in the context of an NHS encounter, this event is bizarre. Patients there rarely make the first utterance, not do they carry around with them their own data. We will later return to such features. For the moment, let us consider the mention of the 'cheque-book'.

One of the major issues that was raised with both GPs was the patient's desire to stay 'private' in relation to the cost of the service. The following exchange was noted with the second GP, again in the absence of the patient and his wife:

(P:5)
1. D: How do you want him treated? Is he so short of cash that he would want to come to (NHS) Hospital?
2. GP: Yes that's exactly what I'd like you to do and I've no doubt they'd be willing

In both these encounters, transfer to the NHS was accomplished without difficulty. In another case, where the doctor raised the question of costs, he received a similar answer from Mr G.

(P:6)
1. D: What do you want to do?
2. G: If it will speed things up, we will pay
3. D: Well there's not much difference. It depends how you are placed financially
4. G: (I am out of work)
5. D: Well, then, it's best to come on the NHS

An exception to the selection of NHS care arose in one case where the patient (Mr H) was covered by private insurance. Here his only concern was whether the costs would fit within his cover:

(P:4)
H: We would prefer the private sector — if you can find a cheaper place than Grace.

Here the patient is referring to the private Princess Grace Hospital. I will later comment on the truncated title.

Since most British private patients *are* covered by insurance, a complementary problem for them can arise where a transfer to another clinic might mean the loss of private rights. For instance, where the doctor has agreed to see a patient in his home town on the same date as he holds an NHS clinic, the patient (Mr I) strikes a note of caution and gives us an insight into what private patients think they are paying for:

(P:5)
1. I: Would I have to wait hours?
2. D: No . . .
3. I: Does this put me in the NHS system and subject to strikes?
4. D: No, it doesn't affect us by definition.

Insurance matters were raised on two occasions via the presentation of a claim form to the doctor. On one such occasion, we catch a glimpse of the personalized service that the doctor is offering:

(P:4)
1. J: I'm a member of PPP and so if you send them the account they will pay . . . They asked for a report if you can send one
2. D: What shall I say?
3. J: Whatever you think
4. D: No, what you say. I'm your agent. I'll write whatever you want.

The cash-nexus adds to the normal character of a 'professional' relationship in providing for the doctor's presentation of himself as the patient's agent. It also creates special matters for the agenda. For instance, on one occasion, I was asked to wait outside because a patient was coming 'to discuss financial matters'. On another occasion, the representative of a foreign patient was directly asked whether the latter wanted to settle his bill now. When the representative was non-committal, the doctor encouraged early payment because the patient was returning home. Finally, there was one instance of the secretary buzzing the doctor to ask for cash to give change to a patient.

Having described the setting, we now have to ask about its impact on the ceremonial order of the clinic. Put more bluntly: exactly what are private patients buying?

2. The Doctor's Role

Three relevant quantitative measures are available: the length of consultations, the scope of consultations (i.e. whether they are widened to include non-clinical matters, such as the practicalities of patient attendance) and the extent of social elicitation (i.e. personal remarks and enquiries about the patients and/or their families). According to Strong's hypothesis of 'product differentiation', we might expect private consultations, compared to similar NHS clinics, to be longer, to have a wider scope, and to contain more social elicitation. Examining the evidence, however, we find a more mixed picture.

At first sight, there is a striking difference in length between private and NHS consultations (see Table 4).

TABLE 4
Length of Consultations (in minutes)

	Private Clinic (n = 42)	NHS Clinics (n = 104)
Total length of all consultations	862	1198.5
Mean length	20.5	11.5

(difference significant at 0.001, $\chi^2 = 69$, 1 d.f.)

This is probably, however, an unfair comparison as consultations in the NHS Leukaemia clinic are very short. If we compare patients seen by the same doctor in the NHS Hodgkin's Clinic and the private clinic, the difference, while still significant, shrinks considerably — from nine minutes to under three minutes. Finally, if we compare only new patients, NHS consultations actually last longer by just over four minutes. This is a fascinating direction of difference which may be accounted for by the tighter scheduling of private appointments.

On the other two measures, the data are unequivocal. In the private clinic, the doctor is far more likely to discuss the arrangement of appointments at the patient's convenience and, with the patient, to engage in social elicitation (see Table 5).

TABLE 5
Non-Medical Matters

	Private Clinic (n = 42) (%)	NHS Clinics (n = 104) (%)
Discussion of practicalities of treatment or attendance	15 (36)	10 (10)*
Social elicitation by doctor and/or patient	25 (60)	31 (30)**

*difference significant at 0.02, $\chi^2 = 6.3$, 1 d.f.
**difference significant at 0.05, $\chi^2 = 4.1$, 1 d.f.

The more equivocal comparative data on the length of consultations is not so important if we recognize that a long consultation might still be bureaucratic and doctor-centred in form. Because the data relating to timetabling appointments and social elicitation touch upon how the doctor is defining the patient, they are more reliable measures of his ordering of ceremonial forms. Such ordering is quite subtle and, therefore, often difficult to quantify. It is now appropriate, therefore, to consider the qualitative data.

a) *The personal service*

(P:3)
1. D: Where do you want to see me, here or (NHS) Hospital?
2. (Discussion of patient's insurance cover)
3. C: We'll do whatever you think is best
4. D: (No practical difference) You won't necessarily see *me* if you come to (NHS) Hospital (explains that there can be over eighty patients at a clinic there)
5. C: No I do like to speak to you

Why do patients 'like to speak' to a private physician? One answer, especially in the case of serious illness, must clearly be their faith in his strictly clinical ability. Another answer seems to lie in the 'personal' service he offers.

Such a form of service is contexted in the features of the setting already discussed. It is manifested in the doctor's behaviour from standing up and shaking hands with patient, family and retainers at the beginning and end of each consultation to helping patients on with their coats ('It's all part of the service' he joked to one such patient who thanked him).

The frequent social elicitation in these private consultations usually turns upon questions of business and family. In one admittedly extreme case, I counted eleven instances of social statements or questions (eight from the doctor, three from the patient). These ranged from a discussion of the patient's business ('Farm doing OK?') and family ('How's your brood?') to the doctor's leisure activities (shooting, dining) to an anecdote from him about the sudden death of the owner of a cafe he went to, complete with homespun philosophy ('Life's so capricious', 'it just makes me think').

Apart from business, family and social life, the doctor may initiate discussion about past gifts received from the patient:

(P:7)
D: Thank you for the beef
P: You cooked it well?
D: It cut so beautifully

As we shall also see, trips abroad, sponsored by patients, on three occasions became a subject for discussion.

Most of the wider scope of these consultations arises through the doctor discussing how treatment can best be arranged at the patient's convenience. Patients expect to be seen at a convenient time:

(P:4)
L: [*referring to his mother*] I'm off this week if you can see her then.

Invariably such requests are granted. For instance, appointments are arranged at longer intervals so as not to exceed the number of consultations allowed each year on private insurance and earlier so as to come before Christmas and thus permit the patient to indulge his taste for alcohol over the festive season.

Here are three further examples of deference to patient's wishes:

(P:1)
    D: [*to patient living abroad*] What's your programme (during your stay here)?

(P:4)
    D: Have you got next year's diary with you? . . . Is there a time that is best for you?
    J: (names date)
  Secretary: What sort of time?
    J: (names time) If for some reason I want to change it, I'll know in a couple of weeks.

(P:8)
[*Patient is contemplating travel abroad*]
    D: Just tell me when you want to go. I'll just send a summary to go with you.

Since a sizeable proportion of the patients are foreign nationals, the personalized service is given an additional gloss for them to help put them at their ease. For instance, a Greek patient was asked 'How are you?' in his own language. More striking was this exchange with a daughter of a Syrian patient which occurred directly after the doctor had been making a valiant effort to read the papers the patient had brought with her:

(P:3)
1. D: I wish my Arabic were better. Damascus is a beautiful city.
2. Daughter: You have been there?
3. D: Yes
4. Daughter: Do you have many Arab patients?
5. D: (Quite a few).

b) *Individual authority*

(P:3)
1. D: Have you had occasion to see Smith at all?
2. E: He's very good
3. D: I thought you were seeing Jones. He thought Smith didn't have anything to contribute.

What is striking here is the doctor's reference to other doctors without using their title. The anonymous, collegial authority of the NHS clinics is replaced here by a form of individualized medicine where: (1) medicine is associated with named individuals (2) these individuals, since they are paid for their services by the patient, can, like Marks & Spencer, be referred to by their surnames. As an extreme example, we have already seen how one patient refers to the Princess Grace Hospital simply as 'Grace'.

Another basis for dropping the title is in the context of talk between doctors: in the NHS clinics, titles of other doctors would not be used in case conferences or in consultations involving medically qualified patients. Private consultations seem to approximate more to these peer-group situations.

This means that taking a history at this clinic often means taking a list of names. For instance:

    (P:4)
    1. D: You've been seeing Jones and Smith
    2. L: Mostly it's been Jones
    (P:9)
    1. M: I went to see er ...
    2. D: Jones
    3. M: Mr Jones
    4. D: Are you still seeing Smith?
    5. M: No I moved to Dr Jones from Dr Smith.

Here Mr M, unlike the doctor, uses titles before surnames (although he is uncertain about which is the right title!) Elsewhere, patients show greater familiarity with their doctors:

    (P:4)
    1. D: Have you had occasion to see Smith? (The blood count looks
              good)
    2. F: Well that's what John Smith said to me

Such individualization of medicine is accompanied, as Strong (1982) predicts, by the sanctioning of patient evaluation of other doctor's performance. Notice, for instance, how in the extract from P:3 above the patient feels free to make a comment on another doctor. Of course, such a favourable comment ('He's very good') is not unknown at NHS clinics. What is most distinctive about this private clinic is that complaints against other doctors may be legitimated.

The most striking instance of this occurred when a patient (Mrs F) complained that her NHS GP had taken both herself and her husband off his list when told that they had sought a private opinion. She then adds a complaint that previously the same GP had not taken action when the presence of high blood pressure had been noted in hospital. This now continues:

    (P:3)
    1. F: I've been left to sizzle
    2. D: Well I'm not prepared to let that happen.

Sometimes the doctor himself initiates this critique. Notice the note of sarcasm present in this question.

(P:5)
[*The doctor has just put the patient's X-rays upon the screen*]
1. D: And what are these clever doctors seeing in these X-rays
2. N: Well they told me I've got a chest infection.

c) *Orchestration of care*

(P:4)
1. L: (Can you name a doctor?)
2. D: [*writes two names on a piece of paper*] These are two gentlemen of different ages. Dr Smith is sixty, Dr Jones is about my age . . . If you'd like me to arrange the appointment, I can do that . . .
3. D: After your mother has seen the rheumatologist I will see you again to interpret his report for you.

Two common features of these consultations are present here: the doctor actively co-ordinates care across a number of specialists and communicates the overall picture back to the patient. Although this is specialist medicine, the private doctor nonetheless assumes much more the role of a GP. For instance:

(P:6)
    D: I've been keeping in touch with Dr Smith. I'm just reading the letter from the skin specialist.

But this is a more committed, rapid service than that normally expected from a GP. For instance, where information is needed, he telephones, in the patient's presence, to another doctor. While waiting on the phone, he tells the patient:

(P:6)
    D: They're calling him out of a meeting to talk about the results.

Not only is quick action taken but the patient is kept informed at all times about the state of his case. A Greek patient is told that he will be sent a report in Athens about 'the whole story' (P:6). Leukaemia patients are called at home with the results of blood tests — good or bad. At the NHS clinic, however, the call is only made in the event of bad news.

In some respects, there is one tangible expression of this personal service, based on individual authority and orchestrated via the private doctor. This is the commitment of records and X-rays to the home care of patients. Although unthinkable in NHS medicine, this is recommended in private medicine — 'it's safer' one patient is told (P:3). Possession of one's own 'data' highlights the personalized, non-bureaucratic character of the doctor-patient relationship. Here the patient (Mr N) is depicted as owning his own 'data' whatever official agencies may prefer:

(P:5)
1. N: The hospital wants my X-rays back today. What shall I tell them?
2. D: Tell them they can't have them.

However, what is a right is also an obligation, so patients are expected to arrive complete with their own data. In one case (P:9), where an elderly patient had arrived without his X-rays, the son was politely ticked off by the doctor.

3. The Patient's Role
The quantitative measure of the patients' role are even more limited than those used earlier. We have crude counts of the numbers of questions and unelicited statements made by patients or those accompanying them. Combining questions and statements together gives a simple measure that I have called a Patient Participation Index (PPI). Once again, at first sight, patient behaviour seems significantly different at the private clinic (see Table 6).

TABLE 6
Patient Participation Index: All Patients

	Private Clinic ($n = 42$)	NHS Clinics ($n = 104$)
Total PPI	340	567
Mean per consultation	8.1	5.5

(difference significant at 0.001, $\chi^2 = 22.5$, 1 d.f.)

TABLE 7
Patient Participation Index: Patients seen by the Same Doctor

	Private Clinic (n = 42)	NHS Clinics (n = 29)
Total PPI	340	228
Mean per consultation	8.1	7.2

(difference *not* significant at 0.10)

If, however, we compare like with like, examining consultations taken by the same doctor in the two sectors, the difference shrinks considerably (see Table 7).

Once again, although these figures tell part of the story, we must rely on qualitative data to obtain a broader picture of patient behaviour.

a) *Self-orchestration of care.* Only in private clinics do encounters typically begin with the patient handing over a bundle of charts and X-rays. Patients expect both to bring such materials and to organize their own X-rays and tests. For instance

(P:8)
1. E: I've had the X-ray done
             . . .
2. E: What we could usefully do is to pop round to the lab and have some blood taken
             . . .
3. D: Are all these your X-rays?
4. E: I brought the lot. Did I do right?

While this degree of patient orchestration is unknown in our NHS clinics, one patient goes still further. He maintains his own records of the dates and quantities of his chemotherapy (P:8). Where the doctor is in doubt about the history of treatment, he turns to the patient who refers to his own charts. In this private clinic, health care is an individualized matter for both doctor and patient. Where, on one occasion, the doctor cannot obtain an early appointment with another doctor, he leaves the patient 'to apply pressure' himself (P:9).

b) *Territorial control.* In the NHS clinics, the patient is very much on foreign territory. Once seated, she remains fixed to her chair, not moving until sanctioned by the doctor. In only one case (H:10), did an NHS patient appear to take a territorial initiative. When re-entering after an X-ray, she sat on the corner of the doctor's desk. Curiously, however, this patient had already mentioned to the doctor her desire to transfer to private care.

In the private clinic, patients routinely exhibit territorial control. Three instances will serve to illustrate this: (1) A patient stood up and went over to examine his X-ray on the display unit while the doctor was talking about it (P:5); (2) While the doctor was out of the room, the patient's husband got up and walked around the room, looking into the bookcase and picking up a book from the coffee table. He was joined by the translator and they engaged in conversation while standing up (P:6). No NHS patient was ever seen to stroll around the consulting room even when the doctor was absent; (3) Another patient, asked about her leg, stood up unexpectedly and walked around the room to show how well she was able to walk (P:7).

Even though this is still medical territory (at both clinics, the doctor sits behind or next to his desk), private patients have far fewer qualms about claiming a measure of control. Perhaps, by paying, they have a rental claim not only on the doctor's time but also on his territory?

c) *Controlling the agenda*

(P:6)
1. B: Now where do we go from here?
2. D: May I ask you something?
   (after a further 10 minutes)
3. B: [*standing up*] Thank you for your kind attention

Viewed in comparison with the NHS consultations, this extract is remarkable in three ways: (1) The patient herself raises the question of the agenda; (2) The doctor has to ask permission to ask a question (it is worth noting that the consultation had *begun* by the patient asking a stream of questions; and (3) the patient signals the end of the consultation by standing up. Nonetheless, this consultation only depicts, in a slightly more exaggerated form, the *rule* at the private clinic.

Other patients make the first statement after a greeting sequence. For instance:

(P:7)
F: I wasn't sure what you were going to do with me so I had lunch.

They also indicate when the consultation is at an end, standing up like Mrs B.

(P:7)
O: So that's fine.

Or, picking up their charts like Mr P.

(P:8)
P: Well that's all good news.

Or, in Mrs F's case:

(P:7)
F: Alright I feel very optimistic

Patients also end particular stages of the consultation, like the elicitation sequence:

(P:7)
1. G: Anything else?
2. D: No
3. G: Good

They also summarize the state of play, like Mr O:

(P:7)
O: So we can be satisfied with that. Things are moving in the right direction.

However, these quite amazing interactional rights are not all. Patients not only *order* the agenda, they also introduce topics not routinely raised at NHS consultations. For instance, they are not afraid to ask about the doctor's note-taking:

    (P:5)
        H: What are the little cubes?

They also regularly ask biological and clinical questions. For instance:

    (P:5)
        H: What is the spleen's function?

    (P:6)
    1.   Q: I was wondering what the output of the scan looked like.
                . . .
    2.   Q: Is that because there are lymphatic glands there?

However, these patients' questions are not limited to the diagnosis and treatment of cancer. Sometimes they introduce non-cancer questions at the end of the consultation. For instance:

    (P:1)
        I: Whilst I'm here I wanted to ask you about . . .

Such an attempt to raise what turned out to be a trivial, non-cancer related matter would never be seen among NHS patients. It fits here within the broader, quasi-GP role that the doctor adopts. In three cases among the sample, such non-cancer matters were raised.

Sometimes, however, entirely non-cancer matters are brought to this clinic. We have already noted how Mr L's mother has been brought suffering from rheumatism. Nonetheless, after specialist assessment, she is to be brought back to this clinic. It seems that Mr L's only link with private medicine is via this doctor. His visit is solely to receive advice about referral to a good rheumatologist.

Finally, in two cases, patients are seen with symptoms that potentially might relate to cancer although they normally would be treated by a GP: swollen glands on an otherwise asymptomatic child, and a blocked salivary gland in a patient successfully treated for Hodgkin's disease. In accord with the pattern of speedy service, the latter gets an appointment made with an ENT surgeon while he waits.

Private patients thus possess an unusual ability to refer themselves to a specialist clinic and to control the agenda once they are there. One final example will illustrate how such a patient is able to pursue his own 'theories' of cancer at far greater length than I have observed in the NHS clinics. He has been referred with a 'lump' in his back that is almost certainly insignificant. Yet instead of the speedy dismissal of such a clinically uninteresting case that one might expect, he pursues his own 'theories' almost unimpeded:

(P:9)

1. R: One interesting thing about the cause of cancer — is it changes of temperature?
2. D: [*Humours the patient — refers to the lack of research*]
        I don't close my mind to your suggestion
3. R: What about blood cancer — could it be a knock?
4. D: Well there is so much evidence that there's a viral origin
        [*The patient is allowed to rattle on for five minutes. Only then does the doctor close the topic*]
5. D: Now with regard to yourself . . .

This degree of patient control of the agenda, especially by a well patient, would not be seen at busy NHS clinics. Once again, however, if you are paying for the doctor's time, you may expect such a measure of control.

d) *A master-servant relationship?*

(P:7)

G: [*referring to the doctor's secretary*] I had ordered tea from the waitress outside

(P:6)

B: Oh you lovely man!

Although, since the advent of private health insurance, only a minority of patients come from aristocratic backgrounds, several consultations give the impression of an encounter between the landed gentry and a tradesman. Of course, since times have changed, this impression is limited to a tongue in the cheek caricature — two extreme examples of which appear above.

Extracts from another patient's (Mrs F) consultation give further examples of this caricature, reading rather like the dialogue from a Noel Coward play:

(P:7)

1. F: I haven't had anything to drink since I saw you
2. D: Oh dear
3. F: May I have the occasional glass of champagne?
        . . .
4. D: And how have you been?
5. F: I've been quite well . . . not exactly frivolous
        (later she says she feels 'frisky')
[*Doctor exits*]
6. F: [*turning to husband and pointing to researcher with whom she shook hands earlier*] This young man's hand is lovely and warm.

If we pursue this questionable analogy a little further, another feature of a master–servant relationship is the gifts that the master can bestow upon the hard-working servant. Would an equivalent here be the offer of trips overseas, to give medical papers, offers which were made by two patients?

What we have here are little more than residual elements of gentility, deriving from a greater equality of social status of doctor and patient than is normally found within NHS medicine. We find no trace of the ability of the patient to evaluate the doctor's character characteristic of the earlier 'aristocratic' form described by Strong (1982).

Conclusions

1. A Distinctive Product?

The debate about private medicine often centres upon the issue of resources. On one side, there is the argument that (like private education) the more money is ploughed into private medicine, the more resources are freed for the public sector. This is countered by the claim that the growth of private medicine will establish a two-tier standard of treatment and that private medicine has high administrative costs and high rates of (possibly unnecessary) clinical tests and surgery.

For instance, the *New Statesman* (19 September 1986) reported an *Economist* estimate in April 1984 that, although the USA spends around $1,500 a year per head on health care, nearly four times what Britain spends, its people are no healthier. Indeed, the health-care in countries like the USA seems increasingly polarized between extensive services offered to those who can pay and very limited services for the poor.

The Guardian (5 August 1985) headed a report from Washington 'Hospitals offload poorer patients'. It went on:

> A growing number of poor patients are being dumped — often in need of emergency care — on to public hospitals because they cannot afford treatment at private hospitals. In the hospital jargon their 'wallet biopsies show a low green count'. Dollar bills are green.

Conversely, GP care, for those who can pay is being redefined as a medical industrial complex. In Australia, we read that:

> the traditional suburban surgery is being metamorphosed into the 'boutique practice' in which perhaps two GP's offer an intensive service to patients who are prepared to pay high fees. The personalized doctor–patient relationship remains and there is an emphasis on preventive care with a wider range of strictly non-medical services such as counselling. (*Sydney Morning Herald*, 5 November 1986)

The evidence gathered from this London oncology private clinic cannot arbitrate between these arguments about inequalities of health care. The NHS clinic, where the doctor works, has no waiting list and the resource impact of his private practice is unclear. We can be a little clearer about what is, rather than what ought to be: about individual gains and losses, rather than social utility. The market principle is sometimes used in support of private medicine. People will only pay for a product that they regard as distinctive and worthwhile. The data give us an opportunity, on an objective basis, to answer the question: precisely what are these patients buying?

In brief, we have shown how these private patients buy a setting which is territorially and socially organized to provide for a personalized service, based on an individualized, non-bureaucratic authority and personally orchestrated care. In social terms, these patients seem to obtain the best kind of individualized, GP service in the context of highly-qualified, specialist treatment for life-threatening conditions.

These gains are balanced by potential and real losses. Socially, isolation can be the other side of the coin to this kind of individual care. Because these patients do not attend large clinics, they cannot call upon the kind of peer-group support that I have observed in the NHS leukaemia clinic. They simply do not see other patients on a regular basis and so cannot share their burdens or appeal to a comparative reference group.

The argument is problematic in the same way as the choice between public wards and private rooms: what is support to one patient may be intrusion to another. All we can objectively say that these patients are losing is the opportunity to observe the peer-group relations that arise in the NHS clinics and to become involved if it should suit them.

Even on the medical side, there are three problematic aspects of private care: (1) Unlike the NHS clinic, other appropriate specialists, like radiologists and pathologists are not at hand. Much of the orchestration of care that develops here is necessitated by the isolated form of consultation. As the doctor concerned has told me, at this clinic it is much harder to sort out the patient's treatment programme very rapidly. (2) The doctor also feels that, ironically, he is 'not on such a tight schedule' in his NHS clinic and so can give more time to patients there. At the private clinic, the perceived need to avoid keeping patients waiting produces a much more uniform consultation length, perhaps less responsive to the special needs of new patients who, as we have seen, actually get slightly shorter consultations than NHS patients. (3) The patients at the private clinic have a broader range of cancers, as well as other conditions, than those seen at either of the NHS clinics. There might be an issue of losses and gains in less specialized, more diffuse medicine versus highly specialized medicine.

2. A Continuum of Ceremonial Forms

It would be completely mistaken to assume that the ceremonial forms observed here are unique to private medicine. Nearly every one has a parallel in the NHS clinics. Four factors, in particular, seemed to push the NHS consultations observed here in this direction:

a) The type of setting. The leukaemia clinic discussed in another paper (Silverman, 1982) was composed entirely of patients who had survived their first treatment. It was an informal clinic where the patients, who all knew the ropes, took on the role of 'old lags'. There was extensive social elicitation and patients were seen to evaluate medical work, to influence the agenda and, like the private patients, were expected to orchestrate some of their own care.

b) The patient's occupation. As is commonly suggested, doctors who are patients, are given a position of much greater interactive equality than others and this can lead to the kind of personalized encounter found in the private clinic (for instance, the definition of medical history by citing doctors' surnames). Again, certain other professionals may have skills that are relevant in obtaining personalized treatment. A senior social worker, for instance, just 'popped in' to the leukaemia clinic and set up a 'joint chat' with two doctors and himself and his wife to discuss his 'future'.

c) The patient's condition. Where the patient is approaching a terminal condition, all the normal rules may be waived. Such a patient, observed at the leukaemia clinic, broadly defined his own preferred consultation disposal, was more or less in control of the agenda, and was promised a home phonecall that day in response to his requests.

d) The patient's social background. Here the evidence is patchy. Nonetheless at the NHS clinic, one clearly upper-class lady (Mrs J) (who I was told would have been a private patient if the consultant concerned had taken them), got personalized treatment to a degree not seen in other patients. For instance.

> (L:2)
> 1.   D: We've got an audience. I hope that's OK.
>   . . .
> 2.   D: John (the consultant) is in America
> 3.   J: Lucky him

Finally, where a patient at another NHS clinic was married to the son of a surgeon, the husband speedily raised the question of private care and an immediate scan was set up at the BUPA Centre because the NHS hospital had a two-week delay in the pre-Christmas period.

Like many private consultations, the encounter ended with X-rays being passed into the keeping of the patient.

3. Further Research

This chapter began by citing Strong's work which hypothesized that 'product differentiation' based on individual, non-collegial, authority would be the distinguishing mark of private consultations. This small-scale study has largely borne out this hypothesis, although I have added a note of caution about the continuum of forms to be found within NHS medicine. Further research should broaden the data-base to include a range of private practitioners and private practice. A study of private general practice would usefully complement this data on a specialist private clinic. If the former can generate situations, as observed here, in two cases, where the GP accompanies his patient to the specialist, it is likely to offer a data-rich area for comparative study.

II
CONSTITUTING SUBJECTS

With the two chapters contained in Part Two, we make a fairly abrupt change of tack. In Part One, I attempted to ground the concept of 'site' by an examination of a wide range of settings and situations and by the use of conventional qualitative and quantitative methods. Part Two looks at only two situations: Down's Syndrome children with congenital heart disease and cleft-palate teenagers being assessed for cosmetic surgery. A smaller number of consultations is examined much more intensively in order to focus on the language of the encounter.

The position I adopt is that individuals are not pre-defined entities with particular psychological properties but are 'subjects', constituted in specific institutional and discursive practices. This can be clearly demonstrated if we return to the issue of the 'patency' of the child's symptoms. As we saw in Chapter Three, the issue of the wellness or illness of a child is discursively constituted in the consultation. Specifically, children initially conceived as 'ill' by parents (perhaps because of a 'heart murmur') may be reconstituted as entirely 'well' (because the murmur is 'innocent'). Conversely, apparently 'well' children may be redefined as 'well-but-with-an-underlying-heart-problem'.

In both cases, the clinical version of the situation incorporates and transforms the parental formulation. By contrast, in these two chapters, the redefinitional process works very differently. With Down's Syndrome children, a *social* version of childhood is validated as the key way of formulating their character and needs. This normally leads to an avoidance of surgical intervention on the child's heart condition. In the case of cleft-palate teenagers, the decision about cosmetic surgery is turned over to the patient. While the Down's Syndrome children are constituted as social objects, the cleft-palate children become psychological subjects who are expected to formulate their desires and needs.

In certain respects, these are two case-studies of what Byrne and Long (1976) would call 'patient-centred' medicine. Discussion of non-clinical realities is encouraged and decisions are left to the patients or parents. Yet rather than liberating the 'true' feelings of the people concerned, the encounters exhibit an appeal to further discourses (of the 'family', of the 'psyche') with just as many effects of power as clinical discourses.

The conclusion of Part One, that 'better communication' was an inadequate guide to reforming the clinic, is underlined. But it is now revealed that communication techniques are not neutral mechanisms but derive from powerful discourses initiated by the human sciences. Rather than seek to substitute one discourse for another, we must focus on the relations between discourses. For this is where effects of power are constituted and challenged.

6
Coercive Interpretation in the Clinic: The Social Constitution of the Down's Syndrome Child

Introduction

Foucault's (1973) work on clinical discourse implicitly agrees with humanist critiques of medicine by identifying a technicized, clinical language inaccessible to the patient. It also fails to consider systematically exchanges between patients and doctors. Following Foucault's (1977 and 1979) later work, this chapter shows how a more 'socialized' discourse can co-exist with a technical vocabulary, supporting and enlarging medically-approved ways of constituting the child.

Using data drawn from audio-recordings of the paediatric cardiology clinic discussed in earlier chapters, it is argued that the 'normal form' consultation involves an attempt by physicians to supplant parents' 'social' discourse by a 'clinical' discourse. A deviant case is provided in clinics attended by parents of Down's Syndrome children with congenital heart disease. Here doctors conspire with parents to supplant a clinical language by a social discourse which depicts the child's present 'enjoyment of life' within an idealized family setting. This 'demedicalized' model of the child allows the doctor to argue effectively against the cardiac catheterization and surgery that would be employed on children without intellectual handicaps.

Here we see ideological practices of closure at work. The apparently liberating move into social discourse simply institutes a coercive 'interpretation'. In merely reversing the common relation between discourses in the clinic, this 'interpretation' serves to preclude topicalizing the relationship between discourses. The closure cannot be challenged by replacing one discourse by another ('reformism'). Nor will it be challenged by seeking to obtain a mythical freedom from discourse, such as that which would allow a formulation of the 'real' child ('romanticism'). An 'interruption' can interrogate the various relationships between discourses found in the clinic and, thereby, challenge any attempt to fix at the outset a non-discursive reality.

This chapter, then, seeks to develop an analysis of what have been called 'discursive practices of mastery' (Silverman and Torode,

1980: Chapter 1). These arise for us in the form of practices (which we call practices of *interpretation*) which constitute their speech as the reality behind the appearances of other speeches. The aim here is not to substitute one interpretation for another, but to interrogate the relationship between discourses. I believe that this has parallels with Ernesto Laclau's (1981) and Laclau and Mouffe's (1985) important work which so valuably reveals practices of mastery at work in political discourse.

The Structure of the Consultation

Paediatrics is a particularly interesting area to examine in the sense that the child-patient always has a representative and so the social character of the encounter is at least acknowledged. The adult patient is capable of being treated purely as a clinical object (an extreme example of this would be a fracture clinic), but the relationship between the child-patient and the doctor is always mediated by the presence of a third party. The encounter actually cannot get going (the doctor will refuse to proceed) without some representative of the child being present. It does not have to be the parent — it can be another relative or somebody with knowledge of that child who can count as its representative — but this presence of the third party acknowledges that social discourse has potential rights in the setting.

This has two kinds of implications that I will touch upon. First of all, it reveals the clinic as the site of multiple discourses. Hence, one of the concerns of this chapter is to map the relationship between this multiplicity of discourses rather than to focus upon a purely clinical discourse. Secondly, as Foucault (1977 and 1979) has shown in other contexts, the introduction of a social discourse can provide another arm for professional surveillance. As opposed to reformist programmes in the sociology of medicine, which emphasize the need to humanize or socialize the clinic and to train doctors accordingly to understand the social needs of the patients and parents, I want to show the way in which social discourse can be used in a coercive manner.

At the paediatric cardiology clinic discussed in Part One, there is a policy of non-intervention on the cardiac condition of Down's Syndrome children. The normal kinds of tests that are carried out on children with suspected congenital heart disease (in particular cardiac catheterization), are not routinely done on these children. Additionally, surgery usually is only contemplated when there is a minor heart condition which is easily corrected. This is rather curious because the clinic concerned is a high-technology unit which often produces, from parents' points of view, miraculous cures for children. Yet here we see a situation in which doctors are withdrawing from intervention. The rationale which they use privately, when you ask them about this, involves a melange of factors. They talk about clinical factors including the greater risks of surgery on Down's Syndrome children. They stress, to researchers although not to parents, the role of the Down's child's limited intelligence and potential contribution to society. Thirdly, I would guess that perhaps medical intervention on handicapped children has a low medical status and, as a consequence of this, the whole area is not one in which the clinic can advance itself by intervention.

This chapter, however, is not concerned with speculating about the reasons why doctors engage in this policy of non-intervention (for further discussion of this topic, see Silverman, 1981). It is concerned much more with how non-intervention is discursively achieved. What I try to show is that it is achieved through a demedicalization of the clinic by a focus on the child's social features and, hence, upon the inappropriateness of surgery.

I will make two further observations at this point. In studying other clinics, I found variability in policy towards intervention on Down's Syndrome children. This does not seem to be an invariable policy. What seems to happen is that a policy is laid down by the consultant in charge of the Unit and the policy is simply applied by other doctors to all Down's children who enter the clinic. Secondly, I am not questioning the rightness of *this* policy — the rightness of the grounds the clinic uses for non-intervention or of *any* grounds that might be argued for non-intervention. No doubt there are certain abstract grounds in favour of non-intervention on such children. What I am doing is questioning the rightness of *any* clinical policy applied uniformly to a category of children, like Down's Syndrome children. And I want to try to show that the practice of this policy involves the closure of possibilities of dialogue between a range of discourses in favour of a coercive interpretation which appeals to available social stereotypes of children.

What I am doing here is counterposing what happens in the Down's Syndrome clinic to what I would call the 'normal form' of clinic. Now, as I tried to show in Chapter Two, a constant feature of this 'normal form' is that social formulations are interpreted by doctors in terms of clinical problematics. In discussions with parents, the social realm gets constituted as an appearance beneath which is always to be read an underlying *clinical* reality.

For instance, with one child with a minor remediable heart condition (a non-Down's Syndrome child), the doctor at the start of the encounter said to the mother in a questioning voice: 'A well little girl who's got a heart murmur'. And at that point the mother contested what he was saying. She said, 'Well, er, no . . .'. What she may have been implying was that the whole notion of 'wellness' was a problematic one for her. The doctor was calling her child 'well' but presumably she would not have been referred to the clinic if she were well. How could a child with a diagnosed heart murmur be well? The doctor's response to this was to reassert his notion of wellness, the clinic's version of wellness. He put it this way: 'But in the way the child was picked up, she's basically a well little girl'. Notice his reference to 'the way in which the child was picked up'. The parent's common-sense conception of illness which identifies a sign — a murmur — as a symptom is displaced. The doctor is pointing out that the heart murmur is only a sign to be read in conjunction with others. Consequently, a child with a heart murmur can still be well for clinical purposes. As it turns out, the child does indeed, on examination, seem likely to require surgery and is brought in for a catheterization.

There is a certain irony here because the consultant is disagreeing with the mother in order to locate the child as well. He will later, as a result, have to persuade the parents into surgery. But because his location of the child as well occurs in clinical terms (in terms, as he says, of the way in which the child was 'picked up'), it allows the triumph of a clinical formulation over the parent's social formulation of the child. In terms of the clinical formulation, the child can later be reconstituted as an asymptomatic child but in need of treatment.

The rest of the encounter turns out to be a process by which the doctor overwhelms the parents' social formulations of their child by a presentation of clinical data, ultimately leaving him to present them with a decision which is formulated in this way: 'What I think we should do is', where the 'I' appeals to the clinical team, the voice of the 'we'.

Now this normal form is also demonstrated throughout the various stages of the consultation. For instance, I took a sample of twenty-two non-Down's encounters. At the early stage of the clinic, invariably there is what we call an 'elicitation sequence'. Here doctors ask questions about how the parents view the child. Now, a curious thing happens if you look at non-Down's cases. In half of them, eleven out of these twenty-two, the elicitation question is something like 'is he or she well?' So there is a reference to wellness in half of these. In another two as well, there is a question by the doctor 'From your point of view, a well baby?' So certainly, in a majority of these cases of non-Down's children, there is a reference to the child's wellness by the doctor.

With a sample of ten Down's children, the initial elicitation question 'is he or she well?' was never used. In six out of the ten cases we found a question in the form 'How is he?', 'How is she?'.

At this point let me speculate about this empirical finding. A discourse of wellness would seem to imply a willingness to restore an unwell child to health or to use the clinical gaze to discover a possible future unwellness lurking beneath the surface. This indeed is the case with the child that I looked at for the child is constituted as a well child by the doctor but ultimately needs surgery.

By avoiding 'wellness' with Down's children, the path is cleared for the physician to constitute the Down's child not in terms of a remediable status of unwellness but in entirely different *social* terms. As we shall see shortly, this social constitution of the child relates to such matters as enjoyment of life within a highly idealized version of the family.

This difference between Down's consultations and others can be seen if you take the consultation through later stages. For instance, at the diagnosis stage which invariably follows the examination, in fifteen out of the twenty-two 'normal' cases, the doctor referred to the child as being well or doing splendidly or some other form of reassurance. On the other hand, in a sample of twelve Down's Syndrome cases, nine parents received no reassurance. There was again no reference to wellness. We simply found a straight statement of the diagnosis. What seems to be happening there is that with the normal child the doctor's strategy is a step-by-step revelation of the clinical situation as symptoms and the treatment unwind over several years. This allows the clinical discourse to be fully in control. The doctor uses reassurance to get parents through difficult stages. Parents must become attuned to the dominant truth of clinical formulations.

With a Down's child, the clinical situation has fully unfolded at birth for doctors. Hence, all can be revealed at once without any need for reassurance because no more could be said and nothing more needs to be done. The consequence is also that clinical discourse has lost its association with a magical power to make the child well. The notions of wellness and unwellness must be avoided in favour of social formulations. This has a certain irony. The full clinical disclosure that we find with Down's Syndrome consultations, involving a revelation of the full irretrievability of the clinical situation, allows for a speedy move into non-clinical territory as a medically-sanctioned way of formulating the child.

A final feature that we find with Down's consultations is that the doctor appeals much more to the parents' wishes than elsewhere. As we saw in the case of the child who was constituted as 'well' but needing treatment the normal form is to say something like 'What I think we ought to be doing here'. In Down's cases, he will say 'Well, normally at this stage we leave it to parents to decide'. This occurs in the context of heavily loaded advice against intervention based in terms of largely social stereotypes. The appeal to democracy allows the doctor to avoid appearing to 'play God'. The reality, as I will show, is, however, of coercive interpretations.

Comparative information on the potentially touchy subject of preserving seriously handicapped children is notoriously difficult to gather. Understandably, hospital records do not reveal very much of what is going on. Where the law is a potential threat, the tendency is also to keep silent. Often we have to rely on the occasional outburst from an insider, as in this extract from *The Sunday Times* of January 1981:

> It is becoming clear that the practice of allowing 'hopeless' babies to die is widespread. Dr John Freeman, a leading American paediatrician, said in a recent broadcast: 'it concerns me greatly that a given (spina bifida) child, if born in Sheffield, has a 75 per cent chance of being dead. That same child, were he born in Baltimore, has a 95 per cent chance of being alive. That's scary.'

The clearest evidence about the overall picture and the reasons for it is provided by Diana Crane (1975) in her book *The Sanctity of Social Life: Physicians' Treatment of Critically Ill Patients*. This American study reveals clearly the role of social factors in medical decision-making. As she puts it, doctors evaluate a patient: 'not only in terms of the physiological aspects of illness but also in terms of the extent to which he is capable of interacting with others' (p.11).

This crucial study was based on a large sample of American hospitals, including a number of children's heart units. Surgeons at these units were sent questionnaires which presented contrived case histories and asked them if they would be likely to operate. For all levels of severity of heart conditions, Diana Crane found that surgeons said they would be more likely to operate if the child had only a physical handicap (the instance given was 'a urogenital anomaly') than if he had a mental handicap (the instance given was Down's Syndrome). Broadly speaking, 90 per cent of the surgeons would do heart surgery on a child with a physical handicap but only 50 to 60 per cent would do the same for a child with Down's Syndrome. Even this figure assumed a 'favourable family attitude'. Where the family was stated to be unfavourable, only 10 to 20 per cent of surgeons would want to operate on the Down's child.

As a competent researcher, Diana Crane knew that what people *say* often bears a limited relevance to what they actually *do*. Consequently, she went beyond questionnaire responses and looked at hospital records in one teaching hospital. She made a complete listing of all Down's Syndrome children who were given heart catheter tests over a five-year period. Overall, she found that, when the heart condition was held constant, 39 per cent of Down's children had surgery compared to 65 per cent of non-Down's. Looking only at the severe condition that affects many Down's children (atrial-ventricular canal defect), she discovered that 'normal' children were more than three times as likely to receive surgery for it (100 per cent for non-Down's as against 29 per cent for Down's).

Overall, Diana Crane found that surgery occurred *less* often in practice than doctors had said in reply to her questionnaire. Even variation in the treatment of particular Down's children suggested that doctors were primarily paying attention to social factors. For instance, an only child or a first-born child were more likely to be operated upon than other Down's children. So Crane concludes: 'Social variables play a more important role than medical variables in determining whether or not such operations are performed' (p.100).

'However, doing nothing she may have a virtually normal childhood'

(Consultant talking to parents of a Down's child)

So it seems we will have to look closely at these 'social variables', as distinct from medical ones, in explaining the decisions which are taken about treating Down's children. Let us do this by looking at a typical Down's consultation at the unit.

Helen, the child concerned, is one year old. Her Down's Syndrome is combined with serious congenital heart disease which has already caused some damage to the lungs. This has been diagnosed at a local hospital, some 150 miles away, but she has been referred to our unit for a specialist opinion. Both her parents are in their forties. They have four other children, all in their teens, from earlier marriages.

After the normal exchange of greetings, this is how the consultant gets down to business:

> D: Well, how is she? Dr X has written to me and has also sent the catheter films that were done in Othertown. Um, can I ask you a few questions? How is she in herself?
>
> M: Well, I've been pleasantly surprised to be quite honest. (She goes on to relate details of colds, chest infections and episodes of breathlessness)

Notice the format of the doctor's question: he does not ask 'is she well?' but 'how is she?', and, afterwards, 'how is she in herself?'. As a discourse of 'wellness' is avoided, so the ground is prepared for other, non-medical, formulations of children.

Parents of Down's Syndrome children usually conspire with doctors to avoid reference to 'wellness'. Notice, for instance, how Helen's mother simply talks about being 'pleasantly surprised'. Not only does this get round the difficult notion of 'wellness', as applied to her child, but it also suggests that Down's parents bring their children to the unit with vastly lowered expectations, since she goes on to relate a whole range of symptoms. She is 'surprised' only because she expected things to be far worse.

Avoiding the delicate issue of 'wellness' also has more long-term implications for the communication between doctors and parents. By sidestepping the possibility of recognizing an 'unwell' child who requires active medical intervention, it prepares the way for discussing the child's symptoms in non-medical terms. The talk begins to centre itself around the home and family. Look, for instance, at how the consultant responds to the mother's account of Helen's breathlessness:

> D: Do you think her breathlessness interferes with her enjoying doing things, or not?
> M: Well, not, not up to the present.

As the consultant later makes clear, the breathlessness that Helen is experiencing is, in the context of her heart defect, an indication of a serious lung condition that is likely eventually to shorten her life somewhat. However, his *initial* reaction is to relate it, not to its long-term effects, but to its immediate impact on Helen's social and psychological capacities. The emphasis is on Helen's social being ('enjoying doing things') rather than her medical problems. However, this is not to say that the medical situation is not fully discussed with such parents, even though the consultation takes a primarily social turn. What happens is that Down's parents get a much balder, less reassuring statement of clinical facts than is normal.

Ordinarily, doctors will start by trying to reassure anxious parents immediately after the examination is completed. For instance, even seriously ill (non-Down's) children can be called 'well' as long as they are temporarily free from symptoms. 'The first thing to say is that he's very well. What we think he has is ... '.With Down's families, however, the diagnosis statement is invariably blunt and to the point. This is how Helen's parents hear the verdict:

> D: We know from the, er, catheter that Dr X sent us that she has a complicated heart abnormality. It's the sort of abnormality that is always difficult to correct.

The consultant continues by reviewing the risks of surgery at some length. He wants to make it clear to the parents that there is no *technical* problem in doing the necessary surgery; the problem only arises in terms of the risks and, if Helen survives, the long-term complications of surgery. The last thing that he wants to do is to let the parents think that his unit is incompetent to do such an operation. It sometimes happens that parents go away to make appeals for funds for 'miracle cures' in other countries. The consultant sees this as wasted effort, as well as unfavourable publicity for the unit.

Here too there is another departure from the 'routine' consultation. Normally, parents of a serious ill child will not be told this at all in so many words, especially at a first out-patients' appointment. The usual tactic is to proceed step-by-step, mixing clinical fact with a measure of reassurance. Parents can elicit more by active questioning but if they appear satisfied with a limited explanation concentrating on the short-term outlook, that is all they will get. The same thing happens with the communication of information to adult patients in the early stages of treatment of fatal illnesses. With Down's families, there is no step-by-step explanation. The whole story is unfolded at the very first consultation.

At first sight, this seems confusing. After all, a parent who knows the full seriousness of the clinical picture may well demand major medical intervention. There are three reasons why this does not usually occur here. First, it allows the doctor to emphasize the risks of surgery. Second, Down's parents get the whole cardiac picture at one sweep because doctors assume that they already have vastly lowered expectations about their child's future and about the prospects of successful medical interventions. Step-by-step explanations allow the doctor gradually to move parents from a social to a medical picture of their child, with a view to persuading them to agree to proposed tests and operations. The bald statement, offered to a parent with reduced expectations, sets the scene for developing alternative, non-medical (hence more acceptable) ways of looking at the Down's child.

This leads on to the third linkage between being told the whole story and non-intervention: the emphasis that has already been implied on the *social* life of the Down's child. As the consultation proceeds, this social picture of a happy child enjoying her life will be developed and embellished. After further discussion of the risks of surgery, the consultant gets back to the social area by means of a rhetorical question:

D: That could be counter-balanced with: what is her life going to be
     without an operation? The answer to that is, probably very good. She
     may well have a relatively normal childhood.
M: Yes.

Here the consultant successfully makes the question one of risky surgery vs. normal childhood. Helen's parents are invited to dwell on the short-term outlook and, viewed in this light, it would be difficult for them to want to request surgery. Even the handicap she will suffer from breathlessness and other symptoms should, it seems, be discounted by looking at things in social terms:

D: (the handicap will be) perhaps not enough to interfere with her pleasure in play and walking and doing things.

However, Helen's mother intervenes to obtain more information about the nature and consequences of her daughter's disabilities. She explains that her interest is in the physical side of things:

M: Um she is likely I suppose to suffer some degree of physical disability um when she gets short of breath and things?

As we know, this appeal to physical symptoms of unwellness might imply an obligation for the doctors to intervene. Even when both parents and doctors know that such intervention is likely to be fruitless, the implied inability of the medical profession to restore a sick child to health is potentially embarrassing for them.

The consultant responds to this by persuading the mother to look at disability in a different way. Don't think about disability in a physical, medical way but in terms of your child's social life:

D: When you say *physical* disability, she may be a bit on the small side and she may get a little bit more puffed than some children. Whether you call that, you know, disability, in inverted commas but I think disabilities are abnormalities if you like that interfere with her pleasure and progress and enjoyment of childhood and, to that extent, no I don't think she will be disabled so that she can't take part.

Drawing on Helen's mothers' lowered expectations, the consultant paints a picture of fairly severe physical symptoms being compatible with 'pleasure and progress and enjoyment of childhood'. Where all else fails, even severely damaged children can still be looked at in terms of the inherent joys of childhood.

Your Down's child probably *is*, at home, happy and good natured. You have looked after the child well. But if you talk about things in this way to a doctor, it follows that nothing needs to be done. The decision about the child's future is effectively made when parents go along with this way of discussing matters. At the actual moment when the decision is formally made, the doctors are careful to avoid appearing to impose a decision on the parents. They do not want to seem to be playing God. Parents of Down's Syndrome children are given extensive 'advice' by the doctor, but are usually told that the actual decision is theirs alone. This is how the decision is handed over to Helen's parents:

D: So I think these are the issues though at that point, having tried to tell you the technical side from our point of view (   ) I mean she's your child
[*laughter*]

M: Well thank you very much. You must appreciate because, um, we felt

that, um, first of all, we didn't really understand what was possible
from the technical point of view and secondly we weren't quite sure
(   ) What you have told us has been very helpful.

As is common in such cases, the consultant then suggests that the
decision is postponed until after 'you and your husband have talked
things over'. The parents gratefully accept the offer. Some weeks
later, the consultant showed us a letter from them repeating their
thanks for his detailed explanation of the situation and informing him
that they did not want an operation.

Readers might not find it very surprising that Helen's parents were
asked to make the choice themselves. After all, parents always have to
sign a consent form for operations on their children. Is it so strange,
you may ask yourself, that parents should be given time to think about
such a decision? At the heart unit, it is in fact most unusual. The
normal pattern would be for the doctor to say something like 'What I
think we should do here ...' or, even more impersonally 'The
management would be ...'. There is normally, then, only the barest
mention of parental consent. For instance, an 'if you agree' may be
inserted somewhere in the doctor's statement of what he intends to do,
without any suggestion that parents might in fact disagree. Indeed, we
have seen no such disagreement in the case of children with serious
symptoms being put up for a catheter test.

With Down's children, complex medical and moral issues have
produced a special kind of consultation. Unusually in a high-powered
technically sophisticated Unit which regularly makes a dramatic
difference to the lives of sick children and their families, the doctors
have stepped aside in order to let people concentrate on a non-medical
world of 'happy children at play'. Doctors mobilize the familiar
descriptions of Down's children in terms of their social life in order to
dissuade parents from medical intervention. In doing this, they
appear to be shifting the balance of decision-making power between
layman and professionals, and, sure enough, the decision almost
invariably turns out to be non-medical. The child is to be left at home
in its social world, rather than brought into the hospital's medical one.

Perhaps Helen's parents seem rather easily persuaded. Their only
attempt to suggest that medical intervention might be needed, by the
question about 'physical' handicap, is easily sidestepped by the
consultant. After that, they go along readily with the doctor's line.
They are not unusual in this amongst the Down's parents we have seen
at the unit. Hardly any need much convincing: in nine out of twelve
conversations we taped, the mother or father has said distinctly that it
seems best to 'leave her alone' or pleaded 'don't mess him about'.

Down's parents don't seem to come to the unit with the high

expectations of the families of otherwise 'normal' children. Why is this, considering that Down's parents have been exposed just as much as others to all the media coverage of 'miracle cures' and revolutionary heart treatment? The answer seems to be that Down's parents have been taught right from their child's birth to think about their child in social rather than medical terms. From the Maternity Hospital onwards, parents will be encouraged to think 'realistically', and to limit their expectations for what can be done medically. By the time they attend the heart unit, Downs' parents will have got used to the idea that they cannot expect their child to live to a ripe old age. Hence it is not such a great shock to be told that his life expectancy may be even shorter, or that he is a little more 'imperfect' than they had imagined.

The parents have already experienced, and come to terms with, the terrible upset of having produced an 'imperfect' child. They have then been told that medicine can only, at best, handle any symptoms that arise but cannot put to rights the genetic defects. They may also have been encouraged to concentrate upon the usually happy personality of such children and upon what they can contribute to family life.

We could say that Down's Syndrome children are 'demedicalized'. This is the reverse of what happens to other children with heart problems. As the otherwise normal child with a heart problem is referred from hand to hand (perhaps from school medical or baby clinic to local hospital and then to the central heart unit), parents are led to see their child more and more in medical terms. They have to gradually give up, for a while, thinking of their child secure at home. The child is 'medicalized' in order to set the scene for restoring him/her to normal. Down's parents are taught to give up the idea of having a normal child. At most, they can think about what would be 'normal for my child'. The outcome of the 'demedicalization' process is that parents' medical expectations are vastly lowered. Even when the decision is apparently thrown open to them, they are not inclined to clamour for medical miracles.

The purpose of this chapter is not to argue that more operations should be performed on Down's children. That is a question which readers will decide for themselves, and which, more importantly, Down's parents and doctors have to make up their minds upon knowing far more about the individual situation. What I am trying to show is that decisions about the future of Down's children are taken under a certain kind of pressure: the 'demedicalization' process, which masquerades as a simple kindness or politeness towards the parents of the Down's child. It is happening whenever everybody is agreeing how happy, good-natured and loving the child is.

However, as already noted, there are exceptions to this co-operative display of social 'enjoyment' without medical intervention. Let us look at what happens when parents actively resist medical non-intervention.

Coercive Interpretation

Gloria is 2¼. Her condition is less severe than Helen: she has a VSD plus some lung damage. Like Helen's parents, Gloria's mother is told that the decision is hers. Although this degree of parental choice would be very unusual in non-Down's consultations, the doctor presents the situation as being entirely normal.

> D: Um I think what we do now depends a little bit on parents' feelings.

He repeats this offer of choice, twice more, and concludes by suggesting, as with Helen's parents, that the decision be postponed until they contact the hospital. Since Gloria's mother has come on her own, this delay will give her the opportunity:

> D: ... to go away and talk about it with your husband

However, this routine unfolding of a Down's consultation is challenged at one point by Gloria's mother. It happens immediately after the consultant has made this typical allusion to Gloria's social life:

> 1.D: I mean do you think a happy child of four, playing and growing up with other children and then, perhaps, you know, either late teens or twenties just peacefully passing away might be (   )

To the average parent, the notion of their child 'passing away', even 'peacefully', around the age of twenty would be horrific. The fact that it can be said to this mother indicates the degree to which Down's parents have already lowered their expectations for their child. Gloria's mother doesn't challenge the doctor's statement of the inevitable long-term outlook. What she objects to is the absence of medical interventions that might make Gloria's limited lifespan more tolerable. Her exchange with the consultant is worth quoting in full:

> 2.M: The only (   ), I expect other children are the same, she gets ill so quickly and we were hoping perhaps if something was done she wouldn't be like, um, like that and she's always just been, you know, in and out of hospital since she was born
> 3.D: Well I think that's a little bit related to her having Down's Syndrome independently of the heart
> 4.M: I see. I'll talk it over with my husband / then
> 5.D: / Yes
> 6.M: And he wasn't keen for her to have an / operation
> 7.D: / Yes

8.M: really. He said even if it came to it he wasn't keen.
       (the doctor returns again to the risks of surgery)
9.D: But I think my own view is if she were my child with Down's
       Syndrome, I think I would adopt the view well, she's a happy little
       thing, she's got plenty of years ahead of her, in any case there are
       going to be problems if she does get to the age of forty or fifty and
       outlives you and your husband
10.M: Yes.
11.D: Maybe the best thing all round is not to distress her with the
       operation and all the things involved, to enjoy her as she is and to
       be pleased that you've got a happy little (   ) fits into the
       family
12.M: Yes.
13.D: And say OK well let's enjoy that and not risk losing you for a
       rather doubtful gain
14.M: Yes, yes. Well thank you very much for seeing her and talking to
       me

In Utterance 1 we find a social formulation of the child which
emphasizes the child's social situation using everyday terms like
'happiness', 'play', 'growing up' which concludes curiously in the
language of obituaries: 'just peacefully passing away'. It is a
stereotype formula response in terms of some kind of formula like:
'It's better to have a happy, if short, life'. It is precisely *not* the
stereotype we find offered to parents of non-Down's children with
suspected congenital heart disease, where the doctor will argue that
the clinic should intervene now despite the lack of symptoms. The
formula that he uses with these parents is that it is better to lose a child
young than grow attached to a dying teenager. With Down's parents
he uses an alternative social formulation which comes to dominate the
encounter.

Unlike Utterance 1, the mother's Utterance 2 seeks to relate this
clinical reality of illness to a social discourse without subordinating
one to the other. Getting ill so quickly is a problem for the parents but
so is the relationship between stays in hospital and the stability of
home life. The mother appeals to the doctor by evincing the hopes of
'we'. 'We were hoping perhaps that something could be done' —
appealing to the family unit as a team which stands in contrast to the
clinical team conjured up by the doctor.

The doctor's Utterance 3 does not really respond to these arguments
but attempts to interpret what the mother is saying in terms of a
clinical formulation. He retreats to the thoughts of the clinical 'I'.
While the mother has proposed that the proper relation between the
world of the clinic and the family should be discussed, the doctor
retreats from an idealized family world into a clinical reality which
offers no hope.

As a consequence of the doctor's coercive interpretation of what the mother has said, the mother does return to the family unit in Utterances 4, 6 and 8 but reformulates her husband's desires. Previously she was talking about what 'we' were hoping for. Now by Utterances 6 and 8, the mother is saying 'he', her husband, was not keen for her to have an operation and in Utterance 8, 'He even said if it came to it he wasn't keen'. What we are seeing is that in the doctor's Utterances 1 and 3, the child can only be conceived as either a stereotyped *social* subject or as an entirely hopeless clinical object. This is repeated in the doctor's subsequent utterances. The doctor's Utterance 9 is prefaced by an account of the risks of surgery on this child which is in terms of the voice of the clinic. But he moves on from there to social formulations of the child. We see in Utterance 9 a reference to 'happiness' again. 'She's a happy little thing', where I take it 'happiness' is an available stereotype for any asymptomatic four year old. What is significant is that it is used here in this particular context. Why formulate the child in terms of 'happiness' rather than in terms of her underlying condition?

There is another stereotype too we find here; 'She's got plenty of years ahead of her', where the maxim seems to be a happy if short life is what matters. All of this is based on an appeal to stereotyped problems of older handicapped people which come out at the end of Utterance 9. 'If she does get to the age of forty or fifty and outlives you or your husband ... ' This move into social discourse as the prevailing way of formulating the child is continued in Utterance 11 where the doctor suggests that the practices of the clinic should ultimately be read in terms of their impact on social and psychological factors. There is here a curious formulation about not distressing the child with an operation which you would never find when doctors talk about children without Down's Syndrome. The clinic is there precisely *to* engage in necessary treatments. Why formulate the situation in terms of not distressing the child?

We see further examples of social formulations of the child in terms of 'enjoying her as she is', 'be pleased you've got a happy little (   ) that fits into the family'. There are also references to an idealized form of the family and the child's place within it as sanctioning this decision. I am stressing the curious nature of this appeal in this particular setting and the coercive work it does by using a stereotype which could be used on any child to argue for non-intervention.

The doctor's Utterance 13 returns to the enjoyment theme 'and say OK, well let's enjoy that and not risk losing for a rather doubtful gain'. The 'rather doubtful gain' to which the doctor refers reflects the relationship his speech has established between clinical and social discourses. For the doctor, the clinic is a site of risks and 'distress'. The social realm of the family, on the other hand, is a site of enjoyment and pleasure. This realm is menaced by unnecessary clinical interventions which may cut short the life of the child. Moreover, should such interventions succeed, they ultimately would propel the child out of the family and into the 'problems' of a handicapped person who outlives her parents.

Each of the doctor's utterances establish paradigmatic oppositions between family life and the world of clinics and state institutions. This can be shown in a schematic form:

TABLE 1
Doctor's Utterances: The Family Versus the Clinic and State

Utterance	Family	Clinic/State
1	Happiness Play Growing up Peaceful death	(Painful death)
9	Happiness	Problems when parents dead
11	Enjoyment Pleasure Happiness Fitting in	Distressing operations
13	Enjoyment	Risks

As Table 1 shows, for the doctor the family is the site of entirely positive activities and sentiments. The outside world, whether clinic or state institution, is treated as entirely a negative entity. Faced with an irreparably damaged child, the clinic and the State hand back the creature to the family. Since the family is a sacred institution, this way of speaking has an inexorable moral logic which commands consent from the child's parents while neatly shedding the responsibilities of clinic and State.

This stress on the family would appear to have one positive consequence. The discourse of family life is a shared social discourse: we can all talk, on an equal basis, about the 'happiness' and 'enjoyment' of children. So it would seem that here parents are on a more equal discursive footing than elsewhere when the voice of the clinic reigns supreme.

As we have seen, this allows the mother to make a claim, in

Utterance 2, for 'something' to be 'done' to allow her child to spend more time at home. This subtle appeal to the (negatively-valued) clinic to be used as an instrument to preserve the (positively-valued) family is undercut by the doctor retreating to his clinical voice.

In Utterance 3, he makes clear that the clinic, although powerless to operate, is still powerful discursively. The master definition of the child ultimately derives from the clinic: the child has Down's Syndrome (posited in Utterances 3 and 9). It is the clinic which possesses both the term for the condition and knowledge of its diagnosis and prognosis, so, although the doctor will appeal to the reality of family life, this is ultimately grounded by an appeal to a further underlying reality of clinical diagnoses.

Both Down's consultations and 'normal' consultations involve a transformation of everyday signs into a clinical discourse of symptoms and diagnoses. Only in Down's cases, however, does this lead to a sanctioning of a discourse of family life as the prime medium for constituting the child. Either way, however, the Down's parent is stuck. She is unable to dissent from moral stereotypes of family life any more than she can contest clinical definitions of her child's 'condition'.

In a sense, this analysis has sought to show how the doctor's speech enters into and *expropriates* the language of family life. This has so far been documented by reference to the stereotypes of emotions used by the doctor ('happiness', 'enjoyment' etc.). It is worth adding, however, that these stereotypes or interpretations gain discursive power by being offered in the context of telling a story.

The narrative structure of the doctor's formulations is clear at the outset. He begins: 'I mean do you think ...' His account of happy childhood appeals to an intersubjective world in which 'You' are able to change places with the subject ('I') who speaks. As Torode (1984) points out, such a formulation asserts and checks the common intersubjective world of speaker and hearer. For the hearer to dissent would imply a moral charge against the speaker's intersubjective competence.

This 'I–You' consensual device is used by the doctor to paint an idealized picture of family life. After resisting the mother's subtle attempt to reintroduce the possibility of clinic intervention, the doctor then retells his story with two important differences. It is now told from the point of view of parental decision-making and the doctor himself assumes the role of a putative parent.

In stating 'my own view if she were my child with Down's Syndrome (Utterance 9), the doctor's speech becomes very powerful. First, it appeals to the presumed concern of parents to do the best for their child. Second, it is made not by anyone but by a subject laying claim to a special competence in clinical matters and a special competence to articulate the relations between clinic and society as a result of his experience of many similar cases. The doctor thus speaks not as, it appears, *any* parent but as a Super-parent.

Moreover, the story that this Super-parent tells is all-encompassing: it provides for descriptions of the child's dispositions and relation to the family ('happiness', 'fitting in'), the mother's proper feelings ('enjoyment', 'pleasure') and even what she should say ('and say OK ...'). It is hardly surprising when the mother immediately terminates the consultation (Utterance 14). The very language of emotions has been expropriated and the child handed back to a family fixed in a clinic-provided set of emotions, sayings and actions.

'I prefer to take the chance but I think you will be doing your job, you see, to save the situation'
(Father of a Down's child)

In our research at the Unit, we have seen only one parent successfully insist on an operation for his child. The grounds for this challenge are, though, very unusual. The case shows how special the case has to be for the parent to overturn the doctor's advice.

John is an African child who is 19 months old. He has a heart defect which, on a scale of seriousness, falls roughly midway between those of Gloria and Helen. It is normally correctable but, as before, the clinic advises against surgery. The communication position has, however, been complicated by the fact that John has been referred to our Unit by a provincial hospital where he has continued to be seen between appointments at the Unit. According to John's father this has led to crossed lines of communication. He thinks that an operation has already been decided upon. However, the consultant at the Unit states that the father has simply been given more time to think and to discuss the matter at his local hospital.

The consultation begins in the way that we have to recognize as typical in these cases. First, the consultant's initial question avoids reference to wellness:

D: How is he?

Second, the diagnosis statement is a bald statement of 'serious' fact. It includes no reassurance:

D: Now, as far as your little boy is concerned, the catheter that Dr um X did in Othertown showed a hole plus an elevated resistance in the lungs

Third, the consultant proposes that the heart condition should be seen primarily in terms of the child's social and psychological state:

> D: The question is, how much is his heart abnormality really interfering with his growth, enjoyment in life and what he can do.

Fourth, a great deal of play is made with the risk to life of surgery (stated to be 25 per cent). This is significantly higher than the normal risk for such an operation because of the lung damage the boy has already sustained. However, it is not higher than the risk involved in many operations carried out at the Unit. Finally, the risk factor is weighed against a picture of normal childhood life which is almost identical to that used with other parents:

> D: I think we have to balance the risk against what happens if we do nothing. And I think if we do nothing he has got many, many years ahead of him of reasonable childhood playing. I mean, there's no reason why he should not be able to play with the other children and to take part in the activities that he would want to, bearing in mind that he does have Down's Syndrome as well which is, to some extent, going to restrict him.

At this point, John's father intervenes to ask the consultant if he has changed his ideas. His understanding from an earlier clinic was that the Unit *was* prepared to operate. He argues that John has consistently done better than doctors have predicted and that, although he knows that John has Down's Syndrome, his life can at least be rid of the 'heart problem'.

The doctor responds by explaining again that he has merely tried to give John's parents more time to think about the matter. He then makes the appeal to parental choice common with Down's parents:

> D: Now my own view is that we have to do, I mean we will do ultimately what you would like us to do, there's no question of that.

When he returns to the issue of the risk of surgery, the following crucial exchange takes place:

> D: And then you're saying, well, is it right to do a big operation with a possible risk of death. Um you get those extra, you know, twenty years at the other end of his life, 10–20 years at the other end of his life. Those are the issues
> F: Yes, because about life (   ) This is why maybe I don't agree with some of the people here. Because er when you report about the condition you see, then there was oppo (   ) I mean somebody said, well he will get on alright. Then why the operation, you see? (   ) in Britain you might have a different family system but at home well, you are just in your family you see? Well he is like a member of the family.
> D: I understand that

F: Like anybody, you see

D: I understand that

F: And er for you in some kind of ways — I think it's wrong. And they asked me who will care for him, you know, if we both go. So I told them that in Africa it's different. See we are a sort of extended family system. That it not a problem

D: Um it's/

F: /it means if you, you know, if we went home, even if say we had maybe four disabled people, that would not be a problem because er we have relatives and our system works different from yours

D: Hm. Hm.

F: So about not having any future, I don't think, I mean what you're saying is not a problem. But medically, perhaps you feel that by operating him you are leaving me a problem. Because no matter what happens, if we say we don't want the operation, he will die. I mean the way I was told at Othertown, someone said well, it's better for him just die in his sleep, you know, even before he is five and that kind of thing. Now, to me, admitting death, to argue that, I think is very painful

D: I understand

F: You see. And this is why we don't want it to happen. We would like him to live in France and go to college. (2.0) It will not be a problem

D: Mm.

F: We would like, you know, to find a solution

The doctor begins by raising the complex moral dilemma which balances a risky operation against a limited lengthening of a life which is, in any event, likely to be shortened. The father's reply highlights different cultural attitudes to handicapped people. At home, in Africa, he will be just like any other member of the family. No problem will arise when John's parents die because 'we are a sort of extended family system'. Hence there is no need to adopt the 'very painful' step of 'admitting death'. The 'solution' that John's parents desire can more readily be found. Consequently, as he will later say, he prefers 'to take the chance'. Faced with this reasoned argument, the doctor agrees.

The convincing argument that John's father mobilizes here is unavailable to British parents. Living in a society which can offer only under-financed institutions for abandoned handicapped people, parents face the heart-breaking dilemma of having to concede that it may be in their child's own best interests to agree not to lengthen his life in order to prevent his institutionalization and decline. They try to do their best for such children but their 'best' is forced to take account of present, unjust realities.

This, then, is not a story of heroes and villains. Consultations at the Unit do not involve a conflict between good and evil. Nor, indeed, is there much conflict of any kind. I selected John's father's consultation precisely because it was so atypical. The encounter between the consultant and Helen's parents is far closer to the normal run of things. Most parents of Down's children seem to come to the cardiac clinic already predisposed against surgery. Faced with a child irretrievably damaged at birth, like one mother at another consultation, they 'don't want 'im messed about with' any more, so consultations proceed smoothly and calmly, with no disagreement.

Conclusion

What I have tried to reveal in these transcripts is a practice of appeals to the realm of social discourse which is at the heart of reformist programmes for change in the clinic. I have shown how these act as strategic means to maintain a particular clinical policy. It seems to me this has certain parallels with my reading of Foucault's work, particularly *Discipline and Punish*. Here we see the humanization that he describes in the context of the prison. As with the reformed prison, humanization operates as a strategy of power. In shifting attention from the body to the soul, or, as we see here, the 'Holy Family', the clinic seems to take control of the potentially independent social discourse and use if for its own purpose.

What I have called 'coercive interpretation' enslaves the speakers to transcendental realities, presented here as the child's 'natural' propensities and features of a proposedly normal family life. Laclau (1981) has called these processes of enslavement the 'articulation of relationships between discourses'. Two forms of that articulation have been observed. Firstly, undercutting the social by the clinical, as I tried briefly to demonstrate in clinics dealing with non-Down's children with suspected heart disease and, secondly, as we have seen with the Down's children, undercutting the clinical by the social. Laclau points out that this articulation of the relationship between discourses, by appealing to extra-discursive realities (the notion of happy family life in the case of Down's children) constitutes other ways of speaking as unthinkable. In the first case, with normal children, the clinical formulation consumes social discourse. And, in the case of Down's Syndrome children, the social formulation consumes the clinical.

In both cases, the *direction* of the interpretation is never topicalized. Nor is the relation of these two discourses to other possible ways of constituting the child: legal, political and moral. For there is no 'pure' discourse of childhood — only certain articulations which fix the child's essential character and needs.

Rather than seeking to speak from within such an articulation, I have sought to interrogate the relationship between discourses that create this unthinkability or unspeakability by fixing the proper forms of constituting the Down's child. It seems to me that issues like this bear both on theoretical debate about ideology and also on a very lively debate within social policy and in the press on the care of children with multiple handicaps.

7

'Consumerist' Medicine in a Cleft-Palate Clinic: Constituting Clinical Subjects

'Consumerism' is a currently popular slogan in health care. It is implied in British programmes for 'patient-centred' medicine (Byrne and Long, 1976) and in American demands for 'patient power' (Wiener et al., 1980). However, there are a great many procedures or devices which could count as 'consumerist' medicine. We need to disentangle fee-for-service medicine, the demand for second opinions, patient-run practices and the tacit threat of legal action from situations where doctors specifically seek to elicit the patient's preference.

Above all, as Van den Heuvel (1980) has pointed out, we lack a theoretical model of the consumer in health care. Following his suggestion, this chapter seeks a tentative understanding of the relation at the micro-level between 'consumerism' and the patient–professional encounter. It focuses on a situation where the importance attached by the doctor to the elicitation of the patient's preference gives the consultation its specifically consumerist form.

I present below an analysis of audio-recordings of out-patients' consultations held monthly at a suburban children's hospital within the British National Health Service. The clinic is concerned with cleft lip/palate children and is run by a consultant surgeon. He organizes children's care from the time they are referred from a Maternity Hospital until they leave school. Other technical specialists such as a dentist, an orthodontist and speech therapist treat the child and usually attend the surgeon's clinic. The clinic was observed over a three-year period (1978–81).

The repair of lip and palate takes place during the first fifteen months of life. At this stage, clinic consultations are unremarkable. The child's lip is repaired in the first few weeks and this usually produces a considerable improvement in appearance and ability to feed.

This chapter is a revised and extended version of a paper published in November 1983 as 'The Clinical Subject: Adolescents in a Cleft Palate Clinic', *Sociology of Health and Illness*, 5 (3): 253–74. It is published here with the permission of the journal.

After successful repair of lip and palate, consultations at the clinic become largely concerned with co-ordinating the work of the specialists dealing with dental and speech problems. When parents raise the issue of the child's appearance, usually with reference to bullying and teasing at school, the surgeon normally seeks to defer any decision about further surgery until the child is older. He appeals to both clinical and psychological grounds: a surgical intervention might have to be repeated because the child's features are not fully formed; moreover, in contemplating cosmetic surgery, it is argued that it is better to wait until the child is able to give his own coherent account of his views.

Only when the child enters his teens, does the surgeon raise the possibility of further cosmetic surgery, usually on the lip or nostril. At this stage, he pays great attention to the child's report of his preferences. I will examine the format and some of the interactional dilemmas in such consultations with children aged eleven or over. A broader picture of the responses of these teenagers and their parents is offered elsewhere (Murphy, forthcoming).

Children and Medicine
Armstrong (1979) has noted that children only become a *distinctive* object for the medical gaze with the emergence of paediatrics in the inter-war years. In some respects, however, the sociology of medicine has still to discover childhood. For example, the classic study of the impact of hospitalization on children by Skipper and Leonard (1968) focused on *mothers'* responses to the work of a nurse/counsellor. Children were only monitored with reference to their physiological and psychological signs. Even important micro studies of the character of ENT and epilepsy consultations by Bloor (1976a, 1976b) and West (1976) have paid little attention to children's interventions, but have focused instead on doctors' decision-making rules and their use of strategies for dealing with parents.[1]

One exception is Strong's (1979) study of the 'ceremonial order' of paediatric clinics. This draws attention to the place of children in the consultation. However, Strong observed that children were routinely excluded from the consultation and had no rights. Even older children were cast as incompetent and subordinate. All that increased age gained for them was a set of interactional duties. Only in the special circumstances of an Accident Department did Dingwall et al. (1980) find that the child's own account was centrally relevant (both for clinical diagnosis and social evaluation of parent's roles).

The distinctive features of the setting studied by Dingwall suggests that the relative neglect of children's roles in most other studies may reflect the fact that much paediatric medicine is carried out in circumstances where (1) children are regarded by adults as too young (e.g. most ENT surgery) or too handicapped (e.g. Strong's study) to participate and/or (2) there is a consensus between adults that medically defined disposals are appropriate (e.g. heart surgery and cleft-lip repairs on babies but *not* cosmetic surgery or the care of handicapped children, where as Strong (1979b) reports, doctors often defer to 'supermums').

The combination of age and handicap suggested in the first variable highlights the fact that physical age is a necessary but not a sufficient basis to be granted interactional rights. As McHugh (1970) has pointed out, a citizen's rights and duties depend upon being treated as a person who, in principle, can recognize commonsense situations of choice and make 'reasonable' decisions. In this sense, at varying ages children may be recognized as theoretic actors who are able, for instance, to be charged with a criminal offence, to drink in a public place and to vote. Theoreticity may, nonetheless, be withheld even when this age is attained, provided that there is evidence of a certain level of mental handicap or illness.

We can now combine both variables in a simple 2×2 table.

TABLE 1

| | | Perceived Status of Child | |
		Non-theoretic	Theoretic
Consensus about disposal	Medically definable	(1)	(2)
	Not medically definable	(3)	(4)

Cell (1) approximates to a decision about a heart-murmur in a young child. Here the child would not participate and parents would be principally involved as informants rather than decision-makers. Where the child with a possible heart-murmur was a teenager (Cell 2), he would take over his parents limited role.[2] Cell (3) would approximate to the handicapped children's clinics studied by Strong. Here where both doctors and families recognize that self-assessment and family-guided disposals are appropriate, one would expect parents, but not children, to be heavily involved in disposal decisions. Finally, Cell (4) would cover situations where there was a consensus that decisions should be made by the patient and where the patient was perceived as a theoretic actor. For reasons that I shall discuss below, cosmetic surgery on a cleft-palate teenager seems to fit nicely into this cell.

The Problem

The table suggests that clinics for cleft-palate teenagers are at one extreme end of the paediatric spectrum, involving children judged old enough to participate and a disposal perceived to imply active patient-participation. A study of cleft-palate clinics thus should bring into clear focus the competing claims of doctors, parents and child patients.

The discussion above allows me, then, to define the three problems discussed sequentially in this paper:

1. The problematic status of teenagers: are they or are they not rational beings who can be trusted to make their own decisions in matters of considerable personal importance?
2. The problematic status of the parents of teenagers: given the 'rights' of their children, what rights do parents retain as informants or advocates? How do they claim them?
3. The policy implications of (1) and (2). What are the limits of 'child-centred' medicine? Do children require social work representatives or advocates?

Given the nature of the analysis attempted, extracts from a limited number of consultations are considered. Five consultations involving teenagers over one three-month period constituted the original sample (one was subsequently excluded for reasons of space). However, these display forms which, with little variation, have been observed by the researcher at a total of nineteen cleft-palate clinics including three clinics in other children's hospitals in London and in Brisbane, Australia. The basis of this apparent invariance cannot be considered within the scope of the present paper.

The method of analysis involves careful examination of the language of the encounter. It draws upon some simple structures discussed by Sacks (1972a, 1972b). However, it follows Dingwall (1980:170) in recognizing the importance of what he calls 'the interpretative context of encounters'. Concretely, this context is subsequently located in the clinical and everyday relevances respected by doctors, parents and children. A further departure from the sequential concerns of conversational analysis is provided by the focus, as in the previous Chapter, on the subjects created within different discourses. Such a focus, with its implicit rejection of appeals to pre-discursive subjects (who are supposed to think and intend *prior* to language) is basic to the very different traditions of Wittgensteinian and Saussurian language analysis (for a recent attempt to develop this approach, see Silverman and Torode, 1980).

The Child as Consumer

In Table 1, I suggested that the status of the cleft-palate teenager, together with a consensus about the basis of the disposal, established the child as centrally involved in the decision-making process. I want to consider now the interactional accomplishment of this involvement and to pick out some traps and limits that arise along the way.

There seems often to be a two-stage process through which this involvement is accomplished. First, direct questions are used to elicit the child's own 'feelings' about looks. Second, the doctor will usually make statements which underline that it is the child's own views that are the ultimate arbiter of the decision.

We can see the use of direct questions in these data extracts drawn from the early stages of four different consultations:

1. C: What about your looks first of all?
2. C: What do you think about your looks Barry?
3. C: Are you happy with your appearance or are you ... ?
4. C2: Do you worry at all about your appearance?
        (child replies)
        And why is it ... What about your appearance is it that you worry about?

The first three extracts are taken from the London consultations and Extract 4 from a cleft-palate clinic in a Brisbane hospital a few months later. Invariably, such questions about looks or appearance are addressed to cleft-palate teenagers.

It still needs to be demonstrated that the children's replies actually had an impact on the decision-making process. In fact, in all such consultations recorded during the study, the disposal decision reflected the child's own reported views. (This excludes those children who remained silent or who gave noncommittal replies.) In the suburban London clinic, the salience of children's consumer rights is underlined in the first three consultations in the following ways:

5. D: I think we can improve that for you. You'd like that would you?
6. D: You're the customer, if you're happy with the way things are then ...
7. D: You're the customer
        (child responds)
        D'you think it's all right?

It seems likely that the special character of the consultations reported here is related more to the perceived status of the condition and of the patient than to the common consulting styles of the two doctors concerned. The uniform character of the question about appearance suggests that 'looks' are constituted as an order available to anyone's gaze. While the condition of bodily organs is treated as only available to the physician's gaze or to his clinical interpretation of the underlying pattern suggested by the patient's answers (Foucault, 1973), looks can be viewed and judged by anybody. Imagine a consultation between doctor and patient which went as follows:

> D: What about your heart first of all?
> P: I'd like something done to my heart(!)

Partly, the availability of 'looks' to the uneducated gaze reflects the fact that they lie on the surface of the body. However, this is equally true of skin conditions, for instance, where the patient's response is treated only as symptomatic of an underlying pattern hidden from him. The difference seems to be that 'looks' are granted no pathology, as they are, by their vary nature, held to be a matter of lay judgment. Clinical ideals here have a very limited relevance — as we shall see later in Elaine and Gillian's cases. Consequently, the condition being treated is placed in a discursive formation which at once elevates the status of everyday 'reality'.

However, 'looks', while available to anyone's gaze, are conceived here as centrally important to a subject who owns them (the 'You' constituted by Utterances 1–7). As many encounters in this clinic show, the child's own conception of looks is crucial to decision-making.

The subject is allocated property rights over looks and the value of his property (and hence the need for repairs to it) is determined by a calculus based on his own assessments.

The *exercise* of property rights is dependent, however, upon the constitution of a 'rational' subject. Where the child's 'rationality' is not recognized, parents or guardians will claim the right to speak 'on his behalf'. In this case, as Blackstone put it, the 'empire of reason' makes way for the 'empire of the father' (or, in most of these cases, the mother) (see Fitz, 1979). We will later examine examples where attempts are made by a parent to negotiate such a transfer of rule.

Having developed the argument about the special status of cosmetic surgery, we will now look in more detail at the interactional work involved and its unintended, as well as intended, consequences. Let us begin with what looks like a straightforward example of consumerism, based on the elicitation of the patient's preferences.

Following normal practice, this boy had his lip and palate corrected in two operations completed by the age of fifteen months. Since that time, he has regularly attended out-patients where the consultant-surgeon checks his development and co-ordinates the work of a speech therapist, dentist and orthodontist, all of whom attend the clinic. From a surgical point of view, the only issue in question is whether A. needs a further 'touching-up' operation to improve his appearance.

(Transcript 14:14)
C = Consultant-Surgeon, A = Boy aged 16, B = Boy's father
[*Following C's question, A has just explained which exams he is taking*].

1. C: Jolly good. Well let's hope you get seven. (2.0) Now then. (1.0) What about (0.5) things nowadays? How d'you feel about this (0.5). What about your *looks*/first of all?
2. A: /Um
3. A: I'd like, I'd like something to be done to my lip.
4. C: Something, yes. It's a bit short, isn't it?
5. A: Yes
6. C: The cupid's bow comes up much too far. We didn't have too much stuff to play with when I did that./ It wasn't a lot.
7. B: / No
8. B: He's very concerned about the (   )
9. C: Yes, yes. I think we can improve that for you. You'd like that, would you?
10. A: Yes please.
11. C: So you'd like that done before you leave school, I expect.
12. A: Yes.
13. C: [*Laughs*]

This extract would seem to illustrate the smooth unfolding of a consultation which gives decision-making power to a patient granted theoreticity. However, it shares in common with medical consultations in other settings, a discursive format, the interview, which as others have pointed out (Bloor, 1976a, 1976b; Drass, 1982), firmly establishes the doctor's claim to autonomy. Let us return to the transcript, listing observations as we go.

1. Within this discursive format, two 'realities' are set into play. The first concerns 'looks', 'feelings' and home-arrangements. We might call this the 'everyday' reality. The second is associated with clinical assessments ('the cupid's bow comes up much too far') and with the possibilities of surgical interventions (parts of Utterances 6 and 9). We can call this the 'clinical' reality. Two preliminary observations may be made about these different 'realities'. First, while all speakers move freely within 'everyday' reality, 'clinical' reality is reserved only for speaker C. While this may not be an exact parallel with Bernstein's contention that only the 'elaborated code' speaker has access to two codes, the discursive range of C is clearly greater than that of A and B.

Second, the boundary between the two 'realities' is often unclear. For instance, it is not clear how the reference to the 'shortness' of the lip in Utterance 4 is to be heard. A consequence is that speakers limited to one reality may mistake one for the other and so intervene unsuccessfully or, more likely, remain silent where they could speak. This uncertainty over boundaries favours the speaker who has access to both discursive 'realities'.[3]

2. As was noted earlier, C's questions about looks (Utterance 1) elicits an answer in terms of a preferred disposal (Utterance 3) which is only an indirect continuation of the topic. Rather than speculate about A's 'motive', it is preferable to treat Utterance 2 as a solution to an interactive problem. The character of the problem and its solution (as a kind of 'pre-emptive strike') will become apparent when we look later at another transcript.

3. Although B makes only two utterances (Utterances 7 and 8), they are addressed to C rather than to his son, A. This can be assumed because C speaks next on the basis of the previous speaker's right to choose the next speaker. The encounter takes the form of a team-game, with C on one side and A and B on the other. Although players may sometimes consult with members of their own team, as we will see in a later transcript, the basic form is alternating utterances between C and *either* A or B. This raises two interesting questions. First, given that C always selects A here, how does B manage to enter the conversation? We have seen in this case that the means of entry is offered by the first of C's utterances which fails to exercise his rights to select next speaker and to extend the question-chain. Other means of entry, still based on the team structure, will be observed in later transcripts.

Despite a decision-making process which is finally sanctioned by a rational subject who is presumed able to judge his present (and preferred) looks, it may be difficult to generate a discussion about looks. A's avoidance of the question about looks in favour of a request for treatment has a parallel in the following example:

(Transcript 29:7)
C = Consultant Surgeon, D = Boy aged 12, O = Orthodontist
                [*D has just entered with his mother*]

1. C: Hello. (1.0) You're *twelve* now, aren't you Barry?
2. D: Yeah.
3. C: And it's two years since we saw you. (1.0) How are things going?
4. D: All right
5. C: All right? Jolly good.
6. O: (   )
7. C: Mm. Jolly good. Let's have a look (C. examines)
8. C: Now then. This has got rather an *ugly scar* line hasn't it? It's rather (1.0) rather a lot of stitch marks. (1.0) Isn't terribly handsome, is it? What do you think about your looks Barry?
9. D: (3.0) I don't know.
10. C: You (laughs) Doesn't worry you a lot. You don't lie awake at night / worrying about it or anything?

11. D: / No.
12. C: No, no. It *could* be improved er because I think that scar line
                     isn't brilliant (1.0) but it's, you're the customer, if you're happy
                     with things the way they are then / that's
13. D: / Well I hope to have it done
14. C: Oh you would, oh. All right well (0.5) we'll see about that
                     (shortly). Now what about this nose of yours, you've got a bit of
                     a . . .

We can observe here a number of interactional traps which work
against the consumerism avowed in the assertion: 'you're the customer'
(Utterance 12). First, the status of the question in Utterance 3 is unclear.
It may be heard as an attempt to commence the elicitation of D's views
about his appearance. Alternatively, it could be heard as a continuation
of the greeting sequence begun with the 'Hello' in Utterance 1. 'How are
things going?' is separated from the 'hello' only by an enquiry about D's
age and can legitimately be taken to continue that greeting work. Hence,
like 'hello', it only requires a formal reply since its prime business is
recognition and greeting rather than a real enquiry. (Recall how
surprised and put out one can be when someone tells us how he *really* is
in response to our greeting: 'Hello, how are you?') This confusion
between greeting and genuine enquiry creates interactional problems in
many medical encounters. How do you show your proper competences
in responding formally, while retaining a right to claim that there is
something 'really' wrong with you?

C's response in Utterance 5 repeats the 'all right' and comments
upon it: 'Jolly good'. So what might have been a formal reply is heard
to represent a genuine statement of D's state of mind. If D later wants
to convey his unhappiness about his situation, he will now run the risk
of seeming to contradict himself.

C now examines the boy and formulates his looks in terms of a scar
line and stitch marks. Although the terms in which these are assessed
are everyday ('ugly', 'a lot', 'handsome'), the ability to assess scars
and stitches can have a clinical basis. To recognize 'a lot of' stitch
marks, depends upon having seen the results of many operations and
having a technical standard to compare them. There arises here an
uncertain boundary between 'everyday' and 'clinical' discourses
which complicates Barry's response to the question about his looks.

The doctor seems to have warranted an expression of lack of
satisfaction by his statement of the technical inadequacies of Barry's
appearance. However, the confusion between the two modes of
discourse means that it may be unclear to Barry whether he can simply
state the everyday 'reality' of his appearance or whether he must offer
a response in terms of the clinical 'reality' of normal scar lines and
stitch marks. In the same way as the extended greeting sequence, the

constitution of a clinical 'reality' prior to the question to Barry partially pre-empts an expression of his everyday 'reality'. To convey dissatisfaction, Barry might have to deny his social competence to recognize a greeting and, later appear to participate in a technical 'reality' in which he cannot claim membership.

A further unintended interactional trap may arise in the direct question about appearance ('What do you think about your looks Barry?'). Since these children and their parents will have been attending the clinic from the child's birth, the family will generally already be aware of the further surgical possibilities. In principle, the child's wishes could be ascertained quite simply by asking him whether he wanted a further operation.

Instead of moving at once to a question on preferred disposal, the doctor raises the topic of 'looks'. In this way, he hopes to be able to infer the child's preferences about disposal. The question about looks is complicated, as we have seen, by the prior statement of the clinical 'reality'. But even without that statement, the question creates difficulties. First, if I am asked about what I think of my looks what standard am I to use to judge? The clinical 'reality' of my looks (as viewed by a surgeon) is outside my competence, while the everyday 'reality' of looks may be relative to any number of standards (do I compare my looks with others, and if so, with which others? Do I operate an absolute standard and see how far I deviate?). Second, I doubt if there is a way of speaking about one's own looks which does not seem to be egotistical and hence morally doubtful — although there may well be culturally-sedimented gender differences here. Others may comment on one's looks and this, given the context, including the gender of commentator and person commentated on, may do the acceptable work of 'complimenting another'. Here one may be expected to respond by a denial and be 'modest'. But making a blunt statement on one's looks makes it appear both that one has other purposes in hand and that one is the kind of person who spends hours contemplating himself in a mirror. Hence, perhaps, A's switch of topic, B's noncommittal answer and his agreement that he doesn't 'lie awake at night worrying about it' (Utterances 10–11). Instead of inferring the child's preferred disposal through his perceptions of his looks, it would be easier to infer his feelings about his looks through his preferences for an operation. Nevertheless, Barry's noncommittal response (Utterance 9) to the looks question, even though it follows a three-second pause, is treated as indicating the absence of worry.[4]

This interpretation will be shown to be mistaken in Utterance 13 when Barry states that he would like a further operation. The confusion seems to arise over two different models of the subject employed here. The doctor formulates his relation with Barry in terms of a version of 'customer'-service ('you're the customer', Utterance 12). In this 'marketplace' model, customers have clear preferences and act rationally when they convey them to the shopkeeper who delivers the service. Hence, when they express no preference this means that they have no particular need for the service. Here the 'empire of reason' is allocated to a subject preconstituted in terms of a marketplace economy.

This, however, fails to take account of the subjects that are constituted within the actual discourse, in particular within the 'realities' which that discourse sets into play. As has been noted, Utterance 8 establishes Barry as a subject awkwardly placed between 'everyday' and 'clinical' realities, with the doctor's clinical standards of judgment super-imposed upon what is anyway a difficult realm for a subject to formulate. Hence 'I don't know' is the 'reason' of a subject who does not know itself. And this uncertainty arises precisely within the practices that we discovered in the utterance that precedes it.

Given this inability to escape the interactional traps created by the putative greeting sequence and the direct question about looks, following the technical assessment, Barry has to resort to an interruption (Utterance 13) in order to convey his real wishes. Following this, the discursive format of the interview is re-asserted by the doctor's exercise of his interviewer's rights to control the agenda by means of closing one topic and beginning another (Utterance 14). This maintains a common pattern of ordering the agenda in this clinic (namely from greeting exchange, to elicitation sequence, to examination, to prognosis, to disposal and then to ending) which reserves statement of the disposal decision until near the end of the consultation.

I have tried to show how the clinical realm operates not simply as an alternative frame of reference to the everyday judgments of the patient, serving to influence disposal-decisions, but also as a discourse which can create uncertainty about the space available for the patient's speech and so can undercut some of the 'rights' of consumerist medicine.

In the further example below, the child's preferences remain ambivalent. The doctor's direct question about 'looks' is once again preceded by a problematic greeting sequence and by what might be a clinical evaluation of the situation:

(Transcript 35:5)
C = Consultant Surgeon, E = Girl aged 16, F = Girl's mother
[*E has just entered with her mother*]
  1. C: Hello
  2. E: Hello

3. C: Come on Elaine. (1.0) Hello Mrs Webb. Well, Elaine, *how are*
           you these days?
4. E: *All right thank you*
5. C: *Very good.* (1.0) Um, (0.5) haven't seen you for a while (C. is
           looking at his notes). Oh is it two years since I saw you? Did I
           see you last year? Oh, here we are (1.0) September '78 was it?
           We did that er (5.0) now then (4.0) there we are, one year ago.
           And we just tickled up, patched up the cupid's bow. What else
           did I do, a bit of the nostril. (2.0) Now it's a very *marked*
           cupid's bow, isn't it, with a little dimple in the middle. What
           do you think about that? [*Elaine looks at her mother*] (1.0)
6. F: Yes,/it's up to you [*laughs*]
7. C: /Yes (   )
8. C: *You're the customer*
9. E: I don't know
10. C: D'you think it's all right? Are you happy with your
           appearance or are you
11. E: (2.0) I really don't know. I don't see any difference at all in it.

I have italicized some of the parallels with the previous transcript.
Notice the 'greeting' sequence which does unintended work
(Utterances 3–5). Here the formal nature of Elaine's reply to the
inquiry about 'things' is stressed by the 'thank you' that she adds to
her 'all right'. Once again, the question about looks eventually elicits a
'don't know' (Utterance 9) which is repeated when the question is
rephrased (Utterances 10–11). Once again, the question is preceded
(Utterance 5) by a formulation potentially based on a clinical
judgment and, despite the interactional complexities of the situation,
the child is formulated as a 'customer' (Utterance 8).[5]

Clinical 'reality' eventually seems to work in this case as a powerful
factor shaping the disposal. Despite Elaine's non-committal response,
the doctor later asks her three times whether she 'would like something
done'. Only at the third time of asking does he obtain a nod of
agreement from her. He seems particularly influenced by his technical
sense of a remaining imperfection and by what he later calls the 'tiny
little operation' needed to put it right. In this case, the 'customer's'
decision looks more like the formal approval required for any
operation than the ultimate determining factor.

The Parent as Consumer
However, in paediatric settings the child never stands alone. Some
adult (usually a mother, sometimes a father, sometimes both parents,
occasionally a grandparent or nurse) will be present at the consultation. Routinely, such adults are treated by medical staff as a source
of information about the child's condition (especially reliable where
the adult is the child's mother) and as a representative of the child's

interests. Consequently, disposals usually occur only after the child's representative has indicated her agreement.

In this situation, two factors change the disposal rule. First, medical staff, like judges, tend to accord greater standing to a child's own account and wishes as he grows older. In a transcript below, we will show how all the adults present refer to this theoretic capacity of the older child. The second factor which here limits parental rights is the assumption that looks and, therefore, decisions about cosmetic surgery, are an area where the subject is best qualified to judge.

Nevertheless, we have seen parents enter the conversation within the context of what we described earlier as a team-game. In principle, given the child's apparent difficulty in formulating his looks, his parents might play an effective role in conveying the reasons behind his diffidence and in arguing that this diffidence did not imply contentment. Let us return to the first and third transcripts, where parents intervene, to see what they accomplish.

In the first transcript (p.164), A's father (B) intervenes at 7 and 8. We have already noted how C's failure to direct a further question at A gives B the opportunity to take the floor at Utterance 8. However, B paves the way for his intervention by Utterance 7. This does some interesting work which is worthy of comment.

In Utterance 6, C enters into what we have called a 'clinical' discourse which formulates a medical evaluation of the child's appearance ('the cupid's bow comes up much too far') and comments on the technicalities of a previous operation ('We didn't have too much stuff to play with when I did that'). At this point, B says 'No'. In agreeing with C's technical formulation (the 'no' agrees with the negative in Utterance 6), the parent B seems to claim entry into the doctor's clinical world. However, he could hardly claim the medical competence necessary for a full entry into that world. Instead, this utterance looks like a claim that he is the more competent member of the patient 'team' to understand such technical formulations. It confirms his ability to 'follow' clinical formulations and his preparedness to accept the doctor's version, and hence to concede medical dominance over the clinical realm. In these transcripts, only parents but not children respond to clinical discourse, they always respond by agreeing with the medical version, and their intervention *can* be used by them to stake a claim to be next speaker.

There is agreement here that one parameter of the conversation is medical dominance over clinical discourse. This is hardly surprising. We would expect it to be a routine feature of medical settings except where the patient or parent was himself a medical worker. In the third transcript we also find a consensus between doctor and parent that the child is the subject best qualified to decide whether anything more needs to be done. When Elaine looks at her mother when the doctor asks her what she thinks about her appearance, her mother says (Utterance 6) 'Yes, it's up to you'. This is confirmed by the doctor's formulation 'You're the customer' (Utterance 7). Both utterances provide for a world in which choices are made by rational consumers. Once again, there is agreement between doctor and parent over the parameters of the conversation: the child is accorded special rights to determine a version of her looks. Such an agreement seems to leave very little scope for parents. Parents are formulated neither as suppliers, nor as consumers of clinical services. Before we can confirm this, we will need to look at what happens when parents take a more extensive part in the consultation than has been seen so far.

In the following transcript, a mother plays a much greater role in the conversation.

(Transcript 14:32–3)
C = Consultant Surgeon, G = Girl aged 13, H = Girl's mother, DT = Dentist
[*C has just begun his examination*]

1. C: Now then Gillian let's have a look, see what (1.0) things look like. The *edge* of that lip is a little bit tucked up. Do you notice that it's not quite symmetrical or does it worry you?
2. G: [*very softly*] it doesn't worry me.
3. C: It doesn't worry you. It's a little bit tucked up there and this is a little bit full, isn't it?
4. H: Yes
5. C: It's *not* bad is it. What do you think? You don't ... you're not/worried about this?
6. H: /Not as bad as it used to be
7. C: Not as (1.0) it's improved with age has it? Yes.
   [*C and H agree that further surgery is needed on Gillian's nostril*]
8. C: Yes, I think we could have *another* go at that. Um (2.0) but you're satisfied with your lip, are you, we don't want anything done to that?
9. H: She doesn't (1.0) it doesn't seem to worry her
10. C: [*laughs*] Don't want anything done about anything?/
11. H: /[*laughs*]
12. C: Not your nose? (3.0) It's still hanging a bit that nostril. Well what d'you you don't want anything done about it yet ... Um you'd rather hang on to things at the moment. OK. When you *want* something done, let me know and um/
13. H: /[*laughs*] She'll never let you know
14. C: /[*laughs*]
15. C: Well we don't wanna have to (0.5) get wild horses to drag her along here./She's old enough now to
16. H: /No. Oh yes
17. C: Do it if she wants to and not if you don't

18. H: But you don't want to leave it too long, really. Want to get it all done
19. C: Yes
20. DT: (   ) She's not really concerned about it
21. H: She's not worried about that, no, at the moment
22. C: D'you, d'you. It's not. Yes [*Recommences examination*] Open wide dear. That's right. She's in a bit there, isn't she? Would that (2.0) um is there anything to be done about this lesser segment? [*Technical talk between C and DT follows*]

In a formal sense, this consultation follows the same pattern as that observed in the first transcript. The mother's (H) utterances begin, as in the first transcript, with a parental agreement over a clinical formulation. In Utterance 4, H agrees with C's observation that the lip is 'a little bit tucked up'. Again, as in the earlier transcript, this entry into the clinical realm serves as a stepping-stone for a claim to be next speaker. In Utterance 5, C comments on the lip in a way which is difficult to locate confidently in either clinical or everyday realms: 'It's *not* bad is it'. As we saw earlier, with C's reference to 'shortness' in the first transcript, the patient–team will have no way of knowing whether 'badness' is intended as a clinical formulation (i.e. compared to other cases he has seen and/or in terms of the surgical realities of the situation).

However, C's request for the child's own view ('What do you think?') suggests that an everyday version of 'badness' may be a preferred hearing. Hence H is able to intervene at Utterance 6 with an observation that draws upon her everyday parental competences to judge her child's changing appearance ('not as bad as it used to be').

Notice how C repeats and accepts this parental version in his next observation (Utterance 7). This implies that a further agreed parameter of the conversation is that parents indeed do possess a special competence to observe their child's progress over the years. This is confirmed by Strong (1979b) and by my own observations at two very different kinds of clinic. There are two limits which medical staff place on this presumption of competence. First, most competence is ascribed to mothers (rather than other family), especially where they have several children or have had previous contact with the unit. Where any of these conditions are not present (e.g. a father, a young mother with only one child), then the degree of competence accorded seems to fall. Second, the attribution of high parental competence does not here lead to a greater parental participation in disposal decisions. Following through the mother's subsequent utterances, we can observe a continued consensus both about the parameters of the conversation and about the state of affairs that is revealed by means of them. So in Utterance 9, H appears to confirm C's sense that Gillian is satisfied with her appearance. She does this by repeating Gillian's own formulation of not being 'worried'. Again at 11, she co-operates in C's version of the light-hearted, consensual character of the situation by joining in his laughter.

On the basis of this consensus, C attempts to terminate the disposal talk: 'OK when you *want* something done let me know and um' (Utterance 12). It is at this point that the mother intervenes to imply that there is more to talk about. Compare the mother's intervention here with the child's intervention after Utterance 12 of the second transcript. Both arise as interruptions to an attempted termination of disposal-talk. While the child intervenes directly with a statement of a desired disposal ('I hope to have it done'), the mother only makes an indirect challenge. The tentative character of her intervention is suggested by her laugh which precedes it, thereby maintaining the lightheartedness begun by the doctor in Utterance 10.

The nature of the mother's challenge is interesting: 'She'll never let you know.' A doubt is implied here about the character of the subject that C has already formulated as 'satisfied', wanting to 'hang on' and able to say something when she 'wants something done'. Unlike C, the mother is casting doubt on the positioning of her child as a rational subject on the market-place. Since this consultation is the only one which we have observed where there occurs such a challenge to the theoreticity presumed by the consumerist language, it will be particularly fruitful to follow it through.

When this moral framework is challenged in Utterance 13, the doctor reasserts the rules of the consumerist game. Action can only be demanded here by the customer not by the supplier: 'Well we don't wanna have to get wild horses to drag her along here'. Moreover, the customer is to be treated as a rational subject, a theoretic actor able to choose the proper services to satisfy her needs: 'She's old enough now to . . .'. The Empire of the Family has, in these terms, given way to the Empire of Reason — 'Do it if she wants', he says. Faced with these powerful moral symbols, the mother's argument that there is an 'objective' case for early treatment (in Utterance 18) has only to be acknowledged but not acted upon (Utterance 19). For the moment, a particular version of everyday 'reality' has been imposed and the medical team is free to return to the technical realm (Utterance 22).

The mother, despite the challenge that she has made to the representation of her child as a fully rational subject is none the less prepared to concede, when pressed, that her child is 'old enough' to be treated as a rational consumer (Utterance 16) who is making no demands on the supplier 'at the moment' (Utterance 20). Even though this mother wants to question the rational character of some of her daughter's statements, she still acknowledges that, *in principle*, children of her age are 'old enough' to make rational choices.

To summarize the argument so far: it has been suggested that parents and medical staff defer to four parameters which define the boundaries of their talk. These are:

1. The assumption of medical dominance over clinical discourse.
2. The assumption that an everyday version of looks can most properly be formulated by the child.
3. The recognition, in principle, that 'older' children are rational subjects, able to theorize alternative courses of action and to make rational choices between them.
4. The assumption that parents (particularly the mother) possess a special competence to monitor the child's 'progress' over time.

If we examine these parameters, it becomes clear that the scope for parental intervention is very limited by (1), (2) and (3). Even if a parent believes that there are grounds for challenging the applicability of these parameters in her own child's case, she is forced to concede that they still apply in principle. Only parameter (4) offers any kind of basis to participate in decision-making.

In the transcript above, Gillian's mother calls on her own assumed monitoring competence to pose a version of Gillian's apparent lack of 'worry' as other than rational consumer choice (Utterance 13). Shortly after, in the talk transcribed below, she tries again to challenge the attribution of theoreticity to Gillian's lack of demand for the product. As in other cases, her point of entry is through an expression of deference to a clinical formulation (here concerning the possible use of an orthodontic appliance for Gillian's teeth). This would be 'a help' the mother agrees (Utterance 2 below). Having established her speaking rights, she pursues her earlier character-work on her daughter:

(Transcript 14:35–6)
1. C: That would be a help / I'm sure, wouldn't it?
2. H: / a help
3. H: I mean you couldn't go on with a gap all this time
4. D: Sorry?
5. H: I said she *can't* go with a gap all this time. I mean she *would*, she's one of those people it don't touch her any more, and that's it, you know. You've gotta give her a bit of persuasion
6. DT: She's not very keen, that's why
7. C: She would, yes
8. DT: She wouldn't be keen
9. C: Yes, it's no good if (0.5)
10. H: Really if she's not that keen, no
11. C: Anyway it can wait can't it?
12. H: Yes

13.	?:	If she changes her mind
14.	C:	Yes, I don't see there's any harm in waiting/
15.	H:	/Waiting (0.5) No.
16.	C:	I shouldn't have thought so. Shall we see you in a year then Gillian?
17.	H:	Yes
18.	C:	Good. Off you go then
19.	H:	Right. Thank you very much
20.	C:	Goodbye.

Here Gillian's mother returns to the theme that she raised earlier of not wanting 'to leave it too long', this time in relation to her teeth rather than her nostril (Utterances 2 and 4). This restatement of the 'objective' case for treatment is coupled with a powerful statement of the possibility that Gillian ought not to be treated as a fully theoretic actor: 'she's one of those people it don't touch her any more'.

However, rather than accept this version of Gillian and, consequently, giving her what the mother calls 'a bit of persuasion', the medical staff continue to assert the sovereignty of her consumer rights. Gillian's diffidence is explained as a lack of 'keenness' for further treatment (Utterances 5 and 7) and this lack of demand for the service legislates what is to be done: 'It's no good if . . . '. Abstaining from action is the proper response where the consumer has made up her mind against it. Despite her diffidence, Gillian is still accorded a rational 'mind' which might change: the treatment can be given, the orthodontist implies, 'if she changes her mind'. Faced by the powerful language of consumer sovereignty, Gillian's mother concurs that action should not be taken 'if she's not that keen' (Utterance 9). Despite her earlier statements to the contrary, she concludes by agreeing that it 'can wait'.

A Parental Pre-Emptive Strike
We have already seen some of the difficulties that a parent faces in contesting a version of her child as a fully rational subject. A second solution would be for the child or parent to pre-empt the questioning about looks in favour of a request for a preferred disposal. We have seen this strategy pay dividends in the first transcript considered where the 'looks' question is answered simply by the statement of a preference for 'something to be done'. In the light of the problems that we saw that Barry had, this early statement by patient A now starts to look like a very skilful accomplishment.

The final transcript to be considered involves such a pre-emptive strike, this time by a parent. We will examine the nature of the devices through which this mother enters the consultation and argues for an

operation. We will also show the mechanism through which her strike
is partially neutralized.

> (Transcript 17:6−7)
> C = Consultant Surgeon, J = Boy aged 16, K = Boy's mother.
> [*Patient and mother have just entered*]
> 1. C: Now, sit down. How's John, all right?
> 2. J: All right thank you
> 3. C: Good. How old are you now? You must be over sixteen, aren't you?
> 4. J: Yes, I'll be seventeen in July
> 5. C: Seventeen in July, goodness. And what's happening about school, have you (0.5) you're still at school, aren't you?
> 6. J: Yes, I'm still there. I'm staying on till next year and I'm taking my exams next year, May.
> 7. C: Your, so you'll be here, not leaving this September, leaving the following, er, July.
> 8. K: No, no, he's leaving June
> 9. C: Oh you're leaving this June, coming June
> 10. K: And, um, he's hoping to start college in September
> 11. C: I see, oh this year, good
> 12. K: And he's wondering whether there's any chance of getting his nose done before 'e starts
> 13. C: Yes
> 14. K: Cos he's going to a business college, he's gonna want to go in hotel management
> 15. C: Oh are you, good. That's a useful job. Tell us where you're working and I'll come and stay with you [*K. laughs*] (2.0). Mm. (1.0) where are you going? Is it away from home or going to ... ?

The encounter begins with the same unintended consequence of the
greeting sequence that has been noted on two earlier occasions: John
says he's 'all right' but, according to his mother, he is anxious to have
his appearance put right. Her point of entry is at Utterance 8. As a
member of her son's team, she has a right to monitor the interview
between C. and J. and ensure that C. understands properly what J.
means (in this case about the year that he will be leaving school). When
C. fails to answer her statements at Utterances 8 and 10 with a further
question the chaining rule which governed Utterances 1- 8 comes to an
end. Moreover, since C. fails to nominate a next speaker at Utterance
11, K. can enter once again.

In Utterance 12, John's mother, having gained the floor, takes over
the initiation of the question−answer chain. In effect, she has used her
original answer, made possible by the team-structure, to generate a
question herself and thus to oblige the doctor to offer an answer. The
arrangement into teams and the possibility of generating a chaining
sequence out of an answer therefore provide two powerful weapons

available to parents who might not otherwise be named as next speaker by the doctor.

Some weaknesses in the mother's conversational position are, however, immediately apparent. First, Utterance 12 is only an *indirect* question. It could be heard by C. to demand an answer to the topic raised, i.e. is there 'any chance of getting his nose done before he starts?'. Alternatively, it can be heard as an observation, requiring acknowledgement but not answer. The 'yes' of Utterance 13 indicates that the second hearing is preferred.

The second weakness of the mother's conversational gambit arises from the way in which all her utterances can be heard as requests which need to be grounded. Here the request for the operation is grounded in John's move to a new school. Unlike the mother, the doctor, as we shall see, feels under no obligation to offer grounds for his observations. Partly, this reflects the presumably secure clinical basis of his speech. Partly, it expresses that he alone offers a valuable commodity (the operation) and hence does not have to be heard as making a request.

So the mother claims to speak rationally not on pre-constituted clinical authority but on demonstrated grounds. The problem this generates for her is that, thereby, she offers *two* topics to her chosen next speaker (C.): namely, her request (or observation) and its grounds. This allows C. to choose to disassociate grounds from request. In topicalizing the grounds, the original request (and the implicit question in which it is couched) becomes lost.

This process is seen here in the way in which the grounds of the request offered in Utterance 14 ('going to business college'), become disassociated and topicalized in Utterance 15 ('that's a useful job'). When the mother enters again into the conversation where C. fails to ask a further question (Utterances 1 and 5 below), the grounds she offers fall prey to the same treatment:

(Transcript 17:7–8)
1. C: Yes. Well it's an interesting job. (1.0) Um.
2. K: (6.0) When we came last time you said/
3. C: [*beginning to examine J.*] /Yes now let's see/
4. K: /you'd see about his (   )
5. C: Mm. Now that *lip*, apart from the little knot in the middle, which is a bit of a nuisance, it'd be better without that wouldn't he, but other than that the lip isn't too bad is it?
6. K: No.
7. C: Er (1.0)
8. K: I was, there was a programme on the television um about people with misshaped jaws / and it showed you where this boy, he'd

9.	C:	/ Mm.
10.	K:	got a top jaw shorter than the bottom jaw/
11.	C:	/Oh yes
12.	K:	And the surgeons had put some in at the side
13.	C:	Oh yes, put a bit in, yes, that's right
14.	K:	To bring it forward to give 'im more/
15.	C:	[*to child*] - /yes, just close
16.	K:	Apparently it's a new one
17.	C:	Oh yes, that's being done, yes. Pretty big stuff. / Now what you
18.	K:	/ Yes
19.	C:	need is to bring it forward, isn't it? This um cupid's bow is a bit short, isn't it? It needs a bit of building up to er bring the, bring the septum forward ...

In Utterances 2 and 4, John's mother argues powerfully (although by implication) for immediate action, grounding her request on what the doctor had said 'last time' about John's appearance. However, C. makes John's appearance rather than his previous promise the topic. He is also able to display his control over the agenda of the consultation by beginning the examination and commenting on that as much as upon the mother's observation. As elsewhere the agenda of the clinic, expressed in what the doctor is doing as well as saying, sets a crucial framework for reading the sense into what is said. For instance, what is appropriate at the elicitation stage or at the time of the statement of the disposal decision might be out of order elsewhere. We see here also, how the doctor's observations are made without grounds (e.g. the comments about the lip, the cupid's bow and the character of an operation) and appeal simply to his presumed technical competence. As elsewhere, the parent is prepared to confirm a medical formulation of her child's appearance, even though it is unclear whether it appeals solely to the clinical realm (Utterance 5).

The mother's further attempt to generate a legitimate ground for immediate treatment (the 'programme on the television') is, once more, made the topic rather than the request it implies and is cursorily dismissed ('pretty big stuff'). Once again, a parent feels constrained to assent to a clinical formulation (Utterance 18).

No commitment to surgery is made by the doctor until later in the consultation. As we saw in the second transcript discussed (29:7), where an early request was greeted by 'well we'll see about that', the clinic agenda usually demands that disposal decisions are left to the conclusion of the consultation. In this case, the decision goes in favour of a further operation but, following the doctor's disposal rule that school-leavers are transferred elsewhere, John's case is referred to another hospital.

It would be wrong to conclude from this that parents are unable to affect disposal decisions. I have shown that mechanisms do exist for parents to enter the conversation even when not specifically requested by the medical team. It is also possible, although the evidence is not clear, that parents' comments, although pushed to one side early on in order to maintain the doctor's desired agenda, do influence his decision, particularly where they formulate a clear impression of the child as experiencing suffering as a result of his appearance. Furthermore, the child's bald statement that he wants an operation appears always to elicit the desired result. This chapter has not sought to deny, then, the possibility of consumer-choice in medicine. Instead, it has argued that this choice is constrained by the discursive format of the interview, by discursive categories like the 'marketplace' and 'looks' and, above all, by the relation between the clinical and everyday 'realities' constructed in medical settings. Even in a clinical context which seems to give many more chips than usual to the patient, consumerist medicine is not all it seems to be.

I want to conclude this examination of my materials by returning to how doctors constitute the clinical subject in the absence of a parent. The consultation discussed below took place in the same year as some of the others. Despite being geographically separated by 12,000 miles from them, it reveals strikingly similar interactional forms.

'Do You Worry at all about Your Appearance?'
(Surgeon at cleft-palate clinic, Brisbane, Australia)
It should first be noted that, unlike other Australian states, Queensland offers a system of free hospital care. This has its origin in the populist politics practised by decades of State Governments — originally Labour now National, or right-wing, controlled. It means that although you pay for a visit to your GP (*if* you have one), operations in hospital are usually free of charge. There is one exception — most forms of cosmetic surgery have to be paid for by the patient. This creates a doubt in the patient's mind at this clinic to which we shall return later.

The clinic takes place in a crowded room. Apart from the patient, there are ten professionals present — four doctors, four speech therapists and two sociologists. It should be stressed, however, that this number is abnormally high. The clinic has coincided with a training session for junior speech therapists and with the visit, for purposes of observation, of the sociologists. The patient, Simon, enters and sits next to one of the doctors who is a surgeon and will lead the discussion. Simon has been investigated a few hours earlier for speech, hearing and ear, nose and throat problems. He has had his lip and palate repaired as an infant. He is now eighteen and the issue is that his lower jaw sticks out.

A preliminary outline by the surgeon (Dr A) of the background to the 'case' is given before Simon enters. It pieces together a picture of Simon's motivations, social background and intellectual qualities which will inform both the question that Simon is to be asked and the sense which we will tend to read into his answers.

Following Garfinkel's (1967) account of the 'documentary method of interpretation', it discovers an underlying pattern which is confirmed in each and every instance; Dr A's outline has a great importance. Its persuasive power is increased by the fact that it is based on long contact with Simon and is buttressed by the case-notes which Dr A has before him. After going through his early case-history, Dr A tells us that, between 1975 and 1980, the hospital apparently lost contact with Simon. There could be a number of causes of this break in the records. However, the implication seems to be that Simon was to blame for it. Dr A refers to Simon as having 'disappeared' from following-up and then having 'suddenly' turned up. Although it is possible to see this choice of words as relating to inefficient hospital practices, a more likely reading is that Simon's absence from care reflected on himself.

Dr A's next comment about 'maturity' makes it clear that he intends to depict Simon as the kind of person who is less than responsible:

Dr A. = D
D: He's er (0.5) it's a matter of deciding whether he should have an operation. And, er, what we are concerned about is his degree of maturity which it will be very interesting for you [*turning to sociologists*] to make a judgment on when he comes in.

Shortly, Dr A will develop his picture of Simon's possible 'immaturity'. Before this, following comment from another doctor, he briefly outlines the family context which, as he describes it, is consistent with an immature personality:

D: I think John's er point is right whether Simon himself will er ... He's very anxious — he's become, er, I don't think he's employed. And he's got a, a mother who was deserted er when he was a baby. And she's er a very immature sort of woman who really doesn't seem to play much role ...

The information about Simon's mother neatly rounds out and confirms what we have already heard about her son's possible inadequate personality. We can easily picture this kind of unsettled home life and its likely impact on a growing child. Simon's reported 'anxiety' and his lack of a job all seem to fit into place.

Now Dr A is in a position to enlarge upon Simon's inadequate personality:

> D: But he still lives with her (i.e. his mother). He's er, he's a simple type (0.5) really kind of general, simple sort of guy. He'll talk to you sort of, you know, all day, and tell you all about it but whether (0.5) He sees it just as something to be done, I think, in a way. He thinks, you know, more free bus passes he can get from (his home town) to (here). [*laughter*]. Er, he'll go through everything.

At this point, I should hasten to add that I am not trying to pick holes in what Dr A is saying, still less to question his good faith. We all attempt to draw brief pictures of other people which are more or less convincing according to circumstances. Indeed, faced with such a snapshot account, there is very little basis for judging it except in terms of whether it fits together.

We can be more sure about the *effects* than about the validity of such character pictures. The first thing to note is that they tend to influence how we interpret the sense of what the character turns out to do and say. And this can continue even where there emerges contrary evidence from his words and actions. Second, it does not seem to matter if the picture is *logically* consistent as long as some elements seem to hold together. This degree of coherence allows the incorporation of such contrary evidence that does emerge.

Now Dr A has drawn a picture of Simon as an immature, unemployed young man with a disorganized family life. It is not his confidence which he questions ('he'll talk to you ... all day') but his reasons for talking and acting. He acts for trivial reasons (having operations in order to get free bus passes) and doesn't seem to have any psychological insights or even responses to his condition ('he sees it just as something to be done'). However, another doctor now seems to contradict Dr A's interpretation:

> Dr B: What I think the interesting thing is the fact that (when) you say simple because (0.5) it's a *sophisticated* sense of humour [*laughs*]
> Dr A: Yeah that's right, oh yeah.

This intervention would seem to cast doubt on Dr A's picture. Can simpletons really have 'a sophisticated sense of humour'? None the less, as we all do in everyday speech, Dr A is able to agree with Dr B's observation without retracting his argument.

Even Simon's willingness to talk about what should be done for him (rare in cleft-palate children) can be interpreted as indicating not that he is a rational person but that he 'grasps' little:

> Dr A: It's just that it's a bit more difficult making a decision in this case

because he um (1.0) he seems very open about it all but er I just don't know how much he grasps.

This kind of picture underlies the consultation that now takes place. As we shall see, Simon too seems to realise that his capacity for rational decision-making is being decided and responds accordingly. However, despite some evidence to the contrary, doubts continue to be stated by the doctors after he leaves. In the morass of communication difficulties potentially endemic in this situation, doctors are unable to avoid using stereotyped psychological pictures to make sense of what a young person means. The only possible irony here is that this consultation *may* involve a rare example of a cleft-palate teenager who says what he means. Consequently, appeals to pathological features of his personality and family life may tend to set the hearer off on a wild goose chase which could be avoided simply by attending to what Simon actually *says* rather than continuing to read it as evidence of his problematic psychological state.

When Simon enters, we see that he is a plump eighteen year old. He adopts a cheery manner at once, greeting everybody and asking 'How have you been?' He jokes about the conflicting measurements of his weight taken in different departments. Although he responds accurately and in detail to Dr A's first few questions, he does so in an informal manner, grinning for much of the time. The professionals laugh at Simon's jokes. Simon has dissolved the formality and tension often present in clinics.

But this, after all, is a serious business. An operation is in prospect and the doctors want to feel that Simon (S) both desires it and understands the discomforts that it will entail. Dr A gets down to business using the question which, in slightly varying forms, we find asked also in clinics in England:

D: Do you worry at all about your appearance?
S: Oh I really notice it but I um if it could be improved. I'd like to get it done. I really worry about it.

In one leap, Simon seems to have overcome the communication difficulties that a question about your appearance usually generates. He freely admits that he 'notices' and 'worries' about his looks and, consequently, would 'like to get it done'. He appears to be making a rational decision. However, we must remember Dr A's earlier assessment of Simon's psychological deficiencies. Viewed in this light, Simon's answer becomes transformed from a rational response into mere chatter coming from a simpleton who can talk to anybody quite freely but whose opinions are often based on trivial grounds (for instance being mainly interested in a free bus-pass). Consequently,

Simon's admitted 'openness' could co-exist with a failure to grasp what is involved (see Dr A's previous comment).

Again, it is worth pointing out the way in which different character assessments can appear equally logical but produce entirely different readings of the impression that someone is giving. In any apparently rational person, the response that Simon gives would settle the matter once and for all, but because Dr A has proposed that Simon's 'openness' may mask an immature personality, he pursues the matter:

> S: ... I really worry about it.
> D: *Really*?
> S: Yeah.
> D: Not really but *really*?
> S: But *really* yes

How can Simon's cheerful, open manner co-exist with his stated deep worries about his appearance? Is he being serious or simply saying what people expect? Consequently Dr A takes up Simon's word 'really' and cross-examines him about it.

I take it that one implication of questioning Simon's use of 'really' is that the questioner has doubts about the speaker's accuracy or sincerity. In this context, Simon's monosyllabic 'Yeah' is not sufficient to convince anybody of his seriousness, so Dr A follows it up with another question 'not really but *really*?' laying a great deal of stress on the final word. It is now apparent that Simon must display the kind of emotional response appropriate to someone who *really* worries about his appearance. A dead-pan answer will not do. So he tries to offer what is required by repeating Dr A's two words 'but *really*'with the same emphasis on the last word.

All of this, however, is inconclusive. The alternative readings of Simon's personality can fit what he is now saying, so Dr A changes tack. He asks Simon:

> Dr A: And why is it (0.5) what about your appearance is it that you (0.5) worry about?

Now Simon responds in a detailed way, explaining how, when he looks at photographs of himself, he sees that his jaw sticks out. Notice, however, that, like most boys, he is not prepared to admit that he looks at himself in the *mirror* — a more obvious place than a photograph in which to contemplate your appearance!

When shown a photograph of himself taken at the hospital eight years earlier, he gives further details of his own sense of his appearance and its deficiencies. However, the questions continue as Dr A and his colleagues try to establish Simon's 'true' feelings. At this point, though, Dr A makes a statement that makes the situation much easier for Simon:

> Dr A: May I explain to you what er (0.5) we're trying to weigh up whether you would *like* to have that jaw fixed up (   )
> S: Yes
> Dr A: And if you thought that you would, whether you understand what would be involved.

Now such an 'explanation' of what is going on usually arises only in 'formal' encounters like medical consultations or job interviews. In ordinary conversation, it may be inappropriate to note publicly that anything *else* is going on other than simple talk between equals. But in formal encounters, we all know that someone is in authority and has certain purposes in hand. In this latter situation, when such a person explains or defines what is going on, it may be done in broadly two kinds of ways. First, the authority-figure may call our attention to the nature of the encounter by saying something like: 'Look, you do realise that *I* am interviewing *you*?' Here we are not given any fresh information. The statement serves simply to re-assert the 'proper' lines of authority. It will be made usually after the subordinate figure has been 'cheeky' (for an example, see Silverman, 1973).

Second, however, the person in authority may explain what is going on so that the 'hidden agenda' of the encounter may become more apparent. As we all know, it is very disconcerting when you have no solid information about an interviewer's motives in asking his question, especially when you want to please.

Dr A's statement seems to be of the second kind. It helps Simon by making the situation more transparent. Simon gets the message, responding in a way which shows that he has indeed thought about what is involved in an operation:

> S: Right, now. I'll tell you my answer, you know. My answer is *yes*. Now you can tell me what's involved (2.0) Yes 'cos er (0.5) anything that could be done I'd like to get done really. I, I don't worry about inconvenience or pain, never worried me yet. So er, that's er, just that I want to know what happens though.

By now, Simon has undergone and apparently passed an extensive examination. He has revealed serious thought about his appearance, and an apparently soundly based consent to surgery, based on a recognition of its unpleasant side. Nevertheless, the doctors seem to be anxious to be sure that Simon *really* understands and so further questions follow. Here are just a few of the ensuing exchanges between Simon and the two doctors:

1.   [*Simon has been joking about how everybody will be delighted during the six-week period that his jaws are wired together*]

Dr A: Now, what, we need to, you know, for you to understand

S: Yes

Dr A: Is, it's a pretty trying sort of a period being wired together for that long

S: Yes

Dr A: And we real- really want you to understand that

S: Yeah, I will — I I will, I shall not joke any more
        [*Dr A laughs*]

Here Simon disarms the implied criticism that he is not being entirely serious about the operation by showing that he understands the implication of what Dr A is saying and stating openly that he is not going to 'joke any more'.

2. Dr B: It's a long time to be wired together

S: Yes

Dr B: And we, you know, we wouldn't want you to get into it unless it's really- feel that you really want it

S: But er, other people, surely, have suffered through the inconvenience somehow

Dr B: Yes

Here Simon appeals to the ability of 'other people' to accept the inconvenience. He asserts his own claim to be 'normal' by identifying with 'other people'.

3. Dr A: Do you think that's all worthwhile?

S: Well, I the er (0.5) well if it looks better and I can speak better in the long run, it would be worthwhile

After an initial hesitation, Simon once again displays his rational thought by appealing to the 'long run' consequences of surgery.

4. Dr A: So you think that would be good?

S: Well um it wouldn't be *good* but er if if it if it was to improve my speech and er er (0.5) the way it looks, being my appearance I suppose, er (0.5) it'd be worthwhile. Also, one thing, one thing, I must ask you this. What does the cost involve?

Simon cleverly detects the trap lurking in Dr A's question. While he appears eager to have the operation on his jaw, it is now clear that the doctors attach great weight to him understanding the painful character of the surgery. So his answer skilfully distinguishes between the short-term and the long-term: the operation 'wouldn't be good', only the long-term improvements will make it worthwhile. Moreover, as a rational consumer, Simon also wants to know what the operation will cost him financially. It transpires that, because this is a children's hospital, even cosmetic surgery is provided on a non fee-paying basis.

Simon succeeds in winning this operation and even, through further questioning, obtains a firm date for his diary for when he has to attend. Although he has learned to play down his jokiness, he cannot resist returning to the same kind of light-hearted banter that he employed when he entered the room:

> D: OK?
> S: Yeah, I'll (   ). Yeah, it was nice coming back to you.
> D: We enjoyed seeing you too, Simon
> S: Oh I enjoyed it too actually, yeah ... (   ) my part

Having obtained his objective, Simon relaxes back into his earlier happy-go-lucky performance, commenting on his 'enjoyment' of the proceedings in a way which patients rarely do. Almost like the character in *Winnie the Pooh* who was too full of himself and so needed to be 'de-bounced', Simon's manner calls forth a cautionary response:

> D: Keep your weight down though. Don't go/
> S: /I'm trying yeah.

After Simon leaves, the doctors speculate about his motives. Their difficulty is summed up by Dr A:

> D: It's very difficult to assess isn't it? Because he's pretty sophisticated in some of his comments and it's er (1.0) it's just the, you know, continuously sunny nature that's troubling me a little bit about the problem as to whether it should be done.

Given Simon's clever responses to a range of questions, Dr A abandons his definition of him as a 'simpleton'. He would now view him as 'pretty sophisticated'. The problem thus shifts away from whether Simon really understands what is going on towards the psychology of a person who can have a 'sunny nature' and yet be very concerned about his appearance.

Eventually, Dr A concludes that Simon's relaxed manner is merely 'a cover-up' for his self-consciousness about his appearance. Although this is rather an odd conclusion since Simon has freely admitted that he is conscious about his appearance, it generates general consent and the doctors agree that Simon is 'motivated' and should have the operation. The psychological discourse, which has been displayed in both the doctors' questions and in Simon's account of his motives, thus provides the grounds for the decision.

Conclusion

In a recent study of paediatric clinics, Strong (1979b) re-emphasizes the need to examine the degree of autonomy possessed by parents even within a framework of medical dominance. This analysis has revealed how, in a cleft-palate clinic, that autonomy may extend to the child, albeit hedged in by a variety of interactional traps. Strong found that his children were excluded from the consultation and that even older children were cast as incompetent and subordinate. Conversely, this study has shown that children *can* be centrally involved in disposal decisions. This variation suggests the need for research to proceed on a comparative basis, examining the different response to a range of illness contexts.

Of course, the degree of the child's participation in decision-making to some extent reflects medical decisions about what is 'appropriate' when treating a particular condition. So children's involvement in decisions about cosmetic surgery partly expresses a qualified 'right' which only testifies to the power of medical staff to dispose of 'rights'. At the same time, parents as well as doctors seem to invoke a consumerist model when discussing issues of 'looks'. This suggests that we are dealing here with a shared expectation that works against the child's exclusion from the clinic.

Elsewhere, when the child is younger or the condition is different, the parents 'stand in' as the child's representative in decision-making. At least at a formal level, within the range of clinics studied by Strong and at paediatric cardiology and cleft-palate clinics examined within our research programme, parents are cast as rational individuals who must be persuaded. Despite their technical and discursive resources, medical staff typically assert and defer to the family unit's 'right to decide'.

I have tried to show how this formal and abstract right can be extended to a child. This child is given the formal rights of a rational subject. However, this consumerist model formulates a purely abstract subject which takes no account of the reality of the uneasy positioning of the child between what I have called 'clinical' and 'everyday' discourses nor the ambiguous nature of a discourse which topicalizes one's looks.[6]

Reforming the Clinic?

One consequence of the practice of consumerist medicine upon children who find it difficult to establish a place for themselves in the talk is, probably, that fewer operations get done that if parental choices or even medical versions of need were to prevail. Undoubtedly, this serves to cut the costs to the NHS. It is possible, for instance, that in private medicine doctors are keener to suggest surgery and probably, therefore, engage in long drawn-out questions to establish a sense of the child's consent to treatment.[7] But it would be wrong to see consumerism as a conscious strategy used for purposes of economy.

First, as in Elaine's case, we have observed consultations where the consultant's opinion on the technical need for surgery makes him pursue the child for approval even where she seems originally not to be very interested. If it were simply a question of time and money, then one would expect doctors to accept gratefully any sign that the patient was satisfied.

Second, doctors may properly see themselves as reflecting the progressive aspirations of movements for 'children's rights' in leaving the ultimate decision to the child who has to live with his present appearance and with the consequences of further treatment. It may well be that parents' judgments about their children's appearance should not be the basis for an operation that is not demanded on purely medical grounds.

A difficulty that constrains all parties arises out of the problems that anybody, but especially an adolescent, has in talking about their looks. In research interviews, as in medical consultations, response is difficult to achieve and often contradictory in content (Murphy, forthcoming). One policy line, suggested by Starr and Zirpoli (1976), involves widening the treatment team. As they argue, the needs of cleft-lip/palate families do vary over a child's life — the cleft-lip baby has very different problems from that of the cleft-lip adolescent. They suggest, therefore, that a fixed team of specialists, headed, as in these clinics, by a surgeon, is too inflexible a treatment format. Instead of a hierarchically organized treatment team, they recommend a constant regrouping of personnel to reflect the changing needs of child and family. In particular, they suggest that a social worker should have a co-ordinating function, liaising with medical staff to help explain social-psychological and economic factors affecting response to treatment. This more flexible organization of treatment seems to be used most in the United States but is worth trial implementation and evaluation in other countries.

However, it is by no means clear that de-medicalizing the clinic in this way would necessarily be associated with greater opportunity for adolescent self-expression. This study has shown already how blurring the lines between clinical and everyday discourses can create confusion. Moreover, as Armstrong (1982) has argued, the outcome of 'whole-child' (or idiographic) medicine as practised in paediatrics is far from clear. Its emphasis on growth and development rather than pathology may actually introduce more subtle forms of patient control compared to nosographic medicine which assigns patients to clear disease classes. As Armstrong puts it:

Nosography was explicit about its boundaries and, in its classifications, only considered circumscribed aspects of the patient. Idiographic medicine, in processing the whole person, offers the potential of total surveillance. Social control becomes truly individualized (p.19).

We have observed this 'individualized' form of social control in which the patient, in Foucaultian terms, is 'incited to speak'. Individuals must declare themselves and, in this discursive self-examination, decisions about treatment will be grounded.

This cleft-palate clinic is fully in line with paediatric medicine as described by Armstrong (1983) elsewhere. It practises a form of 'non-evaluative mapping' in which patients are defined as 'normal children' on the assumption that 'all normal children have behaviour problems' (63).

This fits in neatly with the focus on chronic illness or handicap discussed by Arney and Bergen (1983). Previously hidden handicaps are now made constantly visible and the whole person becomes the object of the medical gaze. As in this clinic, there develop multi-member, health-management teams concerned with 'total evaluation from every standpoint' (18). Patients are incited to speak because their individuality must be surveyed if proper treatment is to be recommended, and they are to be reintegrated into a technically useful place in society.

As Arney and Bergen put it, the 'Elephant Man' is a thing of the past. All handicaps can and must be talked about. Consequently, like these children, we all become 'elephant men'. The humane, liberating impulse sits neatly side by side with total surveillance within a clinic turned a confessional.

It may well be that the only way to oppose this trend is to reject the ever-greater extension of the health-care team in the direction of a further range of psychological expertise. Indeed, might not the whole quasi-psychological interrogation about looks be replaced simply by asking the child whether he or she wants an operation?

Notes

1. West (1976) for instance offers the following exchange from an epilepsy clinic but does not comment on the child's complex response:

Doctor [*addressing patient*]: What would *you* prefer, Sarah, tablets or medicine?
Patient [*hesitates and looks at mother*]: Tablets

As I suggest later, what adults make of children's hesitations and silences can crucially affect disposals (see also note 4).

2. These two situations are discussed in Chapter Three. For a discussion of the range of ways in which children are constituted in this clinic, see Hilliard (1981).

3. It would be wrong to assume, however, that the interview format always leads to medical manipulation of patients. As Hughes (1982) has shown, many communication problems in medical encounters arise simply from the different knowledge-base of the parties.

4. In a study of Scottish Children's Hearings, Smith and May (1980) note the problems created by children's non-response to questions. Silence is invariably treated as evidence of their 'attitude' rather than as interactionally-generated.

5. Strong (personal communication) has suggested that doctors may use different strategies according to gender. Certainly, the words 'ugly' and 'handsome' are only used in a consultation with a boy (Barry). Notice how, in Elaine's case, the reference is only to a 'dimple' in a 'marked cupid's bow'.

6. There is a fascinating parallel here with the account of law by the Soviet legal-theorist Pashukanis in the 1920s. Pashukanis (1978) argues, contrary to Stalinist notions of 'socialist legality', that legal systems cannot be reformed because the very form of law expresses bourgeois economic relations based on abstract subjects engaged in relations of exchange on an abstract market. The clinics considered here seem to take precisely the legal form. An abstract or 'pre-textual' subject (the 'consumer') conceals the real subject (a 'You' positioned between two discourses) constituted by the discourse itself. An abstract market where the consumer is sovereign hides the monopoly of the supplier. Consequently, the vocabulary of children's 'rights' may share the same limits as the legal form itself.

7. 'Over-doctoring' seems to be a consequence of private systems of medicine such as in the USA. The greater use of social workers with cleft-palate cases in America probably has the result of generating more discussion about the psychology of appearance and, thereby, of *increasing* the number of cosmetic operations that take place.

III
THE DISCOURSE OF THE SOCIAL

In Part Two, I sought to demonstrate the nature and consequences of an appeal in the clinic to discourses of 'family life' or 'consumer choice'. Such discourses do not, of course, arise out of thin air but owe a great deal to historical developments, not the least of which was the emergence of the human sciences.

In the next chapter, I examine how the debate about medical reform has centred on the human sciences' discovery of what I call 'the discourse of the social'. This has allowed reformers to develop a number of polarities between 'patient-centred' and 'doctor-centred' medicine and between the voices of 'medicine' and of the 'lifeworld'. I argue against the reformers' demand that we should choose one side or another of these polarities. Each side represents practices which cannot be wished away. The issue remains the articulation of the relation between discourses not the search for a spurious 'discourse of truth'.

The final two chapters take up the argument in the context of a study of clinics for teenage diabetics. Both the doctors and parents of these young people find a need to strike a balance between powerful discourses of adult 'responsibility' and teenagers' 'autonomy'. Chapter Nine shows how even the most liberal kind of doctoring still cannot deny the force of a discourse of 'responsibility'. In Chapter Ten, I examine how mothers skilfully appeal to both discourses, as appropriate, in order to rebut perceived doctors charges of 'nagging' or 'irresponsibility' towards their diabetic children.

In turn, the object of both adults' concern, teenage diabetics, constitute themselves as subjects in the context of the disciplinary gaze or, like many of the cleft-palate teenagers, remain silent. These are not psychological subjects awaiting self-expression, but young people whose subjectivity, like that of adults, is grounded in real social practices.

8
The Discourse of the Social

David Armstrong (1982) has written about a form of medicine primarily concerned with diagnosing and classifying diseases. Such 'nosographic' medicine identifies disease as a pathological disturbance of normal physiological processes, where 'normality' is essentially unambiguous.

Conversely, 'idiographic' medicine treats each patient as a bearer of idiosyncratic problems, has no certain notion of normality and does not clearly distinguish pathology from physiology. As Armstrong points out, we find examples of this latter form in paediatrics' primary emphasis on growth and development (rather than pathology) and in adult 'whole-person' medicine. It is also seen in certain styles of general practice which emphasize 'the patient's environment and/or biography' (Armstrong, 1982:15). Diagnosis becomes of lesser importance and is replaced with the aim of better intersubjective understanding based on the assumption that 'everyone is different'.

At first glance, it might appear that 'idiographic' medicine, as a 'humane' practice, is far more liberating (for both doctor and patient) than the old-style of nosography. However, as an authoritarian version of the doctor–patient relationship, nosographic medicine, Armstrong argues, is relatively explicit about its social control functions. Conversely, in shifting the gaze from the group to the individual, idiography extends the range of its practice and is less explicit about its mechanisms of surveillance. As Armstrong concludes:

> Nosography was explicit about its boundaries and in its classifications only considered circumscribed aspects of the patient. Idiographic medicine, in processing the whole person offers the potential of total surveillance. Social control becomes truly individualized (Armstrong, 1982:19).

Armstrong's comments offer us insight into the nature and consequences of the medical encounters with cleft-palate and Down's Syndrome patients considered in the previous chapters. By constituting these patients as, respectively, psychological subjects and social objects, the doctors concerned combined paediatrics' de-emphasis on pathology with general practice's 'whole-person' medicine. As we saw, many features of these encounters mirrored those recommended by medical reformers. Consultations were unhurried and offered a great deal of choice to the patient or parent. Above all, the doctors involved were very concerned about psychological and/or social aspects of the patient's problem. Yet this humane, idiographic medicine co-existed with precisely the individualized, implicit forms of social control that Armstrong predicts.

In this chapter, I want to explore further the character of the 'whole-person' social medicine observed in these two paediatric clinics, beginning with prescriptive accounts of general practice by Balint (1964) and Byrne and Long (1976) and concluding with the more recent and subtle humanistic work of Mishler (1984). I will then go on to examine the Foucaultian deconstruction of 'whole-person' medicine found not only in Armstrong's (1983, 1984) careful historical analyses but also in the polemics of Arney and Bergen (1984). Finally, I will take up the troubling implications of this latter position for medical practice.

If medical 'reformism' and its partners in the human sciences are inevitably part of the same apparatus of social control that they ostensibly challenge, then we are indeed in deep trouble. My own close involvement with the medical staff, patients and parents in these clinics makes me want to resist the relativist implications that are present in Foucault's recent interpreters. Whether and, if so, to what extent a Foucaultian medical sociology can be at any less than arms-length from medical practice will be the continuing question that animates this last section of the book.

'Patient-Centred' Medicine

Michael Balint was the inspiration behind recent attempts to reform medical practice in the direction of what was to be called a more 'patient-centred' medicine. Balint (1964) argued that medical consultations, particularly in general practice, involved much more than the diagnosis and treatment of physical disease. Patients approached doctors for a range of complex reasons located in their social and emotional existence. Underneath an apparently simple physical symptom, a mass of personal problems waited to be unravelled. Consequently, the medical gaze should be redirected. Not only the interiors of bodies but patients' ever-changing psychology and social life became proper objects of medical perception.

For Balint, diagnosis was as much a study of biography as of pathology. In such biographical studies, a psycho-therapeutic model of 'laying bare' was appropriate. However, as Byrne and Long (1976) were later to point out, doctors were not trained to enact this type of consultation. Set routines of interviewing patients, geared to history-taking, examination and diagnosis, were only adequate in relation to purely physical processes. Such 'doctor-centred' behaviour did not fit with 'non-organic' disease or with the sensitive understanding of psycho-social factors. Consequently, medical education must be reformed. For:

> In our contemporary sick society, the psycho-social factors of our patients' illnesses are becoming more frequently observed and demand the use of skills which we have been formally assisted to acquire (Byrne and Long, 1976:5).

Byrne and Long's language is significant. In a 'sick society', the doctor's gaze can properly traverse every emotional and social space. Nothing is to be hidden from doctor or patient. Instead of each withdrawing into a purely physical realm, medical consultations are to be the site of 'skilful analyses of emotional problems and (the) display (of) skills which psycho-therapists would applaud' (p.15).

In an extensive study of tape-recordings of general practice consultations, these writers ram home their message about the limits of 'doctor-centred' medicine. In almost two-thirds of these interviews, doctors simply announced their diagnosis or limited themselves to an instruction to their patients ('well now take this along to the chemist'). Conversely, in only a quarter of all cases did the doctor encourage the patient to participate in the decision about what was to be done.

For Byrne and Long, patients should be involved in their own treatment and doctors should encourage offers of changed behaviour. Such 'patient-centred' medicine would be characterized by consultation based on open-ended questions, the exploration of patients' own ideas and attempts to negotiate bargains.

'Patient-centred' medicine has made slow progress as a role-model in British medical education. Social science courses are offered to many medical students but, according to two Edinburgh students in a letter to a newspaper, they have little impact because of the negative attitude towards them of medical teachers. They go on:

> Subsequent ward teaching doesn't emphasize sufficiently respect for patients' rights and feelings. In our experience, the decision to consider these fully has been a personal choice rather than a matter of accepted professional conduct.
>
> We feel the issue of future doctors' attitudes to their patients is so vital that the emphasis in medical education must be changed from the study of

isolated disease processes to the concept of the whole patient, including the psychological, social and emotional aspects of their management (*Guardian* letters, 26 February 1986).

These writers use the liberal language of 'rights', 'feelings' and 'choice' as a powerful support for the kind of 'patient-centred' medical education recommended by Byrne and Long and Balint. However, notions of the 'whole patient', like those of a 'sick society' are double-edged. Everything is to be open between doctor and patient but also nothing is to be hidden from the doctor's gaze in the well-intentioned pursuit of the 'management' of the 'whole patient'.

However, the problem is not simply one of a benevolent but totalizing medicine. Throughout the writings we have been considering runs a naive view of the human subject. It seems to be assumed that we are the carriers of unique experiences and that the role of conversation is to discover an authentic language in which these experiences can be truly expressed. Now there are at least two problematic aspects of these attractive assumptions:

1. Are there languages which are more 'authentic' than others? Consider, for instance, how the language of 'emotions' is at once the preferred format of psycho-therapy, popular fiction and tabloid journalism. Is the language intrinsically authentic or rather one historically-located form of sense-production with no intrinsic value?

2. Who are the subjects who speak? When we speak do we express our inner thoughts? Are there, indeed, such private languages or rather, when we speak, do we not invoke one or more of the publicly available ways of speaking? Consider the uniform 'atrocity stories' and 'moral tales' told by parents of handicapped children (Baruch, 1981 and Voysey, 1975).

I will shortly discuss work which considers these issues in the context of medicine as well as the apparently relativistic and disabling implications of this line of analysis. Before I do so, however, it will be worth assessing one final, and far more subtle, version of patient-centred medicine.

Elliot Mishler (1984) is rightly critical of the normative character of many studies of medical consultations. Commonsense has been used as a tacit resource by many investigators — especially in the coding of passages of talk. Instead we need 'to make explicit how conversationalists themselves make sense of what they are saying to each other' (p.47). Mishler says correctly that this will involve far closer attention to how clinical work is done. Systematic methods for studying the structure of medical interviews (MI's) must be deployed and attention paid to how clinical practice 'shape(s) and organize(s) the MI as a particular type of discourse' (p.5).

For Mishler this discourse, which he characterizes as 'the voice of medicine' has three main features:

1. An interrogative unit structured in the form of Question — Answer — Evaluation/Assessment — Question where open-ended questions are typically absent.

2. Disattendance to the 'life-contexts of patients' symptoms' (p.70) including how the problem developed and how it affects them.

3. Pauses before patients reply. Unlike ordinary conversation, where speakers are mutually attentive and develop the 'topic' together, in MIs the doctor controls the flow of topics. Hence patients are often caught unawares by a switch to a new topic (p.75).

The question at once arises whether Mishler has indeed paid the attention he claims to the role of clinical practice in shaping the special form of the MI. Why should we use a model of ordinary conversation as a baseline for the study of an encounter with a far more sharply defined purpose and with special interactional problems? Hughes (1982) has suggested, for instance, that the use of chains of questions is a useful means of proceeding where parties have different access to clinical knowledge. Given this access, patients may well feel discomfited by a consultation that offers apparently 'democratic' conversational forms. There is some parallel with classroom lessons. Interestingly, Mehan (1981) has found precisely Mishler's interrogative unit at work in 'learning lessons'. In neither case can we assume that there is something wrong simply because there is a departure from ordinary conversational practice.

However, there is a second problem which Mishler himself does raise in an auto-critique which follows. Why should we assume that doctors and patients use only one voice — the 'voice of medicine' and the 'voice of the lifeworld' respectively? Acknowledging Silverman and Torode (1980), he 'interrupts' his previous analysis to affirm that:

> Both physician and patient may speak in either voice and each may switch voices within or between utterances or turns. Furthermore, the discourse is shaped by the ways the voices interrupt and interpenetrate each other (103–4).

Here is a useful advance on the essentialist assumptions found in both Byrne and Long's prescriptions and in Mishler's initial approach. Subjects are no longer seen as coterminous with a single voice which expresses their 'true' experiences. The issue is always the relation between voices rather than the establishment of the single authentic voice.

Conceived in these terms, Mishler finds that MIs display an imbalance between voices. Examining at length one consultation, he discovers that, at the start of his turn at talk, the doctor shifts from the voice of the lifeworld (dependent on the patient's biographical situation and contextually grounded experiences) to the voice of medicine (in which events are de-contextualized by an appeal to abstract rules). The patient answers the doctor's question within her turn and then returns to the voice of the lifeworld 'to maintain coherence and continuity in her account' (p.108).

Mishler finds only one trivial example of a doctor-initiated entry into the lifeworld ('and what happened in January?'). Much more common was either a routine acknowledgement ('Hm, hm') or an interruption followed by a switch to the voice of medicine.

At this point, however, Mishler's diagnosis of the problem and his suggested solutions bear striking resemblances to earlier kinds of medical reformism. When the doctor asks 'response-constraining' questions of the Yes/No? or What/Where? type, we are told that he is proceeding from a biomedical model which 'is invisible and inaudible in the discourse' (p.120). What earlier had looked like an orderly sequence now looks like a tale told by the patient and interrupted by the doctor:

> The net effect of the physician's questions is to strip away the contexts of the patient's experience of her problem. He ignores the causally-structured and temporally-ordered connections that she describes. He focuses on one element in her account, the 'objective' symptom, removes it from the grounding she gives it in her life and isolates each element from the others (p.120).

By now we are into the quite familiar 'doctor-centred' critique of medicine. This becomes still clearer when Mishler develops alternative ways of doing an MI. These include:

1. The use of open-ended questions which 'help to sustain and develop the coherent meaning of the patient's account' (p.153)
2. The explanation of medical agendas
3. Using the patient's own words to ask further questions
4. Listening with minimum interruption to the patient's account

As with Balint and Byrne and Long, the emphasis here is on a rejection of the biomedical model and a call for a more 'democratic' form of consultation dependent on:

> ... the interchange between voices rather than solely on the voice of medicine .... Instead of the interview structure based on the formal features of utterances as questions and responses, the structure of this interview is based on the development of coherent and shared meanings (p.162).

Now it is true that Mishler does distance himself from simplistic calls for 'friendliness' (which 'may still function exclusively within a biomedical model') (p.192) and rejects a psychiatric worldview (perhaps not too far away from some versions of 'whole-patient' medicine) because of its reductionist thrust. Nevertheless, his position shares three basic problems with the other views considered in this section:

1. As already noted, medical interviews may well have *necessary* differences from ordinary conversations. To what extent does the 'voice of medicine' constitute simply another way of speaking which must take its place in a democratic arrangement of voices? Doesn't this ignore the place of medical discourse in modern societies and, indeed, the ways in which it has entered into our own accounts of ourselves, thus making the distinction between 'lifeworld' and 'medicine' itself problematic?

2. Despite Mishler's stress on the importance of the relation between discourses, he appears to identify the voice of the lifeworld as somehow more authentic. In his demand for 'the recognition of the distinctive humanity of patients and respect for the contextual grounding of their problems in their lifeworlds' (p.192–3), he seems to espouse the unthought assumptions of liberal humanism. Yet liberal humanism is the self-understanding of many 'caring' professions. So Mishler's calls for reforms in the training of doctors and for support groups are fully in line with current 'progressive' practice (see also the similar recommendations made by Tuckett et al., 1985).

3. We need to consider carefully Mishler's call for medicine to move away from the biomedical model to 'a social perspective in which patients' relationships and involvements in family, community and work settings have primary significance' (p.194). Such a social perspective seems to offer a totally unrestricted form of surveillance in which the medical gaze can roam freely. It also is naive to assume that a discourse of the social is necessarily liberating — indeed my earlier discussion of the Down's Syndrome and cleft-palate consultations demonstrated a very different outcome.

Perhaps we should take a less prescriptive and a more historical look at medical practice. What is it about current medical practice that incites patients to speak and doctors to listen to them?

The Incitement to Discourse

Medicine is compelled by its own logic to speak *with* the patient and to abandon its arrogant logic of speaking for the patient, who must remain silent. Both doctor and patient are compelled to speak with one another in a common language around which a field of power forms to govern them both (Arney and Bergen, 1984:169).

Foucault (1979) has observed that power works as much through encouraging speech as repressing it. For instance, rather than repressing discussion of sexuality, there has been 'an institutional incitement to speak about it … through explicit articulation and endlessly accumulated detail' (p.18). Similarly, the reforms of the monitorial system in mid-nineteenth century English education sought 'not to exclude or repress the problematic environments of the street and the home, but to draw them into the moralizing space of the school' (Hunter, 1987: 18).

So, in the quotation above, Arney and Bergen are suggesting that the reformism of Balint, Byrne and Long and Mishler is already incorporated into medical practice. However, we should not view this as a subtle strategy used to control the patient. 'Medical dominance' is an inappropriate model of doctor–patient relations for power is not simply a finite quality to be fought over in battles. If the 'voice of the patient' must be heard, it is because doctors, patients and reformers alike recognize themselves within a field of power/knowledge which incites discourse viewed as the expression of subjectivity.

Reformers and social scientists are caught within the web of this knowledge:

> For medical sociology only the self that speaks about what is important can countermand the monopolistic tendency of medicine to define and control the rights of people as patients and citizens (Arney and Bergen, 1984:2).

Yet when the patient speaks, does he or she *dissolve* the workings of power?

Arney and Bergen document how the discourse of medicine now does more than allow patients to speak about their experiences, it incites them to speak. Modern medicine has fused the anatomical gaze of Foucault's nineteenth-century clinic with its earlier attention to the discourse of the 'experiencing person'. Although this fusion is clearest in certain areas of medicine (paediatrics, psychiatry, chronic medicine), Arney and Bergen suggest that the discourse of the experiencing person is forcing its way into even the most recondite strongholds of organic medicine. Consequently, diseases are being displaced by patients with problems related to their entire life. So the modern physician

> 'must take the total situation of the patient into consideration in order to put the patient's life course on a normal if not optional trajectory' (p.87).

As the Edinburgh medical students noted, in their letter to *The Guardian*, patient-'management' must now be conceived in broad terms:

> Medicine transformed the patient's personality from something that at best was irrelevant to medical work and at worse interfered with it, into something that could be said to improve medical work. The management of

the subjective aspects of illness complemented the management and treatment of the traditional objective aspects of disease (Arney and Bergen, 1984:69).

This interest in the 'subjective aspects of illness' was an artefact of changes during this century in the perception of the character of the medical interview documented by Armstrong (1984). In the older format, consultations were viewed as equivalent to an interrogation. The patient was absent as a whole person and the role of the doctor was to look behind the words that the patient spoke to find the lesion that was the true source of the patient's speech:

> When the doctor searched for pathological lesions, the (patient) view was the symptom and the patient was both a receptacle for pathology and an unreliable translator (Armstrong, 1984:743).

The patient's view started to become important because of two new forms of knowledge. First, the discovery of mental and psychosomatic illness meant that doctors had to acknowledge the importance of the emotions. This made the patient a less than perfect setting for the observation of pathology. Second, epidemiology encouraged new notions of people at risk, the influence of social class and family life on morbidity. So it became part of the clinical method to map and monitor the social spaces between bodies and this required an incitement of the patient to speak.

However, the patient-view was now little more than 'a measure of medical effectiveness' (p.741). Only when doctors started to stress the need to understand the patient as a person did the patient-view become a problem in its own right. Now notions of coping and adjustment became central, the patient-view was redefined as the 'lay theory' and doctors were required to pay attention to 'non-verbal communication' as well as to what the patient said. Above all, both doctor and patient were to view each other as experiencing subjects:

> 'The meeting between doctor and patient was not between an enquiring gaze and a passive object but an interaction between two subjects' (p.742).

Elsewhere, Armstrong (1983) has documented the changes in English medical education which were the backdrop to the new emphasis on the patient's view. He notes how the 1944 Goodenough Committee on medical education hardly mentioned the patient except in terms of the need to interrogate him. Less than twenty-five years later, the Todd Committee were to stand all this on its head. Language, culture and social prejudices were recognized as factors that 'distort communication' and even the previously sacred medical history-taking was placed in question marks. The central issue was more the problem of 'patient compliance'.

Speculation about 'non-compliance' centred around methods of communication (tackling the 'deep' problem, ensuring the patient understood the diagnosis and treatment) and situational factors related to the patient's personality and social location. So 'whole-person' medicine emerged and the medical interview ceases to be an interrogation to locate pathology and becomes instead:

> a ... mechanism for analysing ... idiosyncratic patients ... the result is that the patient can no longer be encapsulated in a single gaze; the whole person is a multi-dimensional rather than unitary being (Armstrong, 1983:110).

Medicine has helped fabricate this 'multi-dimensional' being. In the past, the clinical examination had been merely 'a device for ordering bodies' (Armstrong, 1983). Here medicine attended to its Franken-stein's monster, analysing and describing bodies viewed purely as objects. Modern medicine, conversely, surveys around and between subjectified bodies:

> the new body is one held in constant juxtaposition to other bodies, a body constituted by its social relations and relative mental functioning, a body of necessity of a subject rather than an object (p.102).

Two main lines of criticism can be deployed against this line of analysis: its tendency to over-generalize and its refusal to acknowledge any form of 'progress'.

First, how far can it be said that 'the patient's view' is central to modern medicine? Most people's experience of fracture-clinics and many mothers' experience of delivery would hardly support this. However, I have already noted that, for all their rhetorical flourishes, Arney and Bergen are concerned with the *direction* of change rather than a description which is valid for all instances. Similarly, Armstrong recognizes that a state of tension still exists between a 'panoptic' gaze, concerned with bodies viewed through complex technologies, and a 'community' gaze, stressing the patient's view in its social and psychological context. In the next chapter, we shall see the working out of this tension in the conflict between styles of 'policing' and 'self-regulation' in clinics for adolescent diabetics. We also have a recent example in the case brought against an English obstetrician, Wendy Savage, which centred around the conflict between 'patient-centred' medicine and high-technology means of assessment.

So it cannot be argued that these writers have over-generalized if we accept that they are not describing a unilinear development. Apparently more damaging, at least in commonsense terms, is the denial of progress in the practice of medicine which is implicit in their position. This argument has recently been deployed by Bury (1986) who invites us to commit ourselves about whether we would prefer to be treated by a modern doctor who, say, combined modern technical knowledge with a deference to the patient view. There is little doubt that all these writers would prefer such treatment for themselves. However, this fails to answer the point about progress. For how can they or we stand outside the contemporary discourses of the 'patient-view'? The person who speaks and chooses is a construction of such discourses.

Medicine and the social sciences have worked hand-in-hand in discovering such a human subject. The social sciences in particular have presented 'subjectivity as the immanent human condition which the human sciences have succeeded in liberating' (Armstrong, 1983:116). But a science of the subject has merely extended the range and disciplinary power of the professional gaze. So we return to the question with which we began: what sort of space can social analysis occupy in medical practice?

The Place of Social Analysis of Medical Practice

> (Your) Critique had an implacable logic which left . . . no possible room for initiative (Foucault, 1981).

The quotation above is taken from a question addressed to Foucault about the impact of his book *Discipline and Punish* on social workers in prisons. In response to the charge that he had anaesthetized them in their search for prison reform, Foucault replies that the problem of the prisons is not one for social workers but for the prisoners themselves. Consequently, he does not set out to tell professionals 'what is to be done'. Indeed his intentions are quite the opposite:

> My project is precisely to bring it about that they no longer know what to do, so that the acts, gestures, discourses which up until then had seemed to go without saying become problematic, difficult, dangerous. This effect is intentional (p.12).

Unfortunately, this kind of observation only serves to support the prejudices of those critics who regard social science as either trivial or disabling. However, elsewhere, Foucault has suggested what I take to be more productive paths for social analysis.

Central to Foucault's work, and to the positions of Armstrong and Arney and Bergen, is a refusal to accept choosing between the dichotomies in which contemporary debates are couched. One strategy, favoured by Foucault, is a purely tactical identification with older, unfashionable ways. As he puts it:

It is necessary to pass over to the other side — the other side from the 'good side' — in order to free oneself from those mechanisms which made two sides appear, in order to dissolve the false unity of this other side whose part one has taken (Foucault in a 1977 interview quoted by Dews, 1984).

Now although Foucault sees this strategy as part of the work of 'the historian of the present' (Dews, 1984) it has a clear implication for very practical debates. Why should we see the choice for medical practice as lying between 'doctor-centred' and 'patient-centred' medicine? What do the latest fashions conceal both about history and about contradictions and tensions in the preferred form of practice?

Here, indeed, is a fruitful area for professional debate which might be unearthed by social analysis. But we also learn from Foucault that professional debates are only part of the story. In his 1981 interview, he rejects 'prescriptive, prophetic discourse' which buries practitioners under its weight. There is a limit to what theoreticians can and should do:

What is to be done ought not to be determined from above by reformers, be they prophetic or legislative, but by a long work of comings and goings, of exchanges, reflections, trials, different analyses . . . . The problem is one for the subject who acts (Foucault, 1981:12–13).

This is an important anti-elitist message. If prisons are to be reformed or clinics changed it can only come about through practical struggles 'not because a plan of reform has found its way into the heads of social workers (or doctors)' (p.13). This need not mean an arms-length attitude towards reform by social scientists. But it does mean a rejection of social engineering perspectives in favour of a responsiveness to the 'comings and goings' and 'analyses' of the subject who acts. (For a further discussion of this response to social problems, see Silverman, 1985, Chapter 9).

However, we also need to go beyond Foucaultian genealogies based on analyses of texts and reports with a problematic relation to practice. Studies of consultations, geared to identify not 'authentic' voices but the relation between voices, complement structural accounts of institutional and discursive forms.

We must always remember, however, the limits of professional or lay interventions which seek to construct entirely new forms of practice or new discourses. Neither politics nor social analysis are about pure forms or pure truths. Both are concerned with connections and disconnections, articulations and disarticulations between elements having no intrinsic meaning. Here, indeed is a worthwhile strategy for intervention:

Form rhizomes and not roots, never plant anything! Don't sow, graft, make a line, never a point (Deleuze and Guattari, 1981:68).

In the final two chapters of this book, I shall adopt such a response to the discourse of the social.

9
Policing the Lying Patient: Surveillance and Self-Regulation in Consultations with Adolescent Diabetics

> I don't believe a thing
> Who do we believe in this clinic?
> (NT: 18.9)

> We want to give you the correct advice
> but we don't want to tell you what to do.
> (NT: 15.1)

Introduction

The treatment of illness inevitably occurs within a moral framework. In the care of diabetic patients, as with other chronic illnesses, there is a perceived need for sufferers to show that they are doing their best to contain their disorder. Where deviance may be wilful, there is an investigative potential present in the consultation and the corrective strategy may be to address the deficiencies in the socialization of the deviant. A recently instituted measure of blood-glucose level (glycosylated haemoglobin) can be used as a means of policing, as observed in this study of forty-seven consultations with adolescent diabetic patients attending two out-patient clinics. This measure provides a form of surveillance which finds truth inside the patient rather than as conversationally constituted. The implications of this practice will be considered and alternative strategies discussed.

Diabetes mellitus is the most common metabolic problem in childhood (Rosenbloom, 1984). In the United Kingdom it affects 7 out of every 10,000 children (Jones, 1983). Like many other chronic diseases, it presents a problem to medical staff in that no 'cure' can be offered to the patient, only a continuing routine of hospital visits and, in this case, a life-long régime of invasive, self-administered tests and injections and control of diet. This self-administration creates a special problem in itself for it demands a degree of activity from the patient that is very different from the common model of the passive patient and the active physician (Szasz and Hollander, 1956). Not surprisingly, it is reported that in a study of nearly 4000 out-patients from a typical diabetic clinic only about fifteen per cent were 'well controlled' (Gillespie and Bradley, 1983).[1]

Medicine has responded in two kinds of ways to this situation. The dominant biological model of health and illness has led to extensive research to improve measurement and control of blood-sugar levels. Although this has produced improved testing and therapy, a recent review of the literature is forced to conclude that 'strict diabetes control remains theoretical because of our inability to mimic the pancreatic beta-cell response with intermittent insulin injection' (Rosenbloom, 1984). The author goes on to note that widely accepted therapies, like twice-daily injections, have not been supported in controlled studies. This 'seat of the pants' character of diabetes treatment has led one sociologist to emphasize how faith, optimism and ritualistic elements enter into medical practice in this area (Posner, 1977).

A second kind of medical response has arisen from the paediatric 'whole person' model of the patient and also perhaps from the 'chronic disease' model which stresses the role of 'motivation . . . as a major problem in long-term disorders' (Gillespie and Bradley, 1983). This has led to a number of studies of patient and family response to diabetes (Cerreto and Travis, 1984; Lavoie and Barker, 1980; and Ory and Kronenfeld, 1980). The 'chronic disease' model goes beyond purely biological versions of health and illness. It is prepared to treat diabetes as 'about people not pancreases' as one doctor has put it (Newton, 1985). The most recent work also allows for process and change (Bradley et al., 1984). Motivation is now seen as 'a changing interpersonal and cognitive process' (Gillespie and Bradley, 1983).

Such 'liberal' or 'humanistic' imperatives avowedly owe a great deal to the discovery of the 'social' and the 'psychological' realms by the human sciences. One of the themes of this book, however, is that knowledge is never neutral and that 'enlightenment' is invariably double-edged. The focus on anatomy produced an organic medicine which was at once (arguably) more efficient at treatment than the earlier medicine of 'essences' but, also more authoritarian. The still later discovery of the 'social' made medicine less authoritarian but also more intrusive. I will return to this issue later.

Settings and Methods
The study began as a result of a chance meeting with a consultant paediatrician who worked at a General Hospital in a new town some thirty miles from London. Having described my previous work to him, I was invited to observe his monthly clinic with adolescent diabetics. As I later learned, this clinic was held for 'problem cases'. The more routine cases were dealt with by the registrar. In a sense, however, all adolescent diabetics are problem cases, combining the

expectation of psychological problems already discussed in this chapter and the kinds of conflicts between medical expertise and the perceived need for self-regulation that I have just been considering. After observing several clinics, the doctor concerned readily accepted my comparison of diabetics with alcoholics. From the medical point of view, both represent 'no-win' situations. Medical expertise is relevant insofar as patients are prepared to perceive that they have a problem and to become actively involved in its treatment. Unlike much medical practice, the patient's active involvement in decision-making is basic to success. Consequently, often sometimes reluctantly, doctors feel compelled to get involved in what for them are murky, intractable psychological and social issues.

At this clinic, the patients see the health visitor before the consultation begins. This is used to do a blood test (via a fingerprick) and, sometimes, to engage in health education through a discussion of diet, often using teaching materials such as models of different foods. These activities take place in a small room which, like the consulting room, is located next to a children's ward. Consequently, the waiting area is filled with small children's seats, as well as larger adult ones, and has a play area containing a slide as well as a number of toys.

After seeing the health visitor, there is often a few minutes wait before it is time to see the doctor. The consultant sits at the side of a desk at the far side of the consulting room. Against the wall nearest the door there are scales and a device for measuring height. Under a window is an examination couch which is rarely used for these patients. The patient, health visitor and researcher arrange themselves in a semi-circle of chairs facing the doctor. Apart from new patients, who seem always to be accompanied by parents, many patients are unaccompanied. Where parents bring their child to the clinic, they do not enter the consulting room if it is established that the child does not want them to be present. Overall, of the ten patients seen more than once during my observation of the clinic, five always had their consultations without their parents being present and four had their parents absent from at least one consultation. Only one patient had a parent present at all consultations.

In order to allow some comparison, I obtained access some months later to another diabetic clinic held in a General Hospital in a suburb of London. The consultant there is also a paediatrician but the clinic differs in a number of ways. All children attend — there is no special adolescents' clinic — and are seen either by the consultant or his registrar according to the time they arrive. I observed only those consultations involving patients aged between eleven and eighteen. At the time I was observing there was no health visitor present (although one has recently been appointed). Before the consultation, patients see a dietitian and have their weight and height recorded by a nurse. They may also chat to a voluntary worker, herself a mother of a diabetic child, who attends all clinics, keeps tabs on patients and their problems and organizes a parents' group. Although there is a side-room, mostly used by mothers and young children, most teenage diabetic patients wait with other adult non-diabetic patients, seated on chairs placed along the walls of a waiting area, with doctors' rooms on each side.

I observed consultations and made notes. After an initial period of observation, all consultations were tape-recorded with patients' and parents' permission. Due to a lack of resources, however, only three consultations were transcribed in their entirety. The initial aim of the analysis was to establish recurrent interactional forms within a version of the 'ceremonial order of the clinic'. (Strong, 1979b) Since I had no access to patients' own accounts outside the consultation, my interest was in what all parties were *doing* in these encounters rather than in what they *thought* about what they were doing. More specifically, I became interested in the kind of medical dilemmas over patient autonomy and medical control that I have already described.

I sought to find patterns across all consultations, using analytic induction to generate categories and strengthening my analysis via the pursuit of deviant cases (Mitchell, 1983) and the use of simple methods of counting where appropriate (Silverman, 1985, Chapter 7). The analysis came to focus on four areas:

1. A description of the distinctive interactional forms found in these consultations and the dilemmas created for the parties.
2. An illustration of the working out of these dilemmas taking advantage of my longitudinal data on several consultations with the same patient.
3. An attempt to depict different medical 'styles' in the consultation centring around the balance between autonomy and control.
4. An assessment, in the light of this analysis, of a number of practical suggestions to reform diabetic clinics.

I observed the first (new town) clinic over a much longer period than the suburban clinic as shown in Table 1.

TABLE 1
The Data

Clinic	'New Town'	'Suburban'
Period of observation	10 months	3 months
Number of clinic sessions observed	10	3
Number of doctors	1	3
Number of consultations	33	14

TABLE 2
Length of Consultations

Clinic	'New Town'	'Suburban'
Mean length of consultation (in minutes)	24	12
Shortest and longest consultations	14 – 31	6 – 16

As shown in Table 2, consultations at the new town clinic last, on average, twice the length of those at the suburban clinic. The longest consultation at the new town clinic was with a new patient and her parents and the shortest was with an educationally subnormal patient who, unusually, had turned up without his mother. The shortest consultations at the suburban clinic were seen by an elderly locum with no previous knowledge of the patients or their parents.

Interactional Forms
This account is based, almost entirely, on the 'new town' clinic data because of the far larger data-base derived from thirty-three consultations held by a single doctor. Many aspects of these forms are seen in the 'suburban' consultations although, as I suggest later in a discussion of medical styles, there is a tendency here to stick closer to a medical model of patient passivity with lip-service only being given to the complex issues involved in self-regulation of care. This is reflected in the far shorter consultations in the suburban clinic — although it must be borne in mind that, unlike the new town clinic, this is not a clinic for 'problem' patients and that dietary issues are dealt with outside the consultation.

It will be helpful if I locate the forms I have identified in the chronology of events in which they unfold. This chronology is taken from the 'new town' clinic. After the patient enters, she is weighed and measured by the health visitor while the doctor reads the notes.* Following standard paediatric practice, the child's height and weight are then plotted against a normal distribution. The variation between the curve and the actual measurement can be an occasion for compliments — 'You are doing very well'. Sometimes it is used to warn — 'You are putting on too much weight' — and sometimes to encourage. Teenage boys are assured that, if they can control their diabetes, they will grow taller. A link between weight and control is regularly used with girls.

---

*All four doctors that I observed were male. The patients were both male and female. As a convention, then, I have used 'she' to describe the patient group.

The doctor then moves on to the main business of blood-sugar levels. He inspects the results of today's blood and/or urine test and, if available, the more reliable results of the test measuring long-term glycosylated haemoglobin. The patient is told whether the figures have moved up or down since the last visit and may be asked to account for such movements.[2]

At this point, the doctor will ask to see the child's own blood and urine test results. These are supposed to be recorded several times a day in a little book provided by the clinic. Two kinds of issues arise from these sets of figures: the levels of blood-sugar recorded and the frequencies of tests. Where the former is high and the latter is low it will be seen as a problem.

The rationale behind the testing programme is to provide information for the patient so that they can become more aware of variations in blood-sugar levels due to diet, exercise or time of day and adjust their injections accordingly. None the less, both sides treat the figures as an occasion for medical judgment leading to praise, blame or excuses as appropriate. In turn, the testing figures are often more complete in the days immediately preceding the clinic visit. Frequently, the doctor will turn back a page and remark on 'all the empty spaces'.

A parallel is with a visit to the dentist when you may look after your teeth particularly carefully immediately before. As with the dental visit, although both parties theorize the condition of your teeth or blood-sugar level as your own problem to be assessed and acted upon yourself, none the less the practitioner's judgment will be treated as crucial, asserting the moral worth or otherwise of your performance. So both diabetic and dental patients hope to be 'let off lightly' by the practitioner. Once again, the dilemma of the balance between autonomy and professional control is neatly illustrated. Being responsible for your own health, the cherished aim of much health education literature, *may* amount to little more than becoming a target for the degradation ceremonies that are feasible in character work.

As a result of the evaluation of these figures, a series of things may happen. The doctor may suggest a new programme of testing which may be more realistic in the light of the patient's past behaviour. Diet may be discussed in the same terms, calling upon the health visitor's knowledge of meal preparation at home. This may lead on to a teaching session where the child is asked to say what would happen with hypothetical changes in diet or insulin dosage. The aim here is to check the patient's competence in the self-regulation of her condition. The sites of injections may also be examined for the same reason and advice given on varying them. Finally, again drawing upon the inside knowledge of the health visitor, some attempt may be made to explore family relations. The issue of 'nagging' by anxious parents often surfaces. It parallels the way in which health professionals may also be constituted as authority figures by these children. This kind of problem is something of which this doctor was only too aware. I will examine shortly his 'negotiating' strategy for handling it.

Disposals usually centre around a newly negotiated programme of diet, testing or insulin dosage. A follow-up appointment, usually of three to four months, is arranged, with the child sometimes being asked to attend earlier for a glycosylated haemoglobin test so that the results are available at the next consultation. Only in two cases was admission as an in-patient considered. In one case, the child's control had been consistently very poor; in the other it was suggested that he might be admitted to be given a 'hypo' under proper care. The aim was to overcome his fear of 'hypos' which had prevented him from raising his insulin dosage when appropriate.

In the context of this chronology of the consultation, I have identified a number of interactional particulars which distinguish diabetic clinics from other adolescent clinics. I will call these as follows: attributions of theoreticity, locating actions in a moral framework, discussing family relations, discussing the patient's psychology and, finally, negotiating outcomes. Some of these features have been identified in other clinics for adolescents — attributions of theoreticity seem to be a central feature of cleft-palate clinics (see Chapter Seven). Others are less common: a serious discussion of family relations would not normally seem to be appropriate in many other clinics given the predominance of the rule of 'politeness is all' (Strong, 1979b); a moral framework might be central to parents' conceptions of their behaviour or to doctors working in such areas as drug-abuse or alcoholism but it would not usually arise in discussions of purely physical disorders. What is important here, however, is the combination of these five elements into a 'ceremonial order' (Strong, 1979b) which reveals the double-edged nature of appeals to patient autonomy and responsibility.

1. Theoreticity
It is standard practice in diabetic-care to encourage patients to understand and to treat their disease. This is reflected in the educational process that occurs during the in-patient stay after diabetes has been identified. It is recognized that the parents — usually the mother — will be centrally involved up to, say, the age of ten. However, as the child enters her teens, she is treated quite openly as the person to whom medical encounters are directed and the person who should be making the decisions regarding her health-care.

'Theoreticity', then, refers to the attribution of the capacity of rational thought, including the ability to perceive and choose between alternative courses of action (McHugh, 1970).

In the early stages, there will be an attempt to wean the child away from dependence on parents. For instance, in the case of Rajiv, a boy of 14:

(NT:17.7)
HV = Health Visitor; M = Mother
HV: Rajiv, you're doing the testing?
M: Sometimes
HV: Rajiv, it's *your* urine. [*To mother*] He's a young man now. Come on Rajiv do your own wees. It's a bit undignified. It's not your Mum's job.

The issue of the responsibilities of age again surfaces in a consultation with Murray (M), aged 15, who lives in a Children's Home where the staff are reluctant to vary his dosage of insulin:

(NT:15.1)
D: What do you feel about making the decisions?
M: I'm getting to know a lot.
D: So it may be time for you to make the decisions. You're fifteen and a half now. But if you're in doubt you could ask P (the health visitor)
       . . .
D: You're old enough to tell when to put it up.

Overall in twenty-three out of the thirty-three consultations observed at the new town clinic, overt attributions of theoreticity were made. A typical exception was a consultation with a twelve year old, attending for the first time, where management of the diabetes was largely treated in terms of an alliance between the child, her parents and the doctor. Also the educationally subnormal boy of thirteen was sometimes not granted theoretic status, the discussion taking place largely between his mother and the doctor. Even he, however, was reminded on one occasion by the health visitor that he must eventually take charge of his testing: 'You're growing up. You're going to have to do it'. (NT:16.10).

In these clinics then, for quite understandable reasons, patients will tend to be treated as theoretic actors whether they like it or not. The assumption was that making decisions and considering their consequences was for the patients' own good as in this further comment to Murray:

(NT:18.9)
D: Do you know that you're doing the testing for you rather than for me. So you can adjust your insulin. If you only adjusted your insulin every time you came here it wouldn't make sense.

2. The Moral Framework

Once the patient is defined as an active decision-maker, she gains autonomy at the cost of being morally responsible for her actions. If rewards and sanctions are the means of maintaining discipline with young children, then the production of feelings of guilt is a subtle means of control when they are granted autonomy, as these two instances show:

> (NT:11.9)
> D: So long as you know that smoking is not good for diabetic people
> (NT:16.10)
> HV: So we won't nag you. Unless you do it you won't be growing right

Failing to carry out tests and their results when done lead on to implicit moral charges and to expressions of disappointment likely to be associated with the production of guilt. For instance, after a poor blood-test result:

> HV: Over 22
> M: Oh (looks glum)

And later:

> D: Yes, I was hoping that you would have had the (glycosylated) test done
>   [*Murray's testing book is examined*]
> D: Yes, it's just that you've done no urine tests since December and we haven't had any early morning tests (NT:15.1).

Blame can however turn into praise — the doctor later says that Murray's testing programme is 'not going too badly'. Another example of praise, this time within more explicit moral framework ('reformed character') later leads into implied moral charges:

> (NT:11.9)
> J = June
> D: So no sugar in the urine
> HV: No, she's a reformed character
>   [...]
> D: Are you keeping to a reasonable diet or do you just go free?
> J: No I'm keeping to it a bit better now
>   [...]
> D: What about your testing? Have you got any tests for us?
> J: No
> D: When was the last time you did a test?
> J: Not since I was on holiday

Sometimes the interrogation on the blood-test results leads to an attempt to get the patient to condemn herself out of her own mouth:

(NT:18.9)
S = Sylvia M = Mother
D: Well, you've got the record today. 22 per cent
       [...]
D: Would you say the control's good?
S: I don't know
D: Come on!
M: It was good but it's gone off lately
       [...]
D: Well the control's a bit up and down isn't it?
S: Yes

The contrast between the patient's own test-results and what is known from hospital-administered tests provides an important moral lever for medical staff. A very powerful moral charge in this context is cheating via 'cooking the books'. The possibility of such cheating is mentioned in this statement after a big difference has been found between home and hospital test figures:

(NT:20.11)
HV: It's not that we don't believe you, Christine. Some children I wouldn't believe

The following examples of comments made after other patients have left the consulting room show such non-belief:

(NT:16.10)
D: He used to invent results. I find him very frustrating to deal with
(NT:18.9)
D: His voice is getting very guilty. He was caught out
HV: I don't believe a thing

The only case of an implied charge of lying being made, clarified by the child's father (F), arises in this consultation with Alan (A), a boy of fourteen:

(NT:16.10)
D: Alan, these (figures) look too good to be true. Is that right Alan?
A: No
F: What he means is have you been making them up?
       [*no response*]
       [...]
D: Does anybody check them with you?
A: Sometimes
D: Well I think all we can say is that it's unlikely that the results really indicate your control
       [*Alan is fiddling with his sweater*]

In fully twenty-eight out of these thirty-three consultations some sort of moral framework is used in the interpretation of test results. Most of the deviant cases are easily explicable: the twelve year old new patient is barely accorded theoreticity and so cannot be held fully responsible for her actions yet. Again a later consultation with June occurs after she has had a hypoglycaemic attack the day before and reassurance rather than evaluation of her actions follows.

More frequently, however, the moral framework employed comes to constitute the consultation as a kind of trial for the patient in which she is to be held accountable for her actions. It should be stressed that the medical staff here are aware of the possible negative consequences of interrogating their patients as this brief comment to a sixteen year old makes clear:

(NT:15.1)
D: How would you like us to carry out these clinic visits? Sometimes we feel like policemen

The medical staff become policemen as an unintended consequence of their desire to recognize their patients' autonomy, while being committed to their professional role of the detection and treatment of disease. A technical advance, in the form of the glycosylated haemoglobin test, has highlighted the potential conflict between self-regulation of diabetes and medical control. On the surface, the test gives useful information about blood-sugar levels over a two-month period. In practice, it underlines the ability of medical staff to 'see through' patients' behaviour and to dispense praise or blame.

3. Family Relations

As Strong (1979b) has argued, most British NHS consultations take on a 'bureaucratic' format in which doctors limit themselves to highly specialized functions. In this format, the 'body' is an appropriate topic for medical discourse, family relations are not. This split between public and private realms helps to explain why, until recently, casualty doctors seemed reluctant to enquire too deeply into the causes of children's injuries.

In these clinics, family relations were topicalized in fourteen out of thirty-three consultations. This breaching of the bureaucratic format seems to arise because of the recognition by medical staff that their inadvertent 'policing' of patients may mirror, on a smaller scale, what is happening in the home. While doctors *can* limit their involvement with their patient to purely bureaucratic forms, no such space is available to parents. Cultural norms of parental responsibility, revealed most clearly when they are infringed (as in child abuse cases), are given an added twist by the issues of diet, testing, and injecting that are the responsibilities of the diabetic child/parent. When children stray from 'the straight and narrow' responsible adults must intervene:

(NT:16.10)
D: If Tessa is going on the straight and narrow, we'll see her again in
       four months

Being responsible means sternness and policing when appropriate:

(NT:18.9)
       [*Discussion of health visitor's daughter's work, checking up on
       Youth Opportunity Scheme participants*]
D: So your daughter has to act as a policeman
HV: Just like Mum
M: Sometimes you do have to be a bit stern

In such circumstances, the space that society demands be given for
teenagers to develop their autonomy can be circumvented by the
fulfilment of proper adult responsibilities. The uneasy tension
between these conflicting demands is neatly brought out in this
exchange:

(NT:16.10)
       [*The doctor is considering what to do about Tessa, aged 15, whose
       control 'isn't so good'*]
M: She's a big girl
D: She's in-between. There's a bit of her wanting you to take an interest
M: Oh I do. For her own sake. She's growing up fast

Using the insight he has gained in trying to walk the tightrope between
autonomy and control, the doctor here tries to act as a kind of honest
broker. This sometimes involves elliptical attempts to ask teenagers
about family relations:

(NT:17.7)
J = June
       [*Doctor has just gone out to speak to June's mother after June had
       said she didn't want her to attend the consultation*]
D: Sounds like you're having a tough time with your Mum
J: She keeps me in
       [...]
D: I'm going to talk to your Mum about not getting on to you about
       your diabetes

An alternative strategy is to encourage the patient to negotiate an
agreement with the family, while the doctor keeps out of the picture.
For instance, after Martin (M) has conceded that his poor control
might be because he is 'digging in his heels' with his Mum:

(NT:15.1)
D: So would it be worth having an agreement with your Mum and Dad
       about your diabetes?
M: Yes, it doesn't work when they start the discussion
       [...]

D: OK so I think the most important thing to do is to discuss this with
      your parents
      [...]
D: I think the best thing is for us not to have any communication with
      your parents, not to go behind your back plotting to get the better of
      you

In cases like this, the doctor moves entirely beyond the limits of a
purely organic version of medicine, surveying and intervening in
family relations. Ironically, just like parents he must find a middle
way between futile nagging and what society would see as an
'irresponsible' laissez-faire attitude.[3]

4. Psychology
It is likely that doctors generally prefer to stay with an organic version
of medicine partly because it is their own safe territory and also
because of the intractable problems of the social and psychological
world protected, as it is, by the British norm of politeness. This doctor
goes further than most by enquiring into family relations. However,
total surveillance would require investigation of the teenager's
psychology. Only rarely is this explored here — understandably, given
the lack of response shown in this example with Rajiv (R), aged 14:

(NT:19.1)
D: Do you like coming here?
R: No
D: Why not?
      [*Rajiv shrugs his shoulders*]
D: Is it because we embarrass you?
      [*No response and the doctor changes the subject*]

At the suburban clinic, where there is barely any questioning of
patients' motives, an exception arose when one patient, Joan (J) aged
14, was visibly very miserable, having been told that her insulin dosage
was to be increased. The doctor tries to elicit some explanation
without success and changes the subject:

(S:12.2)
M = Mother J = Joan
D: You don't look so happy about it. What's the matter?
J: [*looking down*] Nothing
D: Any hypos at all?
      [*no response*]
D: Are you a bit cross about the number of tests you're having to do
      recently?
J: No
      [...]
D: The blood sugar is really too high
      [*Joan looking miserable*]

M: We have to fight this all the way
D: One or two units, does this really upset you?
      [*Joan is looking down and fiddling with her coat*]
D: All I want to do is to increase your morning Monotard to 28 and the
      evening we'll just increase the Actrapid. That'll just get things over.
      Make them a little smoother
      [*Joan is crying*]
D: Is it the volume in the needle?
      [*Joan is still crying*]
D: [*discusses injection sites with Joan's mother*]

As Joan's mother says, 'we have to fight this all the way'. When it
comes to understanding teenagers, or still worse, encouraging
particular courses of action, doctors and parents may make little
progress. In this situation, it is tempting to treat the norm that
encourages teenagers' own autonomy ('learning by experience') as an
escape-clause freeing adults from the responsibility of intervening in
the child's life.

5. Negotiations

One way of balancing the demands of autonomy and responsibility is
to negotiate a 'contract' based on balancing the patient's perceived
needs with the adult's knowledge of the consequences of courses of
action (or inaction). Earlier, we saw the doctor in the new town clinic
suggesting that his patient come to such an 'agreement' with his
parents. In a majority of these consultations, eighteen out of thirty-
three, a negotiating format is used to work out the patient's own
treatment of their diabetes, particularly their programme of testing.
In this case, a contract looks very much like a last resort:

(NH:17.7)
J = June
D: What should we do about your diabetes? Because you've not been
      doing your testing
      [*no response*]
D: I know at the moment you're feeling sod all this altogether
J: Don't know
D: Would it help if we got off your back?
      [*no response*]
D: Can we make a deal? If you will do some testing twice a week for two
      weeks. If at the end of that four lots of testing P (health visitor) can
      see you

It is unclear here whether June is a partner to this agreement. In this
other example, Tessa seems actively opposed:

(NT:16.10)
T = Tessa

D: I think you ought to have a realistic plan. Twice a week, three times a day. What do you think? Isn't that a bit more realistic for you?

T: [*shrugs*]

D: I'm being generous

. . .

HV: Why don't you just pick two days?

T: Can't be bothered [*looking down*]

Only in one case is the testing programme genuinely self-imposed:

(NT:18.1)

M = Martin

D: Well, what sort of testing would you like to do? Something that's realistic to you

M: Well I could do . . . (suggests testing routine)

D: OK so you think that's reasonable

I will shortly look at the policy implications of patient-defined or negotiated programmes. Compared to the built-in conflict between purely formal assertions of the patient's autonomy or theoreticity and consultations which come to take on a policing function, negotiation seems to offer one practical solution to the doctor's (and parents') dilemma.

Given these dilemmas, how do the doctors I have observed cope? Table 3 shows the varying policy directions used by a New Town doctor with four of the patients on whom I have data from several consultations. In all cases, 'control' improved during the period of the study, although I would make no claims about the representativeness of these four cases. In each case, some attempt at negotiation of testing or treatment was made but this sometimes occurred side-by-side with a policing role. Despite great efforts, little seems to have been achieved, from the doctor's point of view, in improving family relations or in understanding the patient's motives.

Styles of Diabetes Care

The 'negotiating' style just discussed was unique to the new town clinic. I will conclude this description of the clinics with an attempt to depict three contrasting styles of diabetes-care which I observed in both clinics. Each may be seen as an attempt to cope with the dilemmas just considered.

1. Policing

Here the emphasis is on getting good data about the patient's control through investigating the 'truth' of the patient's own figures. An attempt is made to impose rules of good behaviour. Two consultations with Gordon, aged fifteen, illustrate this policing style.

TABLE 3:   Medical Interventions over Several Consultations

Patient	Age	Consultation Number	History	Form of Intervention
Murray	14½	(1)	Lives in Children's Home Poor glycosylated haemoglobin test results	Interrogation about conflict with Murray's own test figures Statement that diabetes Murray's own problem
	15	(2)	Better glycosylated haemoglobin result Doing more testing	Negotiation of testing programme Modest congratulations
Aidan	13	(1)	ESN but has come on own today Poor control	Short consultation Aidan leaves in tears after refusing blood test
		(2)	Mother present Control still poor	Attempts to convince Aidan to do more testing Persuades reluctant mother to increase insulin amounts
		(3)	Been in casualty after a hypo Control better	Negotiates admission to Ward Attempts to convince Aidan to do more testing
		(4)	Mother concerned about his mental and physical well-being	
Martin	16	(1)	Problematic control Lack of regular testing	Interrogation Statement that diabetes is Martin's own problem Suggests Hg test
		(2)	Glycosylated haemoglobin test result poor	Exploration of Martin's feelings and of family 'nagging' — suggests Martin discusses it with them Negotiation of testing programme
		(3)	Glycosylated haemoglobin result slightly better	Encouragement of Martin to change his insulin dose himself Re-assurance about hypos
			Family relations not improved	
June	16	(1)	Good control but poor testing Rows with mother	Negotiates testing programme Encouragement to adjust dosage herself
		(2)	Just had hypo More rows with mother	Exploration of eating habits Negotiation of revised testing programme Unsuccessful attempt to explore family relations
		(3)	Glycosylated haemoglobin test indicates better control Not kept to testing 'contract'	Explanation about complications resulting from bad control Encouragement to adjust insulin dosage herself Re-assurance about hypos

Although Gordon has taken the initiative to vary his own insulin levels between consultations, the doctor concentrates on criticizing him for his smoking habit and pointing out his poor blood test results. The following sequence about Gordon's testing programme illustrates well the investigative stance that the doctor takes. Although Gordon is not actually accused of lying, the doctor's scepticism will be readily apparent:

```
(NT:19.3)
G = Gordon
D:  Are you doing them one a day or are you doing them . . .
G:  Two or three a day
D:  Two or three every day?
G:  Well not every day
D:  Hh hmm
G:  You know something like (2.0 second pause) one day, miss a day and
      then again
          (1.00 second pause)
D:  Uh I mean I'm impressed. I've not er been critical er been impressed if
      you've been doing these
```

2. Avoidance

Another way of handling the dilemmas of caring for these patients is to stay largely in the traditional organic realm of medicine, to concentrate on diagnosing and prescribing and to avoid recognizing psychological and social issues. The consultations at the suburban clinic tended to take this form. As Figure 6 shows, the distinct interactional forms present in the new town clinic were found much less frequently here.

TABLE 4
Interactional Forms at Two Clinics

Form	Suburban Clinic (n = 14)	New Town Clinic (n = 33)
Attribution of theoreticity	4	23
Moral framework	6	28
Discussion of family relations	0	14
Discussion of patient's psychology	1	3
Negotiating format	2	18

Three factors may explain these contrasting figures. First, unlike the new town consultations, they were not part of a 'special' clinic set aside for problem cases. It may have been, then, that the patients seen here did not have the kinds of problems that would justify a departure from the normal (limited) medical role. Certainly, as already noted, the mean length of consultations was only half that at the new town clinic. Second, there was no separate adolescents' clinic here. Given a patient load where a baby may be followed by a seventeen year old, it may be difficult for doctors to switch to a more open-ended role. Finally, during the period of observation, three different doctors (a consultant, a registrar and a locum) saw patients. Consequently, as is often the case in hospital practice, doctors lacked continuous contact over time with patients. This may have led to an imperfect overall picture of the patient's circumstances which would already have been limited by the lack of a health visitor with home contact with the families. The consultation with Joan (on p. 217) is a good example of how doctors at the suburban clinic do not pursue family and psychological issues to a very great extent. Even with some evidence of problems in this area, the consultation lasts the standard twelve minutes, during which there is only a limited attempt to explore the source of these problems. (Note that this is not to imply that this is necessarily a flawed consultation. Quite apart from the dubious politics of surveillance, there is little evidence that the greater involvement of the new town doctor in these matters has any outcome which the suburban doctor would regard as positive.)

3. Self-Regulation

Although the usually stated aim of diabetes-care is patient self-regulation, we have already seen the dilemmas that this can create for doctors. Nevertheless in one or two consultations we see the doctor attempting to allow the patient to define her own version of the 'problem and its management'. Where the discussion is based on the patient's expressed needs, then policing ceases to be appropriate.

Tessa, aged fifteen, has poor control of her diabetes. At the first consultation I observed an attempt was made to get her to suggest a programme of testing that she could live with. Six months afterwards, it was not clear that she had kept to it and her control was still not good. Although there is little attempt to check the veracity of the figures recorded in her book, the consultation concentrates on asking Tessa to specify her feelings about her control and about what she would like to do about changing her monitoring pattern and dosage. It becomes clear that Tessa would like to do more but she is scared to alter her dosage on her own. Consequently, Tessa (T) requests help:

> D: But you need to get some information to help you make the decision
>   eh love?
> T: I'd rather someone help me so I'd know what I was doing

and a little later:

(NT:2.4)
HV: Wouldn't it be worth you finding out for yourself which bit needs putting up?
  T: It would yeah (2.0 second pause) but I'm still gonna need help.

Here medical control is re-established but on the basis of the patient's own request. The patient is encouraged about the prospects of successful control and a new testing programme is negotiated on the basis of options offered by the doctor. The consultation lasts twenty-seven minutes, slightly longer than the average for this clinic.

Reforming the Clinic?
Despite my emphasis on the dilemmas and problems in these consultations, it is important to stress that, by the standards of the literature, the new town clinic is an example of good practice. In particular, the style of 'self-regulation' follows very closely the approach recently recommended by two US paediatricians, offering:

> ... realistic, direct discussions ... between the health professional and the teenager, discussions that empathize with the adolescent, acknowledge his feelings of difference (and) encourage appropriate experimentation with the regulation of his own therapy program. (Cerreto and Travis, 1984:706)

Moreover, the negotiating format we have observed fits neatly with psychological theories of compliance, as advocated by Rosenbloom (1984) By offering realistic goals, rather than by making unrealistic demands, a vicious circle of resistance is avoided and compliance, he maintains, is more likely (Figure 1).

FIGURE 1
Consulting Styles and Patient Response
(adapted from Rosenbloom, 1984: 112–13)

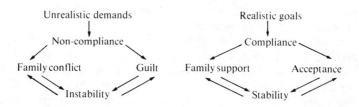

Outside the consultation the new town clinic offers a support system which is fully in accord with current medical thinking. In particular, the use of a health visitor (cf. Jones, 1983) who maintains a link between the hospital and the home and who co-ordinates an educational programme for her clients (cf. Cerreto and Travis, 1984).

This offers not only essential information on diet and the practicalities of testing and injecting but competitions and holidays organized through the British Diabetic Association.

Up till this point, it would appear that we are faced with an easy choice between two practices. This may be simply illustrated in Figure 2.

FIGURE 2
Two Styles of Medical Intervention

Practice A		Practice B
Moral charges	versus	Emphasizing patient's choices
Policing/the search for truth	versus	Negotiating contracts
Surveillance	versus	Self-regulation

Practice A looks like the 'old-fashioned' version of organic medicine. It treats the patient as passive and seeks to impose medically-defined outcomes. Conversely, Practice B has excellent 'progressive' credentials. It represents a newly emerging 'whole person medicine', based on the latest psychological thinking, which respects patients' own expertise and self-knowledge.

It would now follow that the difficulties and conflicts generated in the new town clinic arise from the imperfect adoption by the doctor of Practice B. If only he could remove the traces of 'old-fashioned' organic medicine from his questions, he would avoid these conflicts and offer a self-maintained form of diabetic control. This, indeed, was the doctor's response to reading a first draft of this chapter. At subsequent clinics, he was observed to stick much more consistently to the 'progressive' line. Instead of announcing test figures and querying patients' accounts, he was much more likely to stick to a negotiating format in which patients were actively involved in requesting information and making decisions.

Unfortunately, there are at least two reasons why matters are not quite so simple. First, medicine is constituted by a distinctive (albeit changing) body of knowledge associated with a set of clinical routines. To ask of medicine that it should cease to survey objectified bodies or give up its search for hidden truths concealed in organic processes is to demand that medicine should dissolve itself. This, of course, would be unacceptable not only to doctors but also to lay people who demand of medicine precisely that it should provide such truths. This, then, is why, against all his best intentions, traces of what I have called Practice A remained in the new town doctor's behaviour. Despite all the latest psychological texts that lined his consulting room, despite what he took to be the advice of a researcher offered access for that very purpose, he could not constitute doctoring entirely as non-directive therapy.[4]

The second complication arises from a problem I have already noted. I pointed out that attributions of theoreticity are doubled-edged. On the one hand, the theoretic subject is free to respond and to choose. On the other, she is *forced* to respond and to choose and is held to account for those responses and choices. So the greater involvement of the patient in the consultation is both emancipating and constraining. The mistake is to treat surveillance purely as a function of professionals treating patients as *objects* of the clinical gaze. Surveillance works no less efficiently when we are constituted as free *subjects* whose freedom includes the obligation to survey ourselves. A brief return to one consultation will, I hope, illustrate what I mean.

The Normal, Free Subject

> We are in the society of the teacher−judge, the doctor−judge, the educator−judge, the 'social-worker'−judge; it is on them that the universal reign of the normative is based; and each individual, wherever he may find himself, subjects to it his body, his gestures, his behaviour, his aptitudes, his achievements. (Foucault, 1979:304)

What Foucault calls 'the universal reign of the normative' refers to how effects of power are least visible when free subjects define and assess themselves through professionally-defined bodies of knowledge. In the consultation discussed below, the patient volunteers versions of his behaviour and motivation based on socially approved standards. Moreover, the doctor largely avoids overt policing. Instead, he offers the opportunity for the patient himself to produce the professionally desired response which the doctor then supports and reinforces.

Gordon, aged fifteen and a half, is one of the 'problem patients' seen in the new town clinic. He lives with his divorced mother and during the consultation reveals that his older brother — also a diabetic — has left home and cannot be traced. His diabetic control has been defined as poor. Here is an extract from early on in the consultation following three minutes of assessment and discussion of Gordon's (G) height and weight:

> (NT:19.3)
> D: OK (4.0) When we (0.5) did your blood test last time in September (0.5) the level was (0.5) *not* terribly good. I mean it wasn't (0.5) the worst level we've seen but it could be better
> G: Yes
> D: That's why and we made some changes with your doses last time
> G: Yeah
> D: And I thought it would be useful to check it again to see whether there's been any improvement. Okay?
> G: Yeah

```
*D:  Do you think the control's better?
*G:  Yes I do
```

In *Discipline and Punish*, Foucault (1979) describes how the 'individual' emerged past the threshold of description. For modern medicine (law, prison administration, social work) each individual becomes a 'case' and the case:

> is no longer, as in casuistry or jurisprudence, a set of circumstances defining an act and capable of modifying the application of a rule; it is the individual as he may be described, judged, measured, compared with others, in his very individuality. (Foucault, 1979:191)

So the details of Gordon's blood-sugars must be carefully measured and his individual needs for insulin closely assessed. But surveillance and expert decision-making are alone insufficient. This version of modern medicine 'not only allows the patient to speak as an experiencing person but needs, demands and incites him to speak' (Arney and Bergen, 1984:46). Gordon himself must speak about his diabetic control. All the clinical tests in the world are insufficient without Gordon's own participation and self-assessment (in the asterisked exchange). So Gordon is not pounded into submission or silenced; rather he is incited to speak. He is not repressed; rather he is provided with, and encouraged to demonstrate, his own aptitudes and skills. External surveillance still takes place but not in order to impose purely external standards. In the discussion of smoking, which immediately follows the previous extract, it is clear that, as in Bentham's panopticon, all aspects of the individual are to be made visible. But the strategy is normalization rather than repression. The panopticon works most efficiently when the prisoner turns the warder's gaze upon himself. Here is the relevant passage:

```
 D:  OK. Um (2.0) are you still smoking?
 G:  Well (1.0) not really now
 D:  You were smoking three or four a /day in /September
 G:                                    /yeah  /yeah
 D:  About the same still or
 G:  Well (1.0) hardly ever now
 D:  Why?
 G:  I don't know, I've just stopped
 D:                  /(          )
*G:                  /(          ) Well I don't get much money and I haven't
     got enough money to waste (0.5) really
*D:  Yeah (0.5) Well I, I agree with you it is a waste and
 G:  Mm
 D:  I wouldn't it's not particularly healthy particularly for you (1.0) So
     you mean you smoke other people's cigarettes or (0.5) or are you, have
     you an occasional one of your own
```

G: Occasional one of me own, if someone gives me one
D: If someone else
G: Yeah (1.0) two (   ) after school
   (3.0)

Notice how the doctor makes no moral judgment on the 'facts' as reported by Gordon. Instead, he pursues why Gordon 'hardly' ever smokes. But Gordon's initial response ('I don't know, I've just stopped') does not satisfy the doctor. Gordon must provide a reason for his change of behaviour and this reason must demonstrate Gordon's self-surveillance according to the appropriate moral standards. Only when (in the asterisked passage) Gordon refers to spending money on cigarettes as ' waste' does the doctor start to make moral judgments. But his moralizing draws attention to and embellishes Gordon's own formulations.

This consultation took place after the new town doctor had read an earlier draft of this chapter. As I have already noted, this was followed by an emphasis in his consultations on self-regulation (Practice B) rather than policing (Practice A). But policing does not disappear entirely. The extract concludes with an attempt by the doctor to establish the 'real facts' about Gordon's smoking behaviour which his earlier statement ('hardly ever') glosses over. However, Gordon's further elaboration, vague as it is, does not lead to an additional interrogation. What seems to be most important is that Gordon should speak about his smoking rather than that the 'real facts' should finally be established. In what Foucault has called 'the politics of truth', the facts of individual behaviour are less important than the discovery and *self-recognition* of the person behind the behaviour.

The doctor now elicits Gordon's current dose of insulin and expresses surprise at the amount. It appears that Gordon has adjusted his dosage himself in a reportedly successful attempt to stop bed-wetting. In the light of Gordon's poor control of his diabetes, the doctor implies that the dosage of one form of insulin may now be too low. But Gordon's own change of dosage is not criticized. These encounters are seen by such doctors as concerned with encouraging self-regulation by the patient. When, towards the end of the consultation, the doctor suggests an increase in insulin, Gordon is asked to assess himself ('if you find that they're not being satisfactory'). All he is expected to do is to call the health visitor to discuss 'how you're going to change them again'.

Immediately after Gordon's revelation of his self-assessed change of insulin dosage, the doctor learns that Gordon has left behind his testing book containing the results of his home tests of blood and urine.

D: Um (0.5) have you got some tests there?
G: I left them at home this morning because I was doing I *done* an exam

    today and I was in a bit of a panic
D: Oh dear what exam was that?
    [*discussion of exam and Gordon's performance in it*]

Unlike many of the earlier consultations, there is no suggestion that the doctor is policing the patient. Gordon's account goes completely unchallenged, despite the already stated medical view that patients' records are unreliable and likely to be 'cooked'. Instead, the doctor simply asks for Gordon's own recollection of his test results (in a passage a part of which was discussed earlier):

    D: *Okay* (0.5) so what sort of results are you getting then?
    G: Well (   ) average between ten and six (1.0) not too bad
    D: Blood blood sugars you're talking /about?
    G: /Yeah blood sugars
    D: When when are you doing them mostly?
    G: *Well* I'm doing them before my breakfast, before my tea and er
         (   ) now and again I'm doing them before bed and weekends
         I'm doing them at dinner time and that
    D: Are you doing them one a day or are you doing them
    G: Two to three a day
  *D: Two or three *every day*?
    G: Well not *every* day
    D: Hh hmm
    G: You know something like (2.0) one day miss a day and then again
         (1.0)
  *D: Uh I mean I'm impressed. I've not er been critical er been impressed if
         you've been /doing these (   )
    G: /well I realised (0.5) if I done as I've been told and that
         then I feel a lot better inside
    D: Do you? Do you /really?
    G: /yeah
    D: Feel more energetic
    G: Better than, it's better than /feeling
    D: /Mm. But er so the results are all between
         six what did you say?
    G: Between six and ten but sometimes it goes over ten /it depends
    D: /Mm
    G: What I'm doing really

In the asterisked utterances, the doctor clearly does revert to the policing role found in his earlier consultations. Gordon's story of his testing regimen is closely interrogated ('if you've been doing these'). However, the interrogation melts away with Gordon's revelation that 'I feel a lot better inside' if 'I done as I've been told'. The doctor cannot restrain his admiration ('Do you? Do you really?'). Gordon is saying that he has internalized the medical model: he surveys himself.

I am reminded of Foucault's statement of the major effect of the panopticon:

to induce in the inmate a state of conscious and permanent visibility that assures *the automatic functioning of power*. So to arrange things that the surveillance is permanent in its effects, even if it is discontinuous in its action; that the perfection of power should tend to render its actual exercise unnecessary; that this architectural apparatus should be a machine for creating and sustaining a power relation independent of the person who exercises it; in short, that the inmates should be caught up in a power situation of which *they themselves are the bearers*'. (Foucault, 1979:201, my emphasis)

Practical Implications

At this point, we seem to have come full circle. Reforming the clinic merely appears to reinstate new and, perhaps more subtle, strategies of power. This can be underlined by a brief review of each of the three areas where reforms in diabetic care have been suggested: namely, changing doctors' consulting styles, broadening the care team, and introducing patient support groups.

1. Changing Consulting Styles

I have already noted the new town clinic doctor's change from a 'policing' to a 'self-regulating' style. This is fully in accord with the suggestions made by the psychologists Gillespie and Bradley (1983). They reject what they call 'the traditional confrontational interview' where the patient is told the problem and the solution(s): if the patient fails to comply, then he is defined as 'at fault'. Gillespie and Bradley call instead for a 'motivation enhancing interview'. Here, for instance, the doctor enquires what problems the patient herself has perceived with her diabetes, what she proposes to do about it and whether she would like to see the results of laboratory tests.

Unfortunately, this returns us again to Foucault's 'power situation of which they (in this case the patients) are the bearers'. For discipline as a modality of power is not geared to repression but to the inculcation of aptitude and skills (Foucault, 1979: Part IV, Chapter 3). It is precisely concerned with the person behind the act and is economical and subtle in its functioning. Indeed it is in just such a disciplinary framework that one would expect doctors and psychologists to carry out experiments to alter behaviour and to correct and train individuals. The modern clinic, like the modern prison, is very much a laboratory of power and Gillespie and Bradley's well-meaning proposals resemble those of laboratory experimenters.

2. Broadening the Care Team

There is a broadening conventional wisdom that chronic patients, such as diabetics, need support outside the clinic setting. For instance, Aiken (1976) argues that doctors tend to focus on immediate symptoms and give less attention to the long-term care and adjustment needs of chronically-ill patients. She proposes that nurse practitioners can play a useful supporting role, visiting patients in their home to offer a friendly ear and serving as a patient-advocate in the clinic.

The work of the health visitor in the new town approximates this model. Her role did not seem to be defined as intrusive by either patients or families and she was observed to function as the kind of ombudsman suggested by Aiken. Certainly, the kind of role is less contestable than the suggested involvement of child psychiatrists (Smith, et al., 1984) or the practice of family therapy (Cerreto and Travis, 1984) both of which seem to constitute diabetic people as a deviant or problem group. However, friendly home visitors also clearly function as part of the medical team. They are both patient-advocates and also an additional clinic eye and ear. Broadening the care 'team' also therefore broadens the surveillance of the patient inside and outside the consulting room.

3. Support Groups

An alternative programme would seek to minimize professional involvement and to maximize self-help using peer-group support. One example is provided by the Young Leaders scheme used in Edinburgh (Steel, 1985): patients with good control are offered an adventure holiday together and asked to offer support to their peers when they return.

As Arney and Bergen (1984) note, the support group offers a face of medicine as 'unobtrusive, humane, even liberating' (p.107). At the same time, however, it synthesizes all aspects of the techniques of normalization. It allows individuality to be aired without judgment and enables experts, armed with knowledge of 'the trajectories that constitute the good life' to make the anxieties of the patient inert through normalization and positive imagery. For Arney and Bergen, then, following Foucault, the support group is not an alternative to medical power, it is the new form of medical power:

> the form that ties together the two lines of modern medical thought — that which individualizes and that which maps — and the form that joins together the individual, with his or her unique special concerns and problems, and the expert whose knowledge is redemptive (pp.107–8).

By now, readers with a practical involvement in diabetic care may be more than a little frustrated. Is any attempt to change care doomed to underline professional power?

The social control functions of the old-style medicine of 'policing' are immediately apparent. Yet it is now being argued that the new-style psychology of autonomy and self-expression creates a more subtle practice of 'normalization'. So the links between knowledge and power do not go away but merely take different forms.

This is not, however, just an account of how two paediatricians happen to run their clinics. The practices we have observed here are the end-product of a network of historical and institutional processes. Doctors are expected to be concerned about, say, kidney failure or blindness in diabetic people because their task, in part, is surveying objectified bodies. Especially where these patients are young, we demand that doctors act responsibly towards them. For instance, even the most non-interventionist strategies of diabetic care (e.g. Kinmonth, 1985) draw the line when the patient's life is threatened. It is wrong, then, to criticize medicine as a form of social control when that is partly what it is for.[5] Similarly, if we expect that 'adolescents' or 'young adults' should replace their parents as the source of accounts and opinions, it is because of widely diffused assumptions about the rights attached to advancing years.

The strains between Practice A and B in the new town clinic are the outcome of such historically-sedimented factors. On the one hand, the doctor cannot but be responsive to the psychological development and well-being of his patients. As in education's 'child-care' pedagogy (Walkerdine, 1984), paediatrics wants to concern itself with the 'monitoring . . . and facilitation of individual psychological capacities' (p.162). On the other hand, modern high-technology medical practice must be receptive to 'objective' assessments like the GHg test and to their implications for treatment.

It is not, then, as if doctors face a choice between such practices. Although the new town doctor may give rather more emphasis to overtly psychological strategies than the suburban doctor, both constitute their work through notions of responsibility *and* autonomy.

It would be entirely wrong, however, to view such notions and strategies as ideologies which should be stripped away to allow all concerned to express themselves more 'authentically'. Real subjects are constituted in discourses and these discourses, in turn, are predicated on institutionalized practices in medicine and education. As Walkerdine has put it in relation to the child-centred pedagogy:

> Neither the child nor the individual can be liberated by a medical stripping away of the layers of the social. Such a model assumes a psychological subject laid bare to be reformed in the new order. But if social practices are central to the very formation of subjectivity the laying bare is an impossibility . . . there is no pre-existent subject to liberate (1984:195).

So the dilemmas of medical practice are not to be resolved by constructing a new counter-discourse without any grounding in institutions or subjects. Nor does it pay to assume that any one existing discourse, such as 'child-centredness', is intrinsically more liberating than any other.

It is always a question of the relation between discourses which, in themselves, have no intrinsic value. As Foucault recognized, challenges to strategies of power arise within the very subject positions (or voices) that such discourses create. So a patient can interrupt a discourse of autonomy by a discourse of responsibility, demanding advice rather than self-expression as in the following exchange considered earlier:

HV: Wouldn't it be worth you finding out for yourself which bit needs putting up?
T: It would yeah (2.0) but I'm still gonna need help.

Here Tessa unknowingly follows Deleuze and Guattari's (1981) injunction considered in the previous chapter: she makes a line not a point, she does not sow but grafts. In the next chapter, we will see how the mothers of these young people articulate the responsibility-autonomy couplet.

Notes

1. This relates to the continuing medical concern with patient 'compliance' which extends over a wide range of treatments and illnesses. Gerry Stimson has suggested that it is worth considering why compliance is treated as less of an issue in certain types of treatment, e.g. patients at drug clinics get a urine test to measure compliance but not GP patients taking antibiotics. Of course, drug clinics take patient policing to further lengths than normally observed in diabetic clinics. Patients are nearly always assumed to lie about their condition and a urine test has a purely policing function because self-regulation is not tolerated.

2. Linnie Price has pointed out the similarities with obstetrics where 'objective measures' may be used to displace the mother's account. In both cases we can observe the use of the natural world to support the definitions of one set of actors (see Callon, 1986).

3. Phil Strong has noted that, in American hospitals, adolescents are not seen alone and it is normal for parents to attend until the age of eighteen. Hence a doctor–parent alliance may be much more common in American practice.

4. In the next chapter, we will see how cultural dilemmas similarly delimit the doctor–patient relationship.

5. I am grateful to Robert Dingwall for this way of expressing the argument.

10

Moral Versions of Parenthood: Charge-Rebuttal Sequences in Two Diabetic Clinics

> The study of family order turns on its representation, on its signs, and those whose rhetoric attempts to reveal it for what the latter take it surely to be.
> (Gubrium and Lynott, 1985: 150)

Introduction

The position of this chapter is that 'the study of the family turns on its representation, on its signs' (Gubrium and Lynott, 1985). It follows that to understand inter-generational relations we have no need to 'get inside' families to observe what they are 'really like' since family rhetoric is freely available in a range of settings.

I pursue this position via an analysis of audio-tapes of consultations at out-patient clinics for adolescent diabetics. The analysis is based on a method derived from E.C. Cuff's (1980) development of Harvey Sacks' (1972a, 1972b and 1974) work on Membership Categorization Devices.

My particular interest is how the relational pair mother/adolescent child is constituted by doctors and parents. I show that mothers who define their role in terms of 'responsibility' face the charge of failing to respect the child's 'autonomy' (and vice versa). I also show mothers' artful methods for holding off such charges and/or rebutting them. I conclude by examining the policy implications for medical work with adolescents and their parents.

The Doctor's Dilemma

In the previous chapter, I discussed a 'doctor's dilemma' that appears in a pointed way in the treatment of adolescent diabetic patients. Diabetes is a metabolic disorder resulting in an imbalance of blood-glucose levels. Where blood-glucose is too high (hyperglycaemia), people risk in the short-term only thirst, boils, or possibly coma and, in the long-term, may expect an increased risk of complications involving kidney damage, blindness or damage to limbs requiring amputation.

The doctor's dilemma arises in the following way. Medical knowledge provides for a precise way of establishing haemoglobin levels (via a laboratory blood test). It also offers a set of procedures that should help to maintain good 'control' of such levels (via insulin treatment, diet and exercise) and predictive statements about the likely association between poor control and future complications. As with other conditions, the *application* of medical knowledge to particular cases is often problematic. First, there is always a measure of perceived uncertainty. For instance, complications can arise where diabetic control has appeared to be successful. Or, alternatively, it may prove impossible to maintain good control despite the best efforts of doctor and patient.

A second problem in the application of medical knowledge is whether the patient follows the doctor's advice. The problem of 'patient compliance' arises because, with a few exceptions (drug-abusers, 'sectioned' mental patients), doctors are unable to impose their decisions on patients and, indeed, are prevented by cultural norms of 'politeness' from probing too deeply into the veracity of information that their patients offer.

Knowing what (as defined by medical knowledge) is in the patient's interest and yet being unable to ensure compliance thus provides the classic case of the doctor's dilemma. Yet the treatment of diabetic patients adds a further twist to this dilemma. Diabetes shares with many other chronic conditions a treatment programme aimed at self-assessment of symptoms and self-regulation of the disease. Moreover, the treatment cannot 'cure' the basic problem or preclude the possibility of complications. Consequently, compared to acute conditions where medical intervention can sometimes achieve rapid 'cures' for passive patients, the need for patient compliance is perceived to be far more extensive although the prospect of 'cure' is absent.

The practical requirement to make chronic patients play a substantial part in regulating their own condition is strengthened where that patient is between, say thirteen and eighteen. For 'teenagers', 'adolescents' or 'young adults' are perceived to be in the process of establishing their own identities. Adults then, whether parents or professionals like doctors, come under a culturally-imposed requirement, to encourage autonomy and self-expression. The snag is, of course, that society would also frown upon 'reckless' or 'irresponsible' teachers or doctors who allow a 'young adult' to engage in behaviour which they know is bad for him or her.

The doctor's dilemma with adolescent diabetics is, then, to strike a proper balance between culturally defined norms of 'teenage' autonomy and of professional responsibility. It is, obviously, another version of the dilemma that faces all adults when they deal with young people.

This dilemma arises most pointedly in parent–child relations. Any parent of a teenage child would recognize the potential conflict between acting 'responsibly' (often expressed as passing on one's accumulated experience) and respecting the child's need to express or find himself. This can produce a 'no-win' situation. To act 'responsibly' can lead to the charge of 'nagging'. Conversely, an emphasis on self-expression can be defined by others as uncaring 'permissiveness' and mean that parents can be sharply reminded that 'young adults' still need guidance and support.

Consider the following extract from a diabetic out-patient's clinic in a new town hospital (NT) outside London. Tessa, who is fifteen, has already been told by the doctor that her control 'isn't so good'. At this point, he turns to Tessa's mother (M):

(NT: 16.10)

1. D: How do you think she's getting on?
2. M: Very well (   ) We only have rows about her tests
3. D: (   )
4. M: I mean she has to see you, I don't. She's a big girl
5. D: She's in between. There's a bit of her wanting you to take an interest
6. M: Oh I do. For her own sake. She's growing up fast.

In this extract, Tessa's mother lays herself open to a charge of 'nagging', ('We only have rows about her tests'). Her next turn at talk, however, serves to pre-empt possible criticism by stressing the alternative cultural norms of self-expression appropriate to a 'big girl'. In itself, this is normally laudable according to cultural norms. The catch is that an emphasis on the young person's autonomy can lay oneself open to the charge of irresponsibility, as suggested by the doctor at Utterance 5.

Notice how, at Utterance 6, Tessa's mother's response exhibits her hearing of what the doctor says as a charge and offers a rebuttal: she does indeed, she says, 'take an interest'. I will return shortly to what I take to be the central role of charge-rebuttal sequences in doctor–parent talk here. At the moment, we need only note the neat solution that Tessa's mother goes on to provide to the dilemma of the contradictory cultural norms of 'autonomy' and 'responsibility'. She takes an interest in Tessa, she says, 'for her own sake' (responsibility). But she observes: 'She's growing up fast' (autonomy).

Tessa's mother shows an artful way of juggling with two incompatible principles. Where an assertion of one principle opens the way to a charge in terms of the other, the secret would appear to be to assert both simultaneously. Although illogical in practical terms (but then so is the simultaneous operation of both principles), it is discursively successful. At this point, the doctor stops grilling Tessa's mother, although he will observe to a health visitor after the consultation is over: 'She's a tough woman'.

The question is one of balance. At the other end of the spectrum, parents who simply assert the 'responsibility' principle find themselves reminded of the goal of patient autonomy. For instance, when Sheila (P), aged sixteen, is non-committal about her control, her mother (M) steps in to assert her own active monitoring of the situation.

(NT: 18.9)
    1. D: Would you say the control's good?
    2. P: I don't know
    3. D: (   ) come on
    4.   (2.0)
    5. M: It was good but I think it's gone off lately.

Shortly afterwards, she underlines the 'responsibility' principle applied to parenthood. Her comments arise after the health visitor reveals that her own daughter is a careers officer who has to check up on the working of Youth Opportunity schemes:

    D: So your daughter has to act as a policeman
    HV: Just like Mum
    M: Sometimes you do have to be a bit stern.

Notice that Sheila's mother's stress on responsibility (being 'a bit stern') appears to have been authorized by the health visitor's formulation of her own role as that of a policeman ('Just like Mum'). None the less, a little earlier, when the doctor had asked to see Sheila's testing book and her mother had produced it, the health visitor had defined this as unacceptable. She had pointedly taken the book from the mother's hand and passed it to Sheila for her to pass to the doctor. This little ceremony served to display that testing and keeping test results is the patient's own affair. So, although the subsequent talk affirmed the principle of parental responsibility, the ever-present backdrop was the incompatible principle of patient autonomy.

With younger children, say thirteen or less, as we shall see shortly, this latter principle may be partially waived. For instance, Lucy, aged thirteen remained silent through the first few minutes of her consultation at a suburban clinic (SC). However, when the doctor turned to injecting and testing, Lucy's mother was no longer allowed to act as the surrogate-patient.

(SC: 12.3)
    1. D: How how how are the injections going and how are the sugars going?
    2. M: Well she's just (   )
    3. D: [*to Lucy*] Why don't you tell me? Why don't *you* tell me?

    4. P: (softly) All right
    5.   (1.5)
    6. D: Come on why don't you show me?
    7. M: (softly) Show the doctor (   )
    8.   [*Lucy hands over her testing book*]

Even with a younger child, like Lucy, the principle of autonomy can
become central when the testing programme is discussed. From now
on, Lucy's mother will no longer speak on her behalf but, as at
Utterance 7, will follow the doctor's stated desire to make Lucy an
autonomous subject. Indeed, her 'Show the doctor' looks like another
neat solution to the interactive dilemma we have been considering.
For it seems to reformulate responsible parenthood in terms of
encouraging autonomy through carrying out appropriate adult
functions (such as diabetic patients passing on and discussing their test
results).

As medical staff see it, the major problem is usually too much
emphasis on the 'responsibility' ethic (hence nagging) rather than too
great a stress on 'autonomy' (hence disinterest). In this respect the
exchanges with the mothers of Lucy and Sheila are more typical than
those with Tessa's mother. However, it is important to bear in mind
that we are discussing discourse dilemmas and their resolution rather
than the psychological propensities of particular individuals (except
insofar as the latter are formulated by participants, as we saw in
Tessa's case). Therefore, we shall concentrate on the logic of charge-
rebuttal sequences rather than upon the dispositions of the parties
concerned. For, in the context of this logic, doctors and parents
repeatedly switch from one principle to another. And sometimes
parents find neat solutions to squaring the circle and appear to uphold
two contradictory principles at once.

As I noted in the previous chapter, the doctor's proposed remedy
for the perceived problem of 'nagging' is to propose that patients
should strike up a bargain with their parents. In the sequence below,
he suggests such a bargain, gearing what he says to the 'autonomy'
ethic for the 'agreement' will be initiated by the patient (Martin aged
sixteen). In the meantime, the doctor undertakes to respect the
patient's autonomy by having no independent dealings with his
parents.

    (NT: 15.1)
        1. D: Is it anything to do with (your conflict with) Mum? Are you
                 digging in your heels?
                 [. . .]
        2. D: So would it be worth having an agreement with your Mum and
                 Dad about your diabetes?

3. P: Yes it doesn't work when they start the discussion
       [. . .]

4. D: OK. So I think the most important thing to do is to discuss this
       with your parents [. . .] I think the best thing is for us not to
       have any communication with your parents. Not to go behind
       your back (plotting) to get the better of you.

The consultation below with June, also aged sixteen, has this same
feature of imputed 'nagging' by parents and a proposed bargain.
However, it differs from the one above in that the medical staff also
apply the 'responsibility' norm. First, the health visitor, at Utterance
5, tries to persuade June that nagging is the other side of the coin of
concern or responsibility. Second, the doctor himself opts for the
'responsibility' norm by proposing to talk directly to June's mother
rather than, as with Martin, leaving it to her to do the negotiation
(Utterance 6 below):

(NT: 17.7)

> [*June has said that she doesn't want her mother with her
> today. The doctor has just returned from speaking to June's
> mother.*]

1. D: Sounds like you're having a rough time with your Mum

2. P: (She keeps me in)
       [. . .]

3. HV: What use am I to you?

4. P: Helping me

5. HV: Your Mum's very frightened for you, you do know that? Why
        do you think she's nagging?
        [discussion of the 'bargain']

6. D: I'm going to talk to your Mum about not getting on to you
       about your diabetes.

So, medical staff, just as much as parents, can appeal to the
responsibility norm. As adults and professionals, they are open to the
charge of lack of interest as well as to the charge of 'nagging' or failing
to respect the 'young adult's' autonomy. Moreover, they accept that
recognizing their children's autonomy can be particularly hard for
parents. For instance, after June has left, the health visitor observes:

> HV: I think Mum wants a lot of reassurance that she's not
>   abandoning her.

'Not abandoning' your parent involves maintaining autonomy, while
allowing parental expression of concern. The 'bargains' that this
doctor offers patients and their families try to reconcile this
potentially explosive combination of autonomy and responsibility. In
this consultation with Alex, aged fifteen, after a period of family
rows, and poor testing, a bargain is offered which seems to meet these
conflicting demands. However, although it leads on to a version of

'happy families', apparently supported by Alex's mother, two discursive traps arise which I have marked with asterisks:

(NT: 19.2)
1. D: So we're turning over a new leaf in a new book. So once a week and you can be the person to judge which day and your *parents* can be the ones to just check that there has been a day. How about that?
2. P: Mm
3. D: ( ) OK?
4. P: Yes
5. D: ( ) without getting into scraps
6. HV: You see what we said we would do. He would choose the day and tell Mum and then Mum will remind him on the day /( )
7. D: /Great, excellent
*8. M: That's all I've done I've/
9. HV: /Lovely, super. Nice not to have hassles Alex eh?
10. M: It / makes life so much easier
11. HV: / Yes I thought you would appreciate that
*12. D: It makes life so much easier for both of you. So I mean we can say that although your Mum's done her bit of the job you will have done your bit. So it's at least fifty per cent your doing. It's ninety per cent your doing.

Notice how, despite the general agreement and affability displayed here, the stories that the medical staff are telling could be heard as a charge against Alex's parents. Precisely because a *new* bargain is being specified, the implication is that all was not well in the past. In particular, Alex's mother appears to hear the health visitor's version of the bargain (at Utterance 6) as challenging what she has previously done. For to remind a child too frequently of his tasks is to be over-zealous and to 'nag' rather than to respect his autonomy. Consequently, at Utterance 8, she asserts that what is proposed is no different from her *past* practice. Presumably, because this is the occasion for a display of 'happy families', her version of past events is speedily accepted ('lovely, super'). But notice how even the mother's assent to the proposal (at Utterance 10) can be turned against her. For, as the doctor emphasizes at Utterance 12, from a family perspective, one has to look at things in terms of both the parent's and child's needs. Even though he does not go on to use this observation to engage in character-work, we are reminded of the moral charges that accounts invite in this situation. As Cuff (1980) reminds us, all accounts are able to be treated as mere 'versions' of events. Yet here, where the parties simultaneously assert conflicting norms, the opportunity to generate moral charges and rebuttals is enhanced.

The Moral Adequacy of Accounts

It should already be clear that the focus of this study is on the interactional 'work' done by accounts. I am not concerned with people's underlying motives. However, I am very much concerned with how depictions of possible motives are assembled and challenged. In this section, I will try to specify that concern by showing how it builds upon a very lively sociological tradition. By doing so, I will be able to clarify the conceptual apparatus that I am going to use on these clinic materials.

Almost half a century ago, Mills (1940) suggested that 'motives' are not fixed elements 'in' an individual but 'the terms with which interpretation of conduct by social actors proceeds' (Mills, 1940:00).

The methodological implication of this observation was spelled out by Mills. The imputation and avowal of motives by actors should be treated as social phenomena in need of explanation. Mills said that three major issues then arose:

1. When does motive talk get done? (perhaps in crises or unexpected situations)
2. What motives are available? (the 'vocabularies of motive' appropriate to particular milieux)
3. What does motive talk do? (perhaps influencing others and oneself).

Mills' trail-blazing assertion that, for sociological purposes, nothing lies 'behind' motives encouraged a new generation of researchers concerned with the social organization of accounts. For instance, an interview study of scientists asserted that:

> the goal of the analyst no longer parallels that of the participants, who are concerned to find out what they and others did or thought but becomes that of reflecting upon the patterned character of participants' portrayals of action (Gilbert and Mulkay, 1983:24)

The error was to treat accounts as giving clues to the *causes* of actions. Gilbert and Mulkay demonstrate that this treatment was untenable given the evidence that scientists described their own work differently on different occasions. Instead, they focus on the two repertoires upon which such descriptions drew:

1. An empiricist repertoire which appeals to experimental facts
2. A contingent repertoire which refers to such matters as personalities, politics and finance.

The empiricist repertoire provided the fabric of formal scientific papers. In interviews, however, these scientists were equally at home in both repertoires.

Gilbert and Mulkay's work nicely parallels part of what I have been trying to demonstrate in the diabetic clinic. The twin appeals to 'responsibility' and 'autonomy' can be seen as the repertoires of parent–doctor discourse. As with Gilbert and Mulkay's interviews, both repertoires can be used simultaneously, without regard to their logical consistency.

The leap from 'science' to 'family' is thus possible, providing the enterprise can cohere around a theory of repertoires or discourses and their relations. This hopeful possibility is strengthened by Gubrium and Lynott's depiction of a possible programme of research on the family which would:

> Zero in on family discourse and lay out its rhetorical conditions and representational products, to trace the social organization of concern over the infringement (of family life); indeed, to investigate its native understanding. (Gubrium and Lynott, 1985:150)

To fulfil this ambitious and inspiring programme, we need a conceptual apparatus able to cope with the interpretation of accounts and the moral order. In two papers, Harvey Sacks (1972a, 1972b and 1974), drew our attention to the moral implications and interactional consequences of descriptions. For instance, one of the reasons we may avoid 'name-calling' is that we know that a description using similar categories may then properly be applied to us by the person we have abused. Sacks calls such a collection of categories a Membership Categorisation Device (MCD). Since reality does not come with sub-titles, the use of categories from particular collections constitutes the character of 'reality' and thus displays the teller in a particular light.

E.C. Cuff has used Sacks's work to demonstrate the link between accounts and the moral order:

> The teller, in producing an account of what is happening in the world, is also unavoidably producing materials which make available possible findings about his characterological and moral appearance as displayed in his talk. Alternatively put, in telling about the world he is also inescapably telling about himself: in seeing the world 'that way', he is inescapably open to possible findings that he is 'that kind of person who sees the world that way'. (Cuff, 1980:35)

This immediately suggests that the teller's power to 'constitute' reality is counterbalanced by the ability of hearers to overturn the account and thus cast doubt both on the description it offers and on the moral integrity of the teller. Indeed, as I write, precisely such a possibility is working itself out in disputes in the British Parliament about what 'really happened' at a meeting between a Cabinet Minister and a leading industrialist over the Westland helicopter company.

Cuff's analysis is particularly apposite for our materials because he proposes a development of Sacks's apparatus for analysing descriptions. This highlights the issue of competing accounts in the context of a discussion of family discourse. Cuff discusses a radio programme where a family described their 'troubles' and responded to the advice of 'experts'. He shows the utility of Sacks' MCD scheme in thinking about the collection 'family' and more particularly the husband–wife 'relational pair' from that collection.

Now Sacks maintains that such relational pairs provide linked identities for the parties so described (a standardized relational pair or SRP). Thus, to use the SRP husband–wife implies expectations about the appropriate behaviour and responsibilities of the parties so described. However, Cuff shows that this can imply a social order model where the nature and application of such expectations are not in dispute. Yet this was not the case on this radio programme. On the contrary, while the 'factual nature' of the events described was accepted by hearers:

> what they 'mean', what they 'add up to' and, consequently, what sort of a person 'is doing them' are the prevalent issues for members. These issues appear to concern the 'adequacy' of the inferences made from 'the facts' rather than 'the correctness' of 'the facts' themselves. (Cuff, 1980:73)

In making these inferences, Cuff argues, members were not just appealing to general assumptions about the roles of husband and wife but morally specified versions of being a 'good' or 'bad' wife or husband. This suggests a process of the subversion of accounts very close to what I have called 'charge-rebuttal' sequences. For instance, an appeal to 'what-we-all-know' about the roles of husband and wife (SRP I) can be subverted by a more detailed specification of respective identities (say as a 'dissolute' husband and a 'long- suffering' wife) (SRP II). In turn, this can be subverted through an alternative formulation: a 'nagging' wife and a 'long-suffering' husband (SRP III).

Cuff provides a neat demonstration of how accounts can be defeated through being shown to be partisan or one-sided, i.e. as merely 'versions' of what happened.[1] Where the teller is a member of the unit (s)he describes, the account is particularly liable to be treated as a 'version' because of the party's moral involvement in any unit troubles. Moreover, Cuff shows that the precise character of an expert hearer's expertise may arise in formulating the different 'versions' of events without taking sides. Instead, one 'does' expertise by offering an overall framework which may help all parties gain 'insight' into the events (p.67).

Cuff's paper provides an elegant way of handling the diabetic clinic consultations. It shows how alternative SRP's based on autonomy or responsibility may be used to constitute the discussions of mother/child relations that we have been considering. It also provides a way of understanding the doctor's interventions, particularly his attempts to negotiate 'deals', as exemplifications of expertise involving avoidance of taking 'sides', while attending to the generally available perception of the mothers' moral involvement in unit (i.e. family) troubles.

However, as my discussion of 'rebuttals' has indicated, these mothers are far from being passive recipients of experts' versions of family troubles. Moreover, not only can they rebut charges about their behaviour but their initial accounts often have built into them defences against a subsequent charge of 'one-sidedness'.

Here Cuff is, once again, helpful. He notes that members are aware of the possibility that others might seek to compare their accounts with hypothetical accounts that other members of the family unit might offer. Members respond to the possibility of this comparison in three kinds of ways:

1. By asserting their own share of the responsibility for unit-troubles
2. By taking account of the point of view of other members of the unit
3. By attending to routine knowledge about the nature and causes of unit troubles.[2]

In shifting focus from one source of family troubles to another and from one SRP (husband–wife) to another (parent–child), the issues become still more complicated. First, as I have already argued, moral versions of the parent–child relationship (Cuff's SRP II and III) may be internally contradictory, so that it may be logically impossible to be both a responsible parent *and* a parent who recognizes a child's autonomy. But second, despite this, parents cope by skilfully asserting both norms simultaneously.

The power of Cuff's conceptual apparatus is that it gives us a Durkheimian insight into the power of the moral order without implying that we are 'cultural dopes' unable to 'work the system' to our benefit. It gives us a glimpse of the kinds of dilemmas that doctors and parents may have imposed upon them, while encouraging us to attend to the skills used in finding a way out. It remains to apply the apparatus to the data.

The Case of 'The Neurotic Mother'
I will now look in some detail at one encounter. It is a short meeting between the doctor (D) at the New Town Clinic and the mother (M) of June. We looked earlier at an extract of a previous consultation with June where the issue of 'nagging' had been raised and the doctor had promised to speak to June's mother about it. This encounter takes place seven months later, immediately preceding June's consultation,

when as always, she is seen on her own. As I hope to demonstrate, it shows the fine power of Cuff's adaptation of Sacks's SRP scheme in revealing the interactional dilemmas in parent–doctor talk.

The opening sequence begins with the health visitor (HV) entering the consulting room while the doctor is writing up the notes of the previous patient.

(NT: 19.2)
```
   1. HV:   Could you have a word with Mrs A please?
  *2. M:    [enters] The neurotic mother heh heh
   3. HV:   [softly] No, no
            [HV withdraws to do a blood-test on June]
   4. D:    Hello
   5. M:    Did you hear about our episode yesterday? Did (HV) tell you?
   6. D:    What?
   7. M:    June had a hypo, a very severe one actually
   8. D:    Yes, yes
   9. M:    Worse than she's had before
 *10. D:    Right. Is she outside?
 *11. M:    Yes she's just having tests
```

I previously talked about the 'autonomy' norm that applied to teenagers' management of their diabetes. Let me now reformulate that, following Cuff, as an SRP of the form: autonomous child/non-interventionist parent. If this holds, then June's mother knows that her appearance in the consulting room breaches the expectations of the SRP. Not only are parents of diabetic patients aged sixteen not expected to see the doctor independently of their children but, in the past, June has used her autonomy to request that her mother be excluded from the consultation. This suggestion of a breach is given conclusive support by Utterance 2 ('The neurotic mother').

This utterance neatly copes with the broken expectations of the standard parent–child norms using two devices suggested by Cuff: June's mother asserts her share of the responsibility for unit troubles, while attending to routine knowledge about their nature and cause. We can hear her formulation of herself in terms of a familiar SRP: namely, aggrieved daughter/neurotic mother. Unit troubles in the family ('nagging', 'rows') are standardly retrievable as arising from the action of parents who, neurotically, won't 'let go' of their older children. What Mrs A's utterance skilfully does here is show that she accepts her responsibility for these familiar troubles. Or rather, to the extent that her laughter distances herself from her utterance, that she accepts that a possible *version* of her intervention may be in terms of 'a neurotic mother'. Consequently, since she has shown herself aware of possible unfavourable versions of her behaviour, we may treat her own version with greater respect.

Utterance 2 represents, in my terms, a rebuttal to a charge that is never made. Nonetheless, since the charge is potentially available *in the situation*, the utterance serves as a pre-emptive strike to establish Mrs A's claims to have her version of events taken seriously.

An actual charge and its rebuttal is to be found in Utterances 10 and 11. Here the doctor appeals to the SRP of doctor and patient by making June's absence from the consultation accountable. According to that SRP, it would be quite illegitimate deliberately to exclude a patient. Indeed, the doctor's earlier monosyllabic responses (at Utterances 6 and 8) to Mrs A's tale of her troubles can be heard as refusing to sanction a dialogue until this crucial matter has been cleared up.

Note that Mrs A offers an account of June's absence instead of simply answering 'Yes' to the doctor's question. We may take it that she knows that an unstated second question is implicit i.e. if June is outside what are you doing here without her? Her answer serves as a rebuttal to this implied charge by making June's absence accountable without breaching the norm autonomous child/non-interventionist parent.

The encounter then proceeds with Mrs A re-asserting her share of the responsibility for unit troubles:

   *12. M: I just panicked more than anything
   *13. D: Yeah well (HV) was saying you've been having a bad time
   14. M: [*long account of problems of getting June's dosage of insulin right*] and then one day she's just not (   ). And it takes so much out of her. But yesterday was particularly bad (   ). She was hysterical and I panicked. But she slept it off (   ). But she was still very temperamental. I said one thing and she refused to eat her dinner so I had to sort of coax her
   15. D: Mm
   16. M: Well the whole day she was nonplussed. It was awful really
   17. D: Mm
   18. M: She's still not doing a lot of tests so we're floundering

Once again, acknowledging your share of the responsibility ('I just panicked') serves to prop up your version of events. The doctor responds at Utterance 13 by accepting the legitimacy of her version, using the format that Cuff identified as 'doing expertise'. Rather than 'take sides' in unit troubles, the expert shows his understanding of both sides' versions of events and tries to locate their cause i.e. he engages in what Cuff calls 'doing articulated disagreements' (Cuff, 1980:67).

Mrs A takes the doctor's understanding of her 'panic' as sanctioning a long story of unit troubles. In this story (Utterance 14), she builds on her earlier reference (Utterance 5) to 'our episode'. The pronoun she chooses is curious because the 'hypo' which is at the centre of the story happened, of course, to June. In making the hypo 'our episode' and not 'her episode', we can hear her appealing to a further relational pair: sick child/responsible parent. This SRP supports the tale she has to tell at Utterance 14 by making it into a tale of unit troubles. It legitimates 'panicking' at hypos and hysteria. It justifies 'coaxing' when sick children, whose insulin-balance depends on a regular food intake, will not eat.

Mrs A concludes her story, at Utterance 18, by using another collective pronoun to refer to unit troubles: 'we're floundering' and not 'she's floundering'. This appeal to responsible parenthood, implicated on a child's response to her illness, skilfully legitimates Mrs A's self-confessed states of 'neurosis' and 'panic'. However, it contains the danger of being undercut by the alternative SRP: autonomous child/nagging parent. This is precisely what happens now:

19. D: It sounds as if generally you're having a difficult time
20. M: Her temper is vile
*21. D: She with you and you with her
*22. M: Yes. And her control of the diabetes is gone, her temper then takes control of her.

At Utterances 19 and 21, the doctor displays 'expertise' once more in the form of 'doing articulated disagreements'. But note the charge available in the second of his utterances. Mrs A's claims about her daughter's temper are here constituted as a one-sided version of unit troubles. For 'responsibility' can always be heard as 'nagging' and, consequently, 'necessary' interventions to help a sick child can be retranslated as displays of 'temper'.

In response to this charge, Mrs A concedes the power of this version of events which takes account of the likely point of view of the other party to unit troubles, her daughter. Her rebuttal now takes the form of down-playing her acknowledged irrational outbursts in the context of the greater significance of her daughter's 'vile temper'. Mrs A's 'temper' is reprehensible but understandable in the recognized context of 'having a difficult time'. June's temper is altogether more serious because it is related to her physical well-being, revealing that 'her control of the diabetes is gone'.

Mrs A now pursues this version of responsible parenthood in a way that almost undoes her:

23. M: She's going through a very languid stage (   ). She won't do anything unless you push her
*24. D: So you're finding you're having to push her quite a lot?

*25. M: Mm no well I don't. I just leave her now
26. D: Huh mm
27. M: I've come to a compromise. If she says something (   ) I need to get it under control. I say that's up to you
28. D: Yes
29. M: You see if I mention it she says I'm nagging at her so I don't mention it now
30. D: Yeah
31. M: I think she's got to find out the hard way actually/
32. D: /Mm
33. M: And she has (   ). I feel pretty rotten after she's been through one of these. I don't know what on earth she feels like.

By Utterance 23, Mrs A has built up a version of parent/child relations which extends 'responsibility' to a stage where it may be heard to contradict openly the 'autonomy' of the older child in the management of her diabetes. The hostage to fortune offered by her reference to 'pushing' her daughter is seized upon by the doctor's Utterance 24.

In the rest of this extract, Mrs A skilfully backtracks. Although the doctor's question is really only a re-statement of what she herself said at Utterance 23, she cannot stand by it now that it has been made accountable.

So Mrs A's rebuttal of the charge heard in Utterance 24 functions by rejecting all suggestions of nagging (explicitly rejected at Utterance 29) and appealing to the SRP: autonomous child/non-interventionist parent. Now this directly contradicts the implications for responsible parenthood of her formulation at Utterance 23 that June 'won't do anything unless you push her'. So, without a further gloss, her rebuttal might undercut her earlier versions of her interventions in June's diabetes and her very presence before the doctor today.[3]

The version of responsible parenthood that Mrs A seems to end up with is in terms of respecting autonomy *even if it injures the child*: 'I think she's got to find out the hard way'. This change of tack now allows her to launch into a depiction of June's failure to use her autonomy responsibly. To that extent, it provides a reworked justification for Mrs A's request to see the doctor. Ironically, the sequence below concludes with this new-found recognition of June's 'autonomy' being made available as a charge that Mrs A has neglected the very 'responsibility' from which she has just been forced to withdraw.

34. M: I think she's so mixed up. She's not accepting the diabetes. I mean they've said this at school
35. D: Mm

36. M: I don't think she's really sticking to her diet. I don't know the effect this will have on her. It's bound to alter her sugar if she's not got the right insulin isn't it? I mean I know what she eats at home but outside

*37. D: So there's no real consistency to her diet? It's sort of

*38. M: No well I keep it as consistent as I can at home but

39. D: Yes

40. M: But I wouldn't put it past her having chips but they all do don't they? I can't watch her every (   ). She knows the consequences.

The sequence begins with Mrs A presenting a version of her daughter which appeals to the 'autonomy' norm. June's problem is redefined as not showing the independence and responsibility that autonomy presupposes ('she's not accepting the diabetes'). The version is strenghtened by appealing to what 'they've said ... at school' i.e. 'experts', with no axe to grind in unit troubles, see things this way.

The picture of June's irresponsible autonomy/Mum's responsible surveillance but avoidance of nagging is developed in Utterance 36. Mrs A watches June's diet at home but cannot or will not intervene on what June eats 'outside'. However, the doctor's question at 37 makes 'inconsistency of diet' accountable and, therefore, can be heard as a charge, based on a version of mothers as the family providers of adequate nutrition.[4]

Mrs A rebuts this further charge by re-asserting her modified version of responsible parenthood in terms of surveying and providing but not nagging. Not only is it not feasible to maintain total surveillance over a young adult ('I can't watch her every') but being adult means learning for yourself through bitter experience ('She knows the consequences').

Throughout these exchanges, Mrs A has shown herself sensitive to how her account might be treated as a mere 'version' of events. She has skilfully bolstered her narrative through two procedures:

1. Offering alternative versions of unit troubles that outsiders might infer and asserting her share of the responsibility for them (as a 'neurotic' mother who 'panicked')
2. Perceiving and rebutting charges of *both* 'nagging' and irresponsibility.

As the exchange draws to an end, she seems to have squared the circle of children's autonomy and parental responsibility. Although every assertion of autonomy is still potentially defeasible by an appeal to responsibility and vice versa, Mrs A is now working with a very powerful combination of surveillance *and* respect for autonomy which is harder to challenge.

Yet there remains one further issue through which her account may be subverted. If she so respects her child's autonomy, as she claims, what is she doing here in the first place? After all, autonomous people should not be talked about behind their backs:

41. D: I don't thing we should sit here and talk about her any more if you don't mind
42. M: No I I I feel you need to see her on her own
43. D: No no sure. I don't mind if June wants you to stay.

At Utterance 41, the doctor reconstitutes the potential illegitimacy of a consultation that excludes June. As he had done earlier, at Utterance 10, he is making an appeal to an SRP of doctor/patient, defined in terms of the 'privacy' of a professional relationship.

At this point, there is no way in which Mrs A can continue the interaction. For, when challenged as she is here, she *has* to grant that this version of the SRP is all powerful given the autonomy that she has already conceded to her daughter. Consequently, her only way of rebutting the charge potentially present in the doctor's utterance (that she is prepared to do things behind her daughter's back) is to withdraw.

Finally, note that the doctor doesn't actually demand that Mrs A should withdraw. Consonant with his display of doing expertise, he shows that his concern is to try to accommodate different versions of events (between unit members), subject only to the young adult patient's sovereign right to determine who is present at *her* consultation.[5]

Moral Versions of Parenthood
Having looked in some detail at one consultation, I now want to broaden the data-base again. The issue I will take up here is how these parents use their turns at talk to do displays of parenthood. As before, my analysis makes it clear that the SRP parent–child can be constituted in terms of parental responsibility *or* of children's autonomy. These depictions may be generated by different parents or by the same parents at different times. Since either version can potentially be subverted by a hearer's appeal to the other, in the next section I will set out the variety of rebuttal techniques parents use in these consultations. For the moment, however, I am concerned with the range of obligations that these adults attach to parenthood. To illustrate this, I will use the simple format of a list.[6]

1. Taking Responsibility
As we have seen, parents of diabetic children are held to be responsible, in some respect, for what their child is doing about testing, injecting and dieting. One way to show this responsibility is to display an active involvement in telling the child what to do.

For instance, the mother of Judy, aged fourteen, uses the metaphor of 'fighting' to refer to her involvement:

(SC: 12.2)
1. D: The blood sugar is really too high
2. M: We have to fight this all the way

In another consultation with Angela, aged twelve, a father (F) displays a similar high degree of familial involvement:

(SC: 12.3)
        [*Doctor is looking at the notes*]
1. F: Something her mother is getting /a bit frantic / about
2. D: /Mm   / Yes
3. F: She won't do her b-sticks. She just will will not errmmm I wonder if you could tell her how important it is
4. D: [*shuffling notes*] Right so when did we last have any of these?

Three observations arise here. First, notice how the father nominates Angela's mother as the person who is 'getting a bit frantic', even though it is clear from Utterance 3 that he is concerned too. This is in line with the gender-typing of June's mother's self-characterization as 'neurotic' and 'panicking'. Conversely, no father was heard to characterize himself in this way. This suggests a male/female SRP of 'calm' male/'emotional' female.

Second, although it is not obvious from the doctor's initial response, he will refuse subsequently to 'take sides' in this family dispute, preferring the role of 'articulating disagreements' that Cuff identifies. Finally, Angela's father goes even further than Judy's mother by offering a version of the consultation as some kind of disciplinary occasion.

Now, as we have already seen, 'coming on strong' in terms of parental responsibility can invite the charge of failing to respect your child's autonomy. In the following extract, we see a subtle way of undercutting a display of responsibility by transforming it into inappropriate 'anxiety'. It arises in the context of a heated exchange about the poor control of Alan, an 'educationally-subnormal' boy of thirteen:

(NT: 20.11)
1. M: I know we always discuss this don't we but we never get anywhere do we?
2. D: But you see by you being anxious he's going to have a hypo
3. M: Well of course / I'm anxious
4. D: / I think you're right to be anxious but nevertheless that is interfering with getting his control better
5. M: Well yes I know that as well. I understand all that.

Alan's mother's active involvement in her child's care, displayed in this consultation by her defence of not raising Alan's insulin dose, is thus redefined as 'anxiety' which, ironically, is likely to produce the very 'hypos' that she is trying to avoid. Notice, however, the powerful rebuttal that she uses at Utterance 3. She applies the doctor's formulation to herself as a matter of obvious fact ('Of course I'm anxious').

So one way of rebutting a charge is to argue 'well, of course, this is true, but how else would you expect me to act?' Viewed in terms of the SRP dependent child/responsible parent, 'anxiety' may be heard as entirely legitimate — hence to be implicitly contrasted with 'lack of concern'. So, as Alan's mother acknowledges at Utterance 5, 'anxiety' can, at the worst, have unfortunate but unexpected consequences. It is not, in itself, an inappropriate quality to be possessed by the mother (not the father?) of a handicapped, diabetic child.

Conversely, another way of displaying responsibility is to emphasize the child's autonomy. Take this exchange, involving Averil, an articulate girl of twelve:

(NT: 21.5)
   1. D: Any particular problems?
   2. P: The injections they've been hurting a bit
   3. D: Sometimes it's when you don't inject too deep
*4. M: I'm afraid we've let her get on with it.

Averil's mother's intervention is a neat rebuttal of a charge potentially present in the lack of parental supervision of Averil's choice of injection sites. Following Cuff's scheme referred to above, she admits her share of responsibility for unit troubles ('I'm afraid') while appealing to what everyone knows about families (that older children should be encouraged to 'get on with it').

With younger children, of course, the assumptions about the extent of parental involvement get redefined. Such parents, as in the case below, can successfully rebut a charge of not encouraging autonomy by insisting that any such demand must come from the child.

(NT: 2/4)
   1. D: She's never asked to do her injections or have a go?
*2. F: We don't put any pressure on her
   3. HV: It's not pressure (   ) cultivating the interest. It's just one of my four and a half year olds is doing her own (   )
*4. F: Well if she does that's fine.

Here the father of Norma, who is aged five, redefines the child's autonomy in terms of improper 'pressure' to make her do things for herself. Both his utterances appeal to the moral limits of 'forcing' young children to be 'free'. Since his second utterance is not challenged, we see here a successful formulation of responsibility which runs directly contrary to that proposed by Averil's mother.

2. Surveillance
One aspect of 'responsibility' is monitoring your child to make sure that appropriate behaviour is forthcoming. Of course, such monitoring or surveillance can be displayed far less problematically with younger or handicapped children, like Norma or Alan.

After Alan has had a 'hypo', his mother goes into great detail about the way she has tried to plan and supervise her son's behaviour even though she had had to go to work that day:

> (NT: 2.4)
> 1. M: He was supposed to get up, have something to eat and go to my daughter's to do his injection (1.5). I even left him a note but er whether he got up and went out and came back in I don't know because he was just sort of missing. And when he came back indoors he was a bit vacant. Mind you I've no proof that he actually went out because I was out looking for him, you see
> 2. D: Hh hm
> 3. M: And then he appeared indoors

Alan's mother makes it clear that, if anyone was responsible for his 'hypo', it was not her. Her account displays an irreproachable combination of rational planning (leaving a note), enterprising action ('out looking for him') and calculative enquiry (which demands 'proof'). Her vigilance seems unending. As she says at the end of the consultation:

> M: I watch him (   ). I keep my beady eye on him.

Parents of older children without Alan's mental handicap none the less display a 'beady eye' to detail, whether it's knowing when the last clinic blood-test was done or, as with Lucy's mother, when Lucy's blood-sugars are high:

> (SC: 9.4)
> M: They usually seem to be higher round about four or five o'clockish before the evening meal. She's always had a tendency for high sugars than when she's tested. We've always had that problem.

In the same way as June's mother appealed to the family unit ('our episode', 'we're floundering') as the site of her child's health, so Lucy's mother narrates her story in terms of the problem 'we've ... had'. Given such a site, parental surveillance of a child's test results seems appropriate. Moreover, since everybody knows that, in diabetes, 'control' is a blend of insulin dosage and life-style, other instances of surveillance should be supplied as necessary evidence.

(SC: 9.4)
    M: She hasn't had the exercise since she's been on holiday. The exercise of walking to and fro from school every day she hasn't had that.

Central to this display of parental surveillance is familiarity with the child's blood-test results. This requires inspecting the test figures that the child is expected to inscribe in a book. In a sense, parents take on the role of the 'guardians of the book'. This means ensuring that the book is brought along to each clinic visit. So that, when then there is no book available it is usually the parent who feels obliged to make this accountable.

(NT: 19.3)
    M: But e's come out without the book. Sorry about that, (   ). I said you'd make him come back tomorrow because of that heh heh heh.

Although Patrick is almost fifteen, his mother apologizes for the book's absence. Notice how she allies herself with a version of proper punishment for this absence ('coming back tomorrow'), while showing, through her laughter, that only a minor breach of the ceremonial order is involved.

Elsewhere, as we have seen, too literal an interpretation of the role of guardian of the book can be negatively sanctioned. For instance, Sheila's mother's attempt to pass the book directly to the doctor was rebuffed. Nevertheless, parents regularly feel obliged to make accountable the book's appearance and what appears in the book. In Alex's father's case, this can even mean an alliance with a doctor's suspicions about the figures recorded:

(NT: 16.10)
    1. D: Well let's look at / (   )
    2. F: / I don't think there's much in it
    3. D: (   ) Alex these look too good to be true. Is that right Alex?
    4. P: No
    5. F: What he means is have you been making them up?

More usually, test-figures are believed. Then the issue shifts to what they reveal about the child's attempts to maintain good control. Throughout, parents evince relief and joy at good figures and horror and shock at bad figures. None the less, they regularly produce accounts to explain figures which appear to be bad.

(SC: 9.4)

> [*D is looking at John's book*]

1. M: Heh heh heh / And that was through a cold and this (   )
2. D: / So
3. M: I knew you would like that. Look at *that* that's
4. D: Yes while I've been on holiday / (   )
5. M: / *Yeeahs*. Look at *that* isn't
   that good?
6. D: Oh that's splendid isn't it?
7. M: Mmmm
8. D: That's splendid
9. M: But look at before, the *page* before heh heh heh
10. D: [*to P*] What were you doing there then?

Having produced her account of a poor test result (Utterance 1) John's mother can afford to be relatively light-hearted (Utterance 9). In the context of what we learn elsewhere is generally good control, an occasional slip is cause for no more than a token sanction (like Patrick's mother's response to his absent book).

Elsewhere, the language of 'good', 'like' and 'splendid' and the opposite finds its parallels in parents' responses to news of test figures. Take this comment when Emma, aged four, has the result of today's blood-test revealed:

(NT: 16.10)

1. M: Is that what it is now? That's horrifying
2. D: Did you know the result of that [*earlier*] blood-test?
3. M: Yes it was great
4. D: I think what it means without wanting to take the kudos from you is that she has some of her own insulin.

Proper surveillance involves attending to test-results with due seriousness. 'Bad' figures can potentially rebound on both the child and the parent. So, even parents of older children, like John, want to make poor figures accountable. However, with a younger child, like Emma, moral blame or praise ('kudos') attaches directly to the parent. So doctors must couch their accounts of the body's functioning ('she has some of her own insulin') in terms which show proper respect for the moral character of the enterprise ('without wanting to take the kudos from you').

3. Guardians of the Kitchen

'Thriving', 'well-fed' children testify to the moral worth of mothers. For diabetics, who need to pay close attention to their diet, the issue is more complicated. Irregular eating habits or eating the wrong kind of foods are to be avoided and so even an apparently 'well-fed' child is not, in itself, a testimony to morally responsible parenthood. Remember how, for instance, June's mother expressed her concern about the chips that June was probably buying herself. At home, however, Mrs A tries to keep June's diet 'consistent', doing her best to 'coax' her when she won't eat.

Patrick's mother also provides a version of her son's poor eating habits and her response to it. This occurs when the doctor asks her if anything has changed which might explain his better control:

(NT: 19.3)
1. D: Something has made it better
   (2.0)
2. M: [*softly*] He isn't doing anything different from what he did before. I mean his diet hasn't altered
   [   ]
3. N: I suppose though looking at his meal mind you he says he doesn't *want* any more to eat so I said tell me if you're hungry and we'll see about altering (   ) but compared to what the other boys eat he eats *nothing* (1.0) you know I leave it on his plate and he / (   )
4. HV: / (   )
5. M: So he's evidently getting sufficient for what he needs.

Notice how Patrick's mother immediately turns to his diet when asked about his better control. She shows her concern about his eating 'nothing', compared to his brothers. However, she provides a series of grounds for seeing this as not a report on her inadequacy as a mother. She is fulfilling her role in asking Patrick to 'tell me if you're hungry' and leaving the food 'on his plate'. If he won't eat, it can only be because 'he doesn't want any more to eat' and, anyway, 'he's evidently getting sufficient for what he needs'. If lack of appetite can be heard as a 'unit trouble', possibly casting doubt on a mother's moral status, this mother provides a rebuttal to such a charge displaying her attentiveness to her son's point of view and appealing to what — everyone — knows about children's difficult eating habits.

When children are eating well, however, it is an occasion for displays of parental pride:

(NT: 21.5)
1. D: The diet?
2. F: She's eating more than ever
3. M: We're lucky we've got Jordan Mills near us so we can get wholefoods.

Twelve-year-old Averil is 'eating more than ever'. However, as her mother implies, it is a question of quality as well as quantity. The family may be 'lucky' but this is because, in her account, they know the value of 'wholefoods'.

Elsewhere, a similar display of paternal pride by five-year-old Norma's father temporarily has the wind taken out of its sails:

(NT: 2.4)
1. HV: Smashing. I'd be delighted if she were mine. She's shot up
        Super
2. F: She has a very good appetite
3. D: [*refers to Norma's past state of overweight*]
4. F: It's difficult when you don't want her to go without food for
        too long.

Norma's father skilfully rebuts the charge potentially present in the doctor's reference to her overweight. This breach is redefined as the unintended consequence of zealously following a norm (diabetic children must eat regularly).

4. Seeking out Solutions

Norma's father concludes the consultation by asking a question about the impact of school dinners on Norma's diet and also by observing that a particular type of syringe is 'very good'. He then writes the date of her next appointment into an immaculately kept testing book. The success of his display of responsible parenthood is shown in the doctor's comment to me when this parent is not in the room:

> D: Mr A is a (professional job named) who's done a perfect job. He's coped with a depressed wife and adjusted Norma's insulin when she had flu.

This well-received display of parenthood presents in exaggerated form what is commonly observed in these clinics. Parents show their common attentiveness to their child's problems and to a search for possible solutions to them. For instance, Angela's father, whom we last met asking the doctor to tell his daughter 'how important it is' to do her tests, also seeks solutions via a reference to 'those machines in the newsletter we get from the British Diabetics' (SC: 12.3). When the doctor implies it may be difficult for them to be obtained on the National Health Service, Mr B insists 'that's not the problem'. The only issue is 'Would you recommend them?'

Three final instances show how this active search for solutions is maintained even in the most difficult situations. First, Alan's mother, who has to cope with a diabetic, educationally subnormal child, reveals that she is also worried about a third problem and searching for a solution:

(NT: 19.2)
1. M: Can you tell me what height he is?
2. D: [   ]
3. M: What was he the time before? I don't remember
4. D: [*Alan has grown 2 inches*]

> 5. M: Only he worries about how tall he is. And we did watch this
>   programme and it said you can have something done ...

The second case concerns Matthew, aged fifteen, who is
accompanied by a representative (R) from the children's home where
he lives. Matthew has asked to doctor to examine his foot following an
accident he has had. When no broken bones are found, the
representative makes a rare unsolicited intervention:

(NT 18.9)
> R: If anything had been broken he would have been taken to the
>   hospital

In loco parentis means here maintaining a programme of surveillance
and, when appropriate, resolving problems as they arise. Whether
parent or parent-substitute, you must always be on the watch because
you can always be held to account for your inaction as well as your
actions. Alone among these parents, John's mother takes this to mean
that the researcher (R) observing the consultation must be thoroughly
interrogated:

(SC: 9.4)
> 1. M: Are you the chap we've heard about?
> 2. R: Yes. Is that OK?
> 3. M: What are you going to do with it all?
> 4. R: [*lengthy explanation*]
> 5. M: No I don't like er I didn't like the fact that you're here and I
>   didn't know you were going to be here
> 6. R: Didn't you get a letter?
> 7. M: Yes but I didn't know you were going to be here this visit
> 8. R: Oh I see
> 9. M: Also are you going to use, are you going to write notes and put
>   John (surname)?
> 10. R: Oh I never use any names
> 11. M: That's OK. What are you going to do with all your material
>   afterwards?
> 12. R: [*further explanation*]
> 13. M: OK. Yes fine, mm
> 14. R: Thank you
> 15. M: I just wanted to (   ). No I just think that (2.0) we
>   should have a bit more information.

Remedies and Rebuttals

A continuing theme in this chapter has been that any version of events
can always be undercut. So displays of responsible parenthood, even
in the elaborated form reported above, can be treated as simply
'versions' (just as my letter to parents could be redefined by John's
mother as inadequate).

Up to now, I have examined parents' remedies and rebuttals to such a charge via the apparatus identified by Cuff (1980). I have already remarked, however, that, in the diabetic clinic, the SRP parent–child is complicated by the twin (and potentially conflicting) norms of 'autonomy' and 'responsibility'. I will conclude the presentation of the data by listing the kinds of remedies these parents used to rebut potential and actual charges against their display of responsible parenthood.

1. Natural Facts

A powerful way of handling a trouble is to move it from the moral to the natural universe. For instance, Lucy's mother offers a version of her daughter's bad control due to a 'tendency' for high sugar-levels to arise at a certain time of day:

(SC: 9.4)
> M: They usually seem to be higher round about four or five o'clockish before the evening meal. She's always had a tendency for high sugars then when she's tested

Such potentially inexplicable natural 'tendencies' can make for poor clinic test results even with the most diligent parental surveillance of tests done at home:

(NT: 19.3)
> 1. M: So it was the problems he had with his / (   )
> 2. HV: / Something was throwing the whole lot / (   )
> 3. M: / Mm his tests were OK

While unidentified factors seemed to be 'throwing' Patrick's control, Lucy's mother hits upon a natural fact (the 'growth spurt') as the causal agent in her case even though she elicits a non- committal response:

(SC: 9.4)
> 1. M: So if she if they were growing with quick bursts does that mean that the sugar levels would perhaps fluctuate? (1.5) Quite a bit then anyway?
> 2. D: Yes overall you see [*talks about other factors*]

2. Unintended Consequences of Rational Action

Recalcitrant natural facts can mean that even rational action can have unintended consequences. Lucy's mother had increased her insulin dosage, as instructed by the medical staff, when sugar-levels were high. Unfortunately, as the doctor explains, that may have exacerbated the problem:

(SC: 9.4)

1. M: Actually we have increased the insulin because it's still been high. I think it's because she's been on holiday as well. But I put the whole lot up

     . . .

2. D: [*continuing a long explanation*] Too much insulin around. What you think you've done is to improve her high sugars but what you've actually done is possibly made it worse because what you've done is actually created lower dips so you get higher peaks afterwards

3. M: Oh right

4. D: [*names the syndrome involved*] So actually increasing the insulin paradoxically makes / the instability worse

5. M: / makes it worse

6. M: But she she's put on weight that month

7. D: That's interesting [*changes the subject*]

Notice how the doctor does not question the mother's 'good' motives ('what you think you've done' versus 'what you've actually done'). Lucy's mother accepts this verdict (at Utterances 3 and 5). Because it is 'paradoxical', according to the doctor, no moral blame attaches to her. Faced with this galaxy of medical knowledge, she retreats to her home territory: her own observations of Lucy's weight gain (Utterance 6).

The paradoxes of the body's response to insulin also provide Patrick's mother with a convenient way of accounting for his sickness in the context of raising his insulin dosage:

(NT: 19.3)

1. HV: You can have too much, you can have too little and that's what mucks up (   ) but that's worked very well indeed (   )

2. M: I often wonder about that when you decide to put up their insulin because every time Patrick's has gone up he's been sick you know he's had one of those terrible bad bugs

3. HV: Yes but he could have been sick because it needed putting up

4. M: Maybe

5. HV: Mm

In the temporary absence from the room of the doctor, Patrick's mother voices her fears about raising her son's insulin dosage. However, given the difficult question of finding the 'right' level of dosage (Utterance 1) and the chicken-and-egg character of the whole problem (Utterance 3), the implication is that parents (and children) cannot be held accountable for the negative consequences of dosages given in good faith.

3. Medical Mistakes

Only Patrick's mother's 'maybe' (Utterance 4) suggests that she is not altogether convinced by the medical explanation. Direct challenges to medical versions of the 'facts' are, however, rarely heard in the clinic. One exception is in Alan's mother's negative account of the consequences of following the health visitor's advice to increase her insulin dosage:

> (NT: 20.10)
> 1. M: Once before (   ) he ended up back in hospital with er too much insulin. That's why I've left it alone now because you know he will, he'll start sleeping during the mornings and that's it for the day. He's not too bright (   ) at the moment
> 2. D: Yes
> 3. M: So it's beginning to overact on him
>   (   )
> 4. M: So it seems that he's getting too much insulin
>   (   )
> 5. M: I daren't give him any more
>   (   )
> 6. D: But it might be because he's on the high side so much as on the low side
> 7. M: Yeah
> 8. D: Is that what you mean?
> 9. M: Well (2.0) It could be I suppose really.

Such a direct challenge to the medical version is doomed to failure. Alan's mother's extended account of the negative consequences of 'too much insulin' is stood on its head by the doctor at Utterance 6. Like Lucy's mother when an unknown 'syndrome' was announced, Alan's mother backs down for the moment.

4. Knowing My Child

I referred earlier to Lucy's mother's appeal to her 'home territory' as a far safer site to uphold a parental version of events. While parents must ultimately concede that doctors are expert in medical 'facts', medical staff are reluctant to challenge parents' expertise in assessing how their own child 'seems'. Indeed a question about this is a routine part of paediatric history-taking.

When the treatment programme is in dispute, the question that then arises is whether doctors can successfully treat the parents' accounts as a mere 'appearance' concealing a clinical reality or whether they have to give some ground to the power of parental experience and/or perceptions.

Such perceptions of 'my child' are powerfully deployed by Alan's mother in the consultation we have just been examining. Adding to her ungrounded assertions about the effect of insulin dosage, she notes:

(NT: 20.10)
M: He's coming in from school bad-tempered. He's not as happy as his normal nature is.

The doctor seems to concede some ground in the fact of this mother's unchallengeable knowledge of her son's 'normal nature'. Instead of increasing Alan's insulin dosage, as he had earlier seemed inclined to do, he simply re-arranges the proportions taken in the morning and evening.

Six months later, after an in-patient stay, Alan's control has improved. None the less, his mother continues her battle to reduce his insulin dosage based on her everyday observation:

(NT: 2.4)
1. D: The blood tests then we've got are also good
2. M: But he doesn't seem right. Do you know what I mean? You know he seems all right on that bit of paper but *he* doesn't seem right.

Alan's mother establishes here a neat contrast set between medical territory ('that bit of paper') and maternal territory (where Alan 'doesn't seem right'). When invited to specify her perceptions she is able to develop an extended account about Alan's tiredness which has meant that he no longer resists going to bed at 'proper' times. Although the doctor suggests maintaining the present insulin dosage since there now seems to be good control of the diabetes, he backs down when Alan's mother once again insists that Alan is now 'not so energetic'. The outcome is a reduction in Alan's evening dosage by a minimal amount.

'Knowing my child' is also used by John's mother to influence the outcome of the consultation. Unlike Alan's mother, she wants to *maintain* the insulin dosage despite the doctor's stated desire to reduce it:

(SC: 9.4)
*1. M: Every time we've cut back though John, John feels um (1.0) I can tell / the difference. He just feels
2. D: / Um
3. M: very / (   )
4. D: / I'm (   )
5. M: Isn't that the thing?
6. D: I mean I I'm very delighted by the appearance of his sugars. They're probably the best we've seen aren't they?
*7. M: Oh yes (4.0) Yeah but you know what I'm saying. At the moment I don't like to rock the boat

8. D: Mm I know
9. M: Because we've been through a lot
          . . .
*10. D: OK as we're saying let's not rock the boat and let's leave things as
            they are.

So mothers can 'tell the difference' and only members of the family
unit can know what it's like to have 'been through a lot'. In such a
context, the doctor's appeal to a clinical version (at Utterance 6)
stands for little. By the end, he agrees a policy that is not only in line
with what John's mother wants but adopts her very words ('not
rocking the boat').

Even when they are not used to challenge medical decision-making,
parental accounts of their child's demeanour and appearance always
must be taken seriously. For, in a sense, this is one battle that parents
cannot lose. If they report that their child appears to be not his normal
self, then they are affirming their involvement in appropriate
surveillance and, perhaps, challenging the adequacy of medical
interventions. Conversely, attending to their child's satisfactory
appearance is a tribute to their own good parenting even if, as in the
exchange below, Emma's mother's account does not seem fully in line
with the clinical reality (of 'bad times'):

(NT: 16.10)
1. M: She does look well doesn't she?
2. D: She does. Full of life. Apart from the bad times she's doing well.

Conclusions
In the previous chapter, I sought to show how medical staff were
constrained by the ambiguities of the autonomy/responsibility
couplet. Staff wish to recognize the autonomy of their 'young adult'
patients and know that the prospects of 'good control' of diabetes will
be improved if the patient is actively involved in the treatment.
However, they also know that they are ultimately responsible for their
patients' care and feel frustrated when patients will not comply with
'good' medical knowledge. Given the recent availability of a test to
measure long-term blood-glucose levels, it is tempting to disregard
autonomy and to 'police the patient'.[7]

As I have tried to demonstrate in this chapter, parents are equally
constrained by conflicting appeals of autonomy and responsibility.
Moreover, unlike doctors, they are routinely held to account for
offering versions of their behaviour in terms of one norm rather than
the other.

However, this is not completely a 'no-win' situation for either
doctors or parents. As we have seen, doctors can successfully redefine
the situation by appealing to their clinical knowledge (of 'syndromes'

and the like), to constitute parental accounts as mere 'versions' of events. And parents can buttress their accounts by skilfully balancing logically incompatible norms and grounding their claims on their unchallengeable knowledge of their own children and their ways.[8]

What practical lessons can be learned from this analysis? First, we have moved a long way away from treating doctor–patient communication as a matter of imparting accurate clinical information to the patient. Second, however, the analysis has revealed that what such a treatment excludes is not so much the individual anxieties and needs of the patient (although I don't deny their existence) but shared, cultural dilemmas. In a sense, then, in these medical encounters we are dealing with dilemmas of discourses rooted in a profoundly moral universe. These dilemmas encompass the way in which any account may be rendered a mere 'version' of events (Cuff, 1980) and the likelihood that medical accounts may be heard by parents as a 'charge' against their fulfilment of their parental duties.

The analytic value of this analysis is, I hope, clear. It has developed Cuff's discussion of how to withstand attempts to relativize one's account. It has built upon both his and Gubrium and Lynott's (1985) programme for redirecting research on the 'family'. Finally, it has underlined the pervasiveness of moral forms, while avoiding any characterization of people as mere 'cultural dopes' (Garfinkel, 1967).[9]

As always, the practical lessons are, unfortunately, harder to draw. To treat knowledge as 'enlightenment', while one attractive way out of this problem, has had its appeal tarnished by what Foucault has taught us about the interpenetration of knowledge and power. Consistent with the theme of this book I would, therefore, reject any one-sided attempt to take up this knowledge in order to make doctors experts in social as well as clinical realities.

Instead, my hope is that this analysis will encourage discussion in parents' groups and between medical staff, parents and patients about the dilemmas which so constrain them. This will not, of course, remove these dilemmas. But it should lead to greater awareness that individual parents are not alone in finding it impossible to be 'responsible' without 'nagging' or to respect their child's 'independence' without feeling 'irresponsible'. It might also lead, in a very practical sense, to all parties deciding together that they have no need to defer to *general* moral forms but instead can formulate together what seems appropriate for *themselves*, in *this* situation, at *this* particular time.

Notes

1. Molotch and Boden (1985) suggest another way in which accounts may be subverted. Using a cross-examination of John Dean at the Watergate hearing by a pro-

Nixon Senator, they show how an account is brought into question by demanding of it that it should provide the 'literate truth'. By requiring that a witness should answer 'only yes or no', the interrogator removes the appeal to context which might give weight to the reply.

2. Other discussions of how we attempt to bolster our versions of events are found in Drew (1978) and Watson (1978).

3. As I showed in my discussion of the cleft-palate clinic (Chapter 7), parents of teenage patients are forced to concede their child's autonomy when pressed by the doctor, even if such a concession goes against their sense of the child's present interests.

4. The charge I have identified in Utterance 37 does not *state* the agent to blame. This runs against Pomerantz's (1978) claim that 'blamings' typically name the agent responsible. This would seem to be unnecessary where, as here, the responsible agent may be inferred from the MCD.

5. Once again, as it turns out, June does not want her mother with her during the consultation.

6. Using such a format runs the risk of simply choosing favourable examples. Elsewhere, I have criticized this 'anecdotalism' (Silverman, in press). However, in the context of the earlier close analysis of a simple consultation, listing at least allows extensive comparative analysis to proceed.

7. In the previous chapter I discussed the consequences of this adoption of a 'policing' role by medical staff.

8. See the discussion of 'patency' or the presence of immediately recognizable symptoms and its impact upon medical decision-making in Chapter Two.

9. Although I have only hinted at Foucaultian themes in this chapter, they are clearly implicit in the analysis. Torode (personal correspondence) has suggested that contacts with professionals *incite* the articulation of an 'expert' discourse by these mothers — in the sense of Cuff's account of expertise as juggling with different versions of reality. There is also a parallel between the events in these clinics and Donzelot's (1980) account of the 'policing' of families via a 'tutelary complex', emphasizing family autonomy in the context of hygienist norms, directed at the mother whose rôle is 'preserved, solicited', while the father's role is 'usurped by the judge (and) . . . the educator' (p.104).

Appendix
Paediatric Cardiology Unit Outpatient Clinics: Sites and Action

Our aim was to seek to establish the nature and causes of variation of doctor – parent – child behaviour in these clinics. Robert Hilliard, a research officer on the project, prepared a document to be, as he put it, a set of 'questions-to-be-asked' and 'claims-to-be-tested'. Hilliard began by listing a set of possible stages of the consultation as follows:

1. Greeting exchange
2. Agenda or grounds for consultation
3. Elicitation sequence
4. Examination
5. Talk among doctors
6. Explanation of diagnosis
7. Disposal
8. Question time
9. Social elicitation
10. Ending

This list was based on observation of the routine unfolding of clinic consultations. In any one consultation, some stages may be absent. However, the order of stages is relatively invariant and attempts to change it will normally be made accountable.

Hilliard then considered the situational factors that might be associated with variation in behaviour at each stage. From a long document, I have selected his discussion of two stages: Stage 4 (examination) and Stage 6 (explanation of diagnosis). The discussion of the examination shows the importance of territorial factors as a 'site' of social interaction: for instance, the interactional resources of doctor and parents may vary according to whether the child is examined on the parent's lap or is taken away to be examined on a couch. Hilliard's discussion of the diagnosis stage suggests variability due to other site-specific conditions such as the presence of symptoms recognizable to parents. This section shows the thinking that eventually led to the analysis of decision-making presented in Chapters Two and Three.

Sites and Action

Examination
1. Transition usually explicit, signalled by request for child to be undressed
2. Variability in parental ability to import family structure routines of consultation teaching routines 'ownership' of child, related to *location* of examination, at doctor's desk, at the couch in the same room or in a side room
   a) *Conditions of location*
      desk: 'normal' unless

couch: i. where a small child

           ii. a 'difficult' child

N.B. children with Down's syndrome, though 'oldish' (from 3–4 years) may be seen at couch, more because of i) and ii). i.e. they qualify as honorary babies.

          iii. occasionally for privacy (often nurse-defined)

          iv. teaching: examination by other doctors while next case seen or consultant/parent talk

side room: i. pressure of time (London PCU)

          ii. other clinics; clinic layout

         iii. occasionally for privacy

         iv. to keep talk away from child

Where the child is examined at the couch, the whole consultation is normally there. If the child is examined in a side room, the whole consultation is normally there.

b) *Ability of family to import their own structure*

desk: family structure is family-defined to some extent by seating and handling of child. Not then usually alterable by doctor, except possibly at the beginning: to child: 'why don't you let daddy have the big chair?'

couch: ambivalent in effect: may allow more or less scope for family-definition of family structure

          i. move to couch: an activity and a duty for whoever moves the child (usually the mother) *but* move may involve nurse, to exclusion of family

            move may be linked with feeding or nappy changing

         ii. one parent (or both, where older child) may be left behind at desk sometimes invitation from doctor to 'join us' or 'come to see fair play'

        iii. always more space for a father to remove himself from the goings on at the table, standing to one side

            This is more often optional than unavoidable

         iv. ability of 'extra kin' to be close to scene of events limited

side room: i. scope, as at couch, for family-definition of structure through physical location

          ii. *but* there is a whole room in which to conduct the rest of the consultation. Scope here for doctor to address himself to a particular parent, exclude others etc.

        iii. an extra move then at desk. There, the family seat themselves. Here, they arrange themselves in a room, then doctor enters and chosses a location

c) *Routines of consultation*

desk: usually set order (this one) followed

couch: what happens after examination?

          i. doctor and family move back to desk

         ii. ·doctor leaves the family to consult other doctors or data — then (i) or (iii)

        iii. further talk at couch — usually a move back to desk at some stage

        iv. possibility of separation of parents and child

side room:

          i. doctor doesn't have notes: no 'naturally occurring' pauses in conversation except during examination

ii. separate episode of conversation among doctors unusual in side room

d) *Teaching routines*

desk: commonly an exclusion of family from doctor's talk (see 5 below)

couch: commonly an exclusion of family from the child: (i) Family may have to withdraw from couch to let doctors round it. (ii) Family may return to seats at desk, as the obvious place to go, or to talk to doctor there. side room: often a chance for family to talk to other doctors without presence of consultant (but not usually much significant contact).

e) *'Ownership' of child*

desk: usually firmly parental

an exception: One Registrar, but not the Consultant, sometimes takes child on to his lap for examination

— an appropriation of the child or an opening-up of the doctor's territory? (It seems the latter)

couch: is medical territory

i. nurse from PCU may take child there — away from the father, for instance

ii. where child is accompanied by nurse from other hospital, she may take charge of child

iii. Doctor can sit on couch, and touch child. Less easy for parents

side room: many variations: 'ownership' to be decided and negotiated

3. Other variability

a. how active is the parent(s) part in the examination? apart from   location dependent on child's behaviour

b. how much does the doctor account for what he is doing?

dependent on

i. the parents, their experience, status and knowledge

ii. teaching routines

Explanation of Diagnosis

1. possible transitional move from inter-doctor talk:

'What we've been discussing is ... '

more often no transition, but possible heading:

'Your little child ... '

2. explanation varying in relation to

A. previous treatment history:

no in-patient treatment

post-catheter

post-operative seem to be the distinct stages

B. the disposal the doctor has in mind:

discharge

routine follow-up

further treatment seem to make the difference

C. doctor's perception of parental competence

D. the child's obvious symptoms or debility versus

his medically-defined condition

Then it gets a little bit complicated. The vast variety of explanations seems to be most ordered if we take variables A and B above first, giving nine different conditions, then to see how relevant C and D ('competence' and 'patency' for short) are as salient to varying degrees according to the A and B — derived conditions.

So A and B together give the 'site' of the explanation (as desk, couch or side room give the site of the examination). C and D, are variables whose importance in turn varies with the site.

The Sites (Combinations of A and B)
1. *Pre-inpatient Discharge*
   e.g. innocent murmur
   low relevance of C and D: all patients get much the same explanation, whether they need or want it or not
   D, if invoked at all, is included in a common theme in this situation: the good sense of the referral
2. *Pre-inpatient, Routine Follow-up*
   e.g. closing VSD, mild PS
   concern with lay perceptions of heart disease — 'hole in heart' but lay understandings remedied not through elaborate explanation but through stressing the prognosis and parental action to be taken (the hole will close, penicillin prophylaxis)
   C : not very relevant, as it makes little difference
       (this would be otherwise, I suspect, where it was at issue whether or not the family would come back for the next appointment — i.e. private medicine in USA, versus a GP system)
   D : not very relevant. See above — lay understandings more at issue than visible symptoms. Often other symptoms, unrelated to the heart and not dealt with at the PCU are raised.
3. *Pre-patient, Requiring Further Treatment*
   e.g. most congenital heart disease
   relevance of C and D high
   more variables, and more variety, here than elsewhere
   explanation varies from full to minimal
   (minimal: 'Your child's very well. What we'd like to do is a small test to check . . . ')
   explanation related to (i) securing of agreement — or reassurance if CC not planned yet; (ii) ease with which condition can be explained; (iii) medical certainty; (iv) feeling for parental wishes (Down's syndrome); (v) perception or expression of parental anxiety
   N.B. parents with some kind of medical qualification (nurses) can be expected to get a fuller explanation; they are the only case of pre-inpatient ascribed competence. But they may get less; they are expected to acknowledge that some things can't be known until a certain test is performed.
4. *Post-catheter, Discharge*
   rare: where catheter has revealed no, or a trivial abnormality common theme: the good sense of treatment so far
   trading off parental relief
   C: relevant. A basic (slight) competence is imputed
   D: not so, except where history is to be rewritten
   a full explanation, not oriented to securing a disposal
5. *Post-catheter, Routine Follow-up*
   VSD, PS, Mild AS, closing PDA
   C: relevant

D: less so, unless the story is being changed
some imputed competence, but more a case of parents learning
hence a full explanation, putting the picture together
no need to aim at securing a disposal

6. *Post-catheter, Further Treatment Required*
   C and D highly relevant
   imputed competence, with learning
   2 cases:
   i. where operation is decided on at this consultation:
   explanation linked to securing disposal (but not brief)
   ii. where operation deferred, or all is on course for an eventual operation: space for raising other concerns — physical state of child, his/her development etc.

7. *Post-operation, Discharge*
   e.g. PDA ligated, ASD closed, coarctation resected
   C: parental competence always imputed
   D: an issue only with persisting non-cardiac defects
   de-escalation, reassurance (via common theme of overprotection), stressing success by repetition
   competence (C) is imputed, but social rapport is varying and significant
   a full explanation, unless history and stated expectations have clearly pointed to a discharge now

8. *Post-operative, Routine Follow-up*
   e.g. Fallot corrected
   mostly as in (7)
   C: competence always imputed
   D: this is the optimum time for raising patency, as parents are informed and experienced, and have had plenty of progress to watch.
   social rapport varying and significant
   disposal never a problem, unless parents want 'more', which won't have been raised at this stage in the consultation
   so a full explanation, not oriented to disposal

9. *Post-operative, Further Treatment*
   conditions requiring a shunt, a valve replacement on a small child, a pacemaker (not often at PCU) or multi-stage correction:
   TI, MI, Incuspid Atresia, complex abnormalities, e.g. univentricular conditions.
   C: highly relevant. Competence is imputed with experience, but parents may not decide for the best. So parents very much up for evaluation
   D: highly relevant, as before (3 and 6) where further treatment required. But it's now an issue at a higher level, with a medically experienced family, knowing what an operation entails.

Allied to this, coping with the assumption that operations make you better. So a full but loaded explanation, oriented to securing a disposal which parents have means and grounds for claiming their own say in.

References

Abel-Smith, B. (1976) *Value for Money in Health Services*. London: Heinemann.

Aiken, L.H. (1976) 'Chronic Illness and Responsive Ambulatory Care', *Medicine*: 239–51.

Apley, J. Barbour, R.F., Westmacott, I. (1967) 'Impact of Congenital Heart Disease on the Family: Preliminary Report; *British Medical Journal*: 103–6.

Armstrong, D. (1979) 'Child Development and Medical Ontology', *Social Science and Medicine* 13A: 9–12.

Armstrong, D. (1982) 'Medical Knowledge and Modalities of Social Control', mimeo. London: Unit of Sociology, Guys' Hospital Medical School

Armstrong, D. (1983) *The Political Anatomy of the Body*. Cambridge: Cambridge University Press.

Armstrong, D. (1984) 'The Patient's View', *Social Science and Medicine* 18(9): 737–44.

Arney, W. and Bergen, B. (1983) 'The Chronic Patient', *Sociology of Health and Illness* 5(1): 1–24.

Arney W. and Bergen, B. (1984) *Medicine and the Management of Living*, Chicago: Chicago University Press.

Atkinson, J. and Drew, P. (1979) *Order in Court*. London: Macmillan.

Balint, M. (1964) *The Doctor, his Patient and the Illness*. London: Pitman.

Baruch, G. (1981) 'Moral Tales: Parents' Stories of Encounters with the Health Professions', *Sociology of Health and Illness* 3: 275–95.

Baruch, G. (1982) '*Moral Tales: Intervening Parents of Congenitally Ill Children*', unpublished PhD thesis, University of London.

Bloor, M. (1976a) 'Professional Autonomy and Client Exclusion', in M. Wadsworth and D. Robinson.

Bloor, M. (1976b) 'Bishop Berkeley and the Adenotonsillectomy Enigma', *Sociology* 10(1): 43–61.

Bloor, M. (1983) 'Notes on Member Validation', in R. Emerson (ed.), *Contemporary Field Research*, 156–72. Boston: Little, Brown.

Bourdieu, P. (1977) *Outline of a Theory of Practice*. Cambridge: Cambridge University Press.

Bradley, C. et al. (1984) 'Psychological Aspects of Diabetes' in K. Alberti and L. Krall (eds), *Diabetes Annual, 1984*. Amsterdam: Excerpta Medica.

Bury, M. (1986) 'Social Constructionism and the Development of Medical Sociology', *Sociology of Health and Illness* 8(2): 137–69.

Byrne, P. and Long, B. (1976) *Doctors Talking to Patients*. London: DHSS.

Callon, M. (1986) 'Some Elements of a Sociology of Translation', *Sociological Review* 32: 194–233.

Calnan, M. (1984) 'Clinical Uncertainty: Is it a Problem in the Doctor–patient Relationship?' *Sociology of Health and Illness* 6(1): 74–85.

Campbell, A. and Duff, R. (1979) 'Deciding the Care of Severely Malformed or Dying Infants', *Journal of Medical Ethics* 5: 65–7.

Cerreto, M. and Travis, L. (1984) 'Implications of Psychological and Family Factors in the Treatment of Diabetes', *Pediatric Clinics of North America* 31(3): 689–710.

Clegg, S. (1975) *Power, Rule and Domination*. London: Routledge.

Cousins, M. and Husain, A. (1983) *Michel Foucault*. London: Macmillan.

Crane, D. (1975) *The Sanctity of Social Life: Physicians' Treatment of Critically Ill Patients*. New York: Russell Sage.

Crozier, M. (1964) *The Bureaucratic Phenomenon*. Chicago: Chicago University Press.

Cuff, E.C. (1980) 'Some Issues in the Problem of Studying Versions in Everyday Situations', *Occasional Paper*, No. 3, Department of Sociology, University of Manchester.

Dalton, M. (1959) *Men Who Manage*. New York: John Wiley.

Davis, A. and Strong, P. (1976) *'Aren't Children Wonderful?'*, in M. Wadsworth and D. Robinson.

Davis, A. (1982) *Children in Clinics*. London: Tavistock.

Davis, F. (1963) *Passage Through Crisis*. Indianapolis: Bobbs–Merrill.

Deleuze, G. and Guattari, F. (1981) '*Rhizomes*', *Ideology and Consciousness* 8: 49–71.

Dews, P. (1984) Comment in *New Left Review* 144: 91.

DHSS (1980) *Inequalities in Health: Report of Research Working Party*. London.

Dingwall, R. (1980) 'Orchestrated Encounters: An Essay in the Comparative Analysis of Speech-exchange Systems'. *Sociology of Health and Illness* 2(2): 151–73.

Dingwall, R. et al. (1980) 'Identifying Abuse and Neglect: The Child as a Clinical Entity', mimeo. Oxford: Centre for Socio-Legal Studies.

Donzelot, J. (1979) *The Policing of Families: Welfare versus the State*. London: Hutchinson.

Drass, K.A. (1982) 'Negotiation and the Structure of the Discourse in Medical Consultation', *Sociology of Health and Illness* 4(3): 320–41.

Drew, D.R. (1978) 'Accusations', *Sociology* 12(1): 1–22.

Dreyfus, H. and Rabinow (1982) *Michel Foucault*. London: Harvester.

Earthrowl, B. and Stacey, M. (1977) 'Social Class and Children in Hospital', *Social Science and Medicine* 11: 83–8.

Elling, R. (1980) *Cross-National Study of Health Systems*. New York: Transaction Books.

Fisher, S. (1984) 'Institutional Authority and the Structure of Discourse', *Discourse Processes* 7: 201–24.

Fitz, J. (1979) 'The Child as a Legal Subject', paper presented to BSA Law and Society Conference, Warwick, April.

Forman, Roy (1983) 'Letters', *The Guardian*, 5 February.

Foucault, M. (1973) *The Birth of the Clinic*. London: Tavistock.

Foucault, M. (1977) *Discipline and Punish*. London: Allen Lane.

Foucault, M. (1979) *The History of Sexuality*, Vol. 1. London: Allen Lane.

Foucault, M. (1981) 'Questions of Method', *Ideology and Consciousness* 8: 3-14.

Freidson, E. (1970) *Professional Dominance*. Chicago: Aldine.

Friedberg, D. and Caldart, L. (1975) 'A Centre for Paediatric Cardiovascular Patients', *American Journal of Nursing* 4: 1480–2.

Galbraith, S. (1983) 'Letters', *The Guardian*, 5 February.

Garfinkel, H. (1967) *Studies in Ethnomethodology*. Englewood Cliffs: Prentice-Hall, New Jersey.

Gilbert, G.N. and Mulkay, M. (1983) 'In Search of the Action', in P. Abell and N. Gilbert (eds), *Accounts and Action*. Aldershot: Gower.

Gillespie, C. and Bradley, C. (1983) 'Motivation and the Person with Diabetes', unpublished paper. Nottingham: Postgraduate Medical Centre, University Hospital. 13 December.

Gillespie, C. (1985) Unpublished talk, Symposium on Adolescent Diabetes, Leeds General Infirmary, 1 March.

Glaser, B. and Strauss, A. (1967) *The Discovery of Grounded Theory*. Chicago: Aldine.

Goffman, E. (1961) *Encounters*. Indianapolis: Bobbs-Merrill.

Goffman, E. (1968) *Asylums*. Harmondsworth: Penguin.

Griffith, B. and Rayner, G. (1985) *Commercial Medicine in London*. London: GLC.

Guardian (1981), 'Tory Plan to Scrap Way NHS is Run', December.

Guardian (1982), 'Six GPs in First Private Service', 26 October.

Gubrium, J. Buckholdt, D. and Lynott, R. (1982) 'Considerations on a Theory of Descriptive Activity', *Mid-American Review of Sociology* 7(1): 17–35.

Gubrium, J. and Lynott, R. (1985) 'Family Rhetoric as Social Order', *Journal of Family Issues* 6(1): 129–52.

Habermas, J. (1972) *Knowledge and Human Interests*. London: Heinemann.

Hammersley, M. and Atkinson, P. (1983) *Ethnography: Principles in Practice*. London: Tavistock.

Hilliard, R. (1981) 'Categorizing Children in the Clinic', *Sociology of Health and Illness* 3(3): 317–36.

Hughes, D. (1982) 'Control in the Medical Consultation', *Sociology* 16(3): 359–76.

Hunter, I. (1987) *Culture and Government: The Emergence of Literary Education*. London: Macmillan.

Jewson, N. (1976) 'The Disappearance of the Sick-Man from Medical Cosmology, 1770–1870', *Sociology* 10: 225–44.

Jones, M. (1983) 'Survey of Diabetic Children in the Yeovil Area', *Health Visitor* 5(10): 378–9.

Kinmonth, A.-L. (1985) 'Children into Young Adults', *Practical Diabetes* 2(4): 21–2.

Kornblum, H. and Anderson, B. (1982) ' "Acceptance" re-assessed — A Point of View', *Child Psychiatry and Human Development* 12(3): 171–8.

Laclau, E. (1981) 'Politics as the Construction of the Unthinkable', translated by D. Silverman, mimeo. London: Goldsmiths' College.

Laclau, E. and Mouffe, C. (1985) *Hegemony and Socialist Strategy*. London: Verso.

Lavoie, J. and Barker, M. (1980) 'Psychology of Juvenile Diabetics', *Union Medical of Canada* 109(2): 199–211.

Lynch, M. (1984) *Art and Artifact in Laboratory Science*. London: Routledge.

Manning, P. (1986) 'Book Review', *Sociology of Health and Illness* 8: 178–86.

McHugh, P. (1970) 'Commonsense Conception of Deviance', in H.P. Dreitzel (ed.), *Recent Sociology, No. 2* New York: Macmillan.

Mehan, H. (1981) *Learning Lessons*. Cambridge, Mass: Harvard University Press.

Mills, C.W. (1940) 'Situated Actions and Vocabularies of Motive', *American Sociological Review* 5: 904–13.

Mishler, E. (1984) *The Discourse of Medicine: Dialectics of Medical Interviews* Norwood, New Jersey: Ablex.

Mitchell, J.C. (1983) 'Case and Situational Analysis', *Sociological Review* 31(2): 187–211.

Molotch, H.L. and Boden, D. (1985) 'Talking Social Structure: Discourse, Domination and the Watergate Hearings', *American Sociological Review* 50: 273–88.

Murphy, A. (forthcoming) 'The Cleft-palate Teenager: Child, Familial and Medical Versions of Appearance', PhD in progress. London: Department of Sociology, Goldsmiths' College.

Navarro, V. (1976) *Medicine Under Capitalism* New York: Prodist.

Newton, R. (1985) 'Social Integration of the Adolescent Diabetic', *Practical Diabetes* 2(4): 25–8.

Ory, M. and Kronenfeld, J. (1980) 'Living and Juvenile Diabetes Mellitus', *Paediatric Nursing* 6(5): 47–50.

Pashukanis, E. (1978) *Law and Marxism: A General Theory*. London: Ink Links.

Pomerantz, A. (1978) 'Attributions of Responsibility: Blamings', *Sociology* 12(1): 115–21.

Posner, T. (1977) 'Magical Elements in Orthodox Medicines: Diabetes as a Medical Thought System' in R. Dingwall and C. Heath (eds), *Health Care and Health Knowledge* London: Croom Helm.

Rayner, G. and Stimson, G. (1979) 'A Response to Medicine, Superstructure and Micropolitics', *Social Science and Medicine* 13A: 611–12.

Rayner, G. (1981) 'Medical Errors and the "Sick Role": a Speculative Enquiry', *Sociology of Health and Illness* 3(3): 296–316.

Rosenbloom, A. (1984) 'Primary and Subspecialty Care of Diabetes Mellitus in Children and Youth', *Pediatric Clinics of North America* 31(1) 107–17.

Roth, J. (1963) *Timetables*. New York: Bobbs–Merrill.

Sacks, H. (1972) 'On the Analysability of Stories by Children' in J. Gumperz and D. Hymes (eds), *Directions in Sociolinguistics*. New York: Holt, Rinehart & Winston.

Sacks, H. (1972) 'An Initial Investigation of the Usability of Conversational Data for Doing Sociology' in D. Sudnow (ed.), *Studies in Interaction*. Glencoe: Free Press.

Sacks, H. (1974) 'On the Analysability of Stories by Children', in R. Turner (ed.), *Ethnomethodology*. Penguin: Harmondsworth.

Sacks, H., Schegloff, E. and Jefferson, G. (1974) 'A Simplest Systematics for the Analysis of Turn-taking for Conversation', *Language* 50: 696–735.

Sheridan, D. and Johnson, D. (1976) 'Social Work Services in a High-risk Nursery', *Health and Social Work* 1: 86–103.

Silverman, D. (1970) *The Theory of Organizations*. London: Heinemann.

Silverman, D. (1973) 'Interview Talk', *Sociology* 7(1) 31–48.

Silverman, D. (1981) 'The Child as a Social Object: Down's Syndrome Children in a Paediatric Cardiology Clinic', *Sociology of Health and Illness* 3(3): 254–74.

Silverman, D. (1982) '"Is It Cancer Doctor?" Interpersonal Relations in Two NHS Oncology Clinics', mimeo, London: Goldsmiths' College.

Silverman, D. (1983) 'The Clinical Subject: Adolescents in a Cleft-Palate Clinic', *Sociology of Health and Illness* 5(3): 253–74.

Silverman, D. (1983b) 'Counting Events: Quantitative Analysis of Encounters at Three Oncology Clinics', mimeo. London: Goldsmiths' College.

Silverman, D. (1984) 'Going Private: Ceremonial Forms in a Private Oncology Clinic', *Sociology* 18(2): 191–204.

Silverman, D. (1985) *Qualitative Methodology and Sociology*. Aldershot: Gower.

Silverman, D. (in press) 'Telling Convincing Stories', in B. Glassner and J. Moreno (eds), *The Qualitative-Quantitative Distinction in the Social Sciences*. Dordrecht: Reidel.

Silverman, D. and Jones, J. (1975) *Organizational Work*. London: Collier–Macmillan.

Silverman, D. and Torode, B. (1980) *The Material Word: Some Theories of Language and Its Limits*. London: Routledge & Kegan Paul.

Silverman, D. et al. (1984) 'Factors Influencing Parental Participation in a Paediatric Cardiology Out-patient Clinic', *International Journal of Cardiology* 6: 689–95.

Skipper, J.J. and Leonard, R. (1968) 'Children, Stress and Hospitalization: a Field Experiment', *Journal of Health and Social Behaviour* 9: 275–87.

Smith, G. and May, D. (1980) 'Executing "Decisions" in the Children's Hearings', *Sociology*: 581–601.

Smith, M. Strang, S. and Baum, J. (1984) 'Organization of a Diabetic Clinic for Children', *Practical Diabetes* 1(1): 8–12.

Stacey, M. et al. (1970) *Hospitals, Children and their Families*. London: Routledge.

Starr, P. and Zirpoli, E. (1976) 'Cleft-palate Patients — The Social Work Approach', *Health and Social Work* 1(2): 104–12.

Steel, J. (1985) 'Evolution of Adolescent Diabetic Care in Edinburgh', *Practical Diabetes* 2(4): 29–30.

Strong, P. (1977) 'Private Practice for the Masses: Medical Consultations in the NHS', mimeo. Aberdeen: MRC Medical Sociology Unit.

Strong, P. (1979a) 'Materialism and Medical Interaction', *Social Science & Medicine* 13A: 613–19.

Strong, P. (1979b) *The Ceremonial Order of the Clinic*. London; Routledge.

Strong, P. (1980) 'Doctors and Dirty Work — The Case of Alcoholism', *Sociology of Health and Illness* 2(1): 24–47.

Strong, P. (1982) 'Power, Etiquette and Identity in Medical Consultations', mimeo, Open University.

Szasz, T. and Hollander, M. (1956) 'A Contribution to the Philosophy of Medicine', *A.M.A. Archives of Internal Medicine* 47: 585–92.

The Times (1983) 'Greeks Try to Win Back Trust of Patients', 29 January.

Torode, B. (1984) *The Extra-Ordinary in Ordinary Language*, 2nd edition. Amsterdam: Kontekstan 5.

Tuckett, D. et al. (1985) *Meetings between Experts*. London: Tavistock.

Van den Heuvel, W. (1980) 'The Role of the Consumer in Health Policy', *Social Science and Medicine* 14A: 423–6.

Voysey, M. (1975) *A Constant Burden*. London: Routledge.

Wadsworth, M. and Robinson, D. (1976) (eds), *Understanding Everyday Medical Life*. London: Martin Robertson.

Waitzkin, H. (1979) 'Medicine, Superstructure and Micropolitics', *Social Science and Medicine* 13A, 601–9.

Walkerdine, V. (1984) 'Developmental Psychology and the Child-centred Pedagogy' in Henriques Holloway, Unwin, Venn and Walkerdine (eds), *Changing the Subject*. London: Methuen.

Watson, D.R. (1978) 'Categorization, Authorization and Blame — Negotiation in Conversation', *Sociology*. 12(1): 105–13.

West, C. (1984) 'Medical Misfires', *Discourse Processes* 7: 107–33.

West, P. (1976) 'The Physician and the Management of Childhood Epilepsy' in M. Wadsworth and D. Robinson (eds), *Studies in Everyday Medical Life*, pp. 13–31. London: Martin Robertson.

Wiener et al. (1980) 'Patient Power: Complex Questions need Complex Answers', *Social Policy*, September–October.

Name Index

Subject Index